From Dark Heart To Kalahari

From Dark Heart
To Kalahari

The not-so-ecological adventures
of an Ecologist in Africa

Clive Spinage

Librario

Published by

Librario Publishing Ltd.

ISBN No: 1-904440-74-6

Copies can be ordered from retail
or via the internet at:
www.librario.com

or from:

Brough House
Milton Brodie
Kinloss
Moray
IV36 2UA
Tel / Fax: 01343 850617

Printed in Times.

Cover design and layout by Steven James
www.chimeracreations.co.uk

Printed and bound by
DigiSource (GB) Ltd.

An ecologist's Africa

Contents

List of Black and White Illustrations

List of Colour Illustrations

28. Siapi, the end of the last tall forest in Burkina Faso.

29. The crater of Karisimbi with its bizarre giant groundsel and senecios.

30. A main road in Botswana.

31. Chapman's Pool.

32. The Kalahari Desert.

33. The shape of things to come? Water supply for game in the Gemsbok National Park.

List of Maps

Chapter 1

When the Going was Grim

on becoming an ecologist

Gloom overcame me.

Someone at the end of the table had risen and was addressing the meeting: "For conducting research into wild life we must have people with at least a P-H-D", the speaker pronounced emphatically, leaving no room for doubt that amateurs were not required.

The gathering, ranged either side of the long polished table in the ministry building, nodded their heads sagely. It was a distinguished collection of personalities in wild life circles in those days, dubbed as one of the most elite of gentlemen's clubs. Kenya's Chief Game Warden, Billy Hale; the Director of Kenya's National Parks, Colonel Mervyn Cowie; the Chief Game Warden of Uganda, Major Bruce Kinloch (the only man to hold the post for each of the three East African territories); Gerry Swynnerton, Chief Game Warden of Tanganyika; and Colonel Peter Molloy, Director of Tanganyika's National Parks; plus a collection of veterinary experts and senior government officials. But the speaker was Noel Simon, an amateur himself, founder and first chairman of the Kenya Wild Life Society (later to become the East African Wildlife Society). A farmer from Molo in the White Highlands, he had written to the Kenya Weekly News setting forth proposals for such a society, expressing concern at the destruction of Kenya's big game. Letters to the press on this subject and predictions of the imminent extinction of game were as frequent then as now, but this happened to strike a responsive chord and the reaction was immediate and profound. Within weeks the Kenya Wildlife Society had been formed, with Noel elected as chairman. Now here he was making things difficult for others. For, consumed with an avid interest in wild life, I myself was indeed a complete amateur.

A Ph.D. was a higher research degree awarded after three years of distinguished university research, and not so common in the fifties when money was tighter than it was to become later. But I did not possess even a university first degree.

"Oh well," I thought, looking around at the sombrely nodding heads, "I suppose I shall just have to get a Ph.D.", since by that time I had firmly resolved wild life research was the one thing in life I most wanted to do.

What was I, then, a humble amateur doing taking my place at such a distinguished meeting – the prestigious Regional Meeting of the British East Africa Fauna Conference?

The year was 1958 and the country Kenya. I was employed as a laboratory assistant at an agricultural research station, undertaking the incredibly boring job of analysing soils and plants for minute quantities of chemicals known as trace elements. The Director of the establishment, knowing of my interest in wild life, had sent me along to the conference as an observer. For the Director of a leading research establishment to send along a mere laboratory assistant to such a meeting pleased me, but it also showed that wild life matters had yet to be taken seriously as far as research priorities were concerned.

It was, in fact, all a horrible mistake, my working at this agricultural station anyway. I had mentioned to John Williams, the well-known East African ornithologist, that I wanted to work in wild life, and he had suggested I look for a job at EE-AV-RO, where, he said, they were involved in some wild life orientated research. Hence one day I found myself seeking employment at a research station situated some eight miles outside Nairobi. Here I was informed they would be pleased to employ me, but the only post they could offer was that in which I now found myself. It was not what I wanted and I had disliked chemistry at school, but it might provide the opening for which I was searching. So I took the job. I was well qualified for it as my first appointment upon leaving school at the age of sixteen had been as a Scientific Assistant at Britain's Harwell Atomic Energy Research Establishment in the heady days at the end of the 1940s, joining just at the time that the unmasking began of one of its most senior figures, Fuchs, the atom bomb spy, when despite Britain's post-war austerity, money for nuclear research was no object at the leading establishment in the country. Then I could walk into the main stores and walk out again with any piece of equipment I chose up to one hundred pounds in value, considerably more in today's terms. Anything above that value simply required a signed chit. Research for me was never to be so generous again.

I had been working in my new job for a week when I discovered there was another laboratory, about a mile down the road, called EE-AV-RO, where they were indeed working on some wild life related research. I was at EE-AFF-RO. The former was a veterinary research laboratory and I was in the agricultural and forestry laboratory! I've hated acronyms ever since. But my ineptitude had its advantages, for the establishment boasted an excellent ecological library inherited from the old Amani library. Amani had been an agricultural research station set up in Tanganyika by the Germans before the First World War and moved to Nairobi, lock stock and barrel, after the Second World War.

There were such volumes as Theodore Roosevelt's *African Game Trails* in which a later, English hand, had written in the margin: "This man is a bloody murderer." But it was Charles Elton's landmark work *Animal Ecology*, which really motivated my thinking. Until then I had wanted to work with animals, yes, but it was Elton's absorbing approach, as fresh today as when it first appeared in 1927, which focused my ideas, and made me aware of how little we really knew then about the actual lives of African animals. This was in the days before the word 'ecology' became the cant word for natural history. Mention the word ecology then and few people knew what you were talking about.

I began to read every word on the subject I could lay my hands on, which wasn't much. But the real question remained: how could I get a Ph.D. when I lacked not only a first degree, but A levels as well? I had attended a reasonably sound grammar school, but I saw no career for myself in History, my main school interest; nor did I see any future in Latin or Divinity, considered to be the main passports in life by the beak-nosed canon who guided one's destiny. The only subject that really interested me was natural history. But natural history had not been taught since the science master had gone to the War and never came back again. The old 'museum' cabinets had long since been ransacked by curious schoolboys, and stood empty, their shelves covered in dust in a bleak, seldom-used classroom, appropriately termed 'the Gods' because of its situation on the remote top floor at the back of a stark, ugly, red brick building.

So I had left, at the age of sixteen, confidently thinking my six *Oxford and Cambridge Schools Certificate* passes would suffice as a passport to life. I had now come up against my first obstacle. I needed A levels.

I inquired at the schools' examination centre in Nairobi, to be told there was an examination in six months' time. It took two years' schooling before you sat A levels but, "Why not try? You can always sit the exam again next year if you fail," the receptionist urged. So I registered.

The next step was to find out what one had to learn.

I obtained a correspondence course in botany and zoology, but this gave no inkling as to the actual examination requirements.

So I made my way to Nairobi's principal boys' establishment, the Prince of Wales School. Somehow the headmaster met me outside; perhaps he had been gardening for he was tie-less, wearing a grubby, open-necked shirt with the sleeves rolled up; quite unlike the austere canon of my former schooldays, with his dog collar and obfusc attire.

They did only biology, and not botany and zoology as separate subjects, he informed me. Perhaps the girls' school could help.

When I had plucked up enough courage, I wandered into Nairobi's principal girls' school, the Kenya High School for Girls. The main door was open and walking in I stood momentarily at a loss, for at first the place seemed deserted. Then I heard the noise of a piano and nervously made my way along a bleak corridor towards the sound, finding myself in a large hall where an attractive schoolgirl sat playing in solitary splendour. She looked up and smiled. It seemed the most natural thing in the world to her for a strange man to amble in.

Covered in embarrassment I stammered I was looking for the biology mistress. Thankful for the excuse to abandon her exercises, she jumped up with alacrity and told me to follow her. Passing briskly along several more corridors we emerged at the edge of a quadrangle, where she asked me to wait.

It was lunchtime, and one could not mistake the dining hall at one side from which emanated an indescribable uproar, surpassing anything I had ever experienced at school. Shrieks, laughter, chatter and the rattle of plates, knives and forks, made a deafening row.

I stood there miserably wondering if I should cut and run for it. But what if I got lost in the school building? There might then be even worse embarrassment. Just at that moment two good-looking young teachers with ponytail hairdos walked by:

"There's a very worried-looking father over there," remarked one of them loudly to her companion, glancing in my direction.

I would certainly have had to be a very precocious one! But that decided me. Since the earth would not swallow me up I was just about to make a run for it when my eye caught a figure striding purposefully across the quad, feet at a quarter to three. Dumpy figure, kindly round face wearing a big grin, horn-rimmed glasses, hair tied in a bun, sporting a green porkpie hat, thick tweed skirt, thick men's socks and hefty Oxford brogues: the very caricature of a biology mistress.

"Ha!" she bellowed in a stentorian voice from halfway across the quad, "so you're the feller who wants to do 'bot' and zoo!"

But it was the same story. They only did biology. All the embarrassment had been for nothing.

* * *

I worked away at my correspondence course. Jane, one of the researchers at the veterinary laboratory, tried to guide me in the mysteries of the practical dissections which were an important requirement of the final examination. She produced a white rabbit from the lab and opened it up. I nearly vomited, but persevered.

Getting a white rabbit from a research laboratory was easy; not so easy was finding an elasmobranch fish, more commonly known as a dogfish, or 'rock salmon', an essential element of zoological instruction. I had asked the club caterer if she could oblige, but the answer being in the negative I had forgotten all about it, placing my faith in the lap of the gods.

It was a Saturday lunchtime and I was downing a drink in the club bar as was my habitual wont, when a sudden hush fell over the noisy drinkers. One of the Kikuyu waiters had marched in, attired as usual in flowing white *khanzu* (a sort of ankle-length nightshirt) and red fez, his forearms held out before him like a depiction in Ancient Egyptian tombs of slaves bearing tribute to the Pharaoh, with draped across them a five-foot long shark: dead of course, although from the look on the waiter's face it might not have been. He announced with evident puzzlement that it was for me.

In the afternoon, Jane and I got to work on the dissection of the cranial nerves, the favourite of the biology practical. The shark having been sent up from Mombasa on the coast, 350 miles away in the tropical heat, had been gutted, so the dissection of the cranial nerves was all that was left. I just hoped against hope the final examination would be a rabbit or a frog to dissect.

The day of the exam came, and found me once more suffering acute embarrassment as it was to be held in an Indian boys' school. In those days there was a dividing line between the races, and it was somewhat infra dig for an almost thirty-year-old white to be sitting an examination side by side with eighteen-year-old Indian schoolboys. The boys perhaps thought it strange, but they politely made no comment.

The written papers seemed not too bad, and I awaited the main dissection with trepidation.

I sat on the hard wooden laboratory stool waiting, the question paper lying face down on the bench before me.

The Indian schoolmaster came in carrying a large basin of assorted sharks. I began to feel distinctly uneasy. Well, let's hope that at least it will be the cranial nerves.

Passing along the row of tremulous schoolboys he noisily slapped down a wet shark before each. Passing me he flung down in front of my astonished gaze a large hammerhead shark.

Oh no! Not the cranial nerves! For the hammerhead shark is a grotesque beast with its eyes positioned at the extremities of two long, fleshy flaps, which stick out either side of the head. Only an expert could dissect out the ocular nerve on that!

Hunched on my stool looking glumly at the slimy monstrosity laid before me my heart gradually sank to my boots. It really was too much.

The command came to turn over the examination paper. I looked at it fearfully. It could not have been worse. We were required to dissect out the blood supply to the viscera – guts in simple language. I, of course, had never seen the viscera of an elasmobranch fish before!

There was nothing for it but to have a go. I opened up the belly, pulled bits of the creature's smelly insides this way and that, and stuck marker pins in at random. The Indian schoolmaster walked by, looked, and shook his head in disbelief. Ah well, it was a try anyway.

When the results came out I was surprised and, to say the least, overjoyed, to find I had not done too badly. A grade 'B' pass, as good as most got after two years at school.

The first step on the ladder to becoming a wild life researcher had been overcome – that of qualifying for university entrance; or so I thought.

But above-age students were not welcomed with much enthusiasm at English universities for some reason (although they usually do very well), and only two A level grade 'B' passes was not much of a qualification. Finally I was accepted, after several disappointing exchanges of letters from other universities, by Chelsea College, London, at that time a polytechnic offering London University degrees. Reluctantly kissing goodbye to seven years' government pension, I resigned my post and flew back to England.

In September 1960 I walked down King's Road, Chelsea, not quite yet the King's Road of the 'swinging sixties', and turned into Manresa Road. It was marked at the corner by a bombsite, still untouched fifteen years after the end of the War, a rusty tin helmet and an old enamel chamber pot displayed in the overgrown debris-filled garden. I climbed the steps of the Chelsea Polytechnic and passed through the battered, dingy, dull-green painted doors. Everything had been much brighter in Kenya.

Would-be students were flowing into a large, bleak hall with tables arranged around the sides, behind which sat the heads of departments with their staff. I followed the flow and located the zoology table. The Head welcomed me. He glanced through my application form, approved it and passed me on. I began to feel distinctly better. I was getting there!

I walked to the exit, where an elderly, white-haired man sat behind the final table checking the students' completed application forms as they filed out. The queue shuffled forward, I handed mine over confidently.

The elderly white-haired man glanced at it. Slowly he rose from his chair. Coming from behind the table he placed his arm around my shoulders in a fatherly manner and spoke gently:

"I am afraid you do not fulfil the minimum entry requirements."

"But . . . but . . . I've resigned my job . . . Seven years' pension . . . I've come all the way from Africa . . . They accepted my application . . . " I babbled distraughtly, despair clutching at my heart.

"Well, let's go and see the Head of Department," he replied.

He escorted me across the hall through the milling prospective students, his arm still around my shoulders. They must have thought this display of fatherly affection towards such an elderly student rather strange.

So it had all been for nothing. I had burned my boats in Kenya. I had no job. My future in wild life research in Africa had suddenly vanished. Now what was I to do?

The problem, the elderly man explained, was that I had only obtained the equivalent of an O level pass in mathematics (hated mathematics) 'way back in the forties; but I had always assumed the old Oxford and Cambridge Schools Certificate was a superior examination to the O and A levels the Labour government subsequently introduced. Apparently it was not. Shirley Williams had done her damnedest[1].

I found myself standing before the Head once more. He seemed unconcerned.

"Oh well, there's a maths exam in six weeks' time. Could you pass that?" he inquired breezily.

"No!" I replied emphatically. I wasn't going to go through all that swotting again, as well as attending the botany and zoology courses. And this time for a subject I saw little hope of mastering quickly.

"Well, just carry on as normal then. I'll plead with the Board of Governors."

It was three months later before I was informed the Sword of Damocles had been removed from above my head. The plea had been successful and I could stay on. Two years and nine months after that I obtained a First Class Honours degree in Zoology, and began to think it had all been worthwhile. The lonely digs in bleak Wandsworth, the endless swotting punctuated with Friday night binges at the Six Bells, the sedate Saturday night dances at the Chelsea Town Hall redolent of a bygone age with its elaborate painted friezes adorning the walls: waltz, quickstep, more waltz, and rarely, a jive; but never the girl of one's dreams.

But at least now I stood a good chance of getting a research grant and being able to return to Africa to study wild life. That was the theory. But application after application was turned down. No one was interested in a 30-year-old student, First Class Honours degree or not.

Almost a year had passed in fruitless inquiry and I was wandering disconsolately along one of the dingy passages of Chelsea College, drawn back aimlessly to my Alma Mater like a moth to a candle, when an advertisement for North Atlantic Treaty Organisation scholarships caught my eye. I had nothing better to do so I read it. I learnt that NATO scholarships were not, as one might suppose from the title, for the purpose of studying armaments and military tactics, but were available for almost any subject. The application date had already passed, but I rushed into the office of the now new Head of Department. He said he would see what he could do for me. Once again I was to be pleaded for.

The plea was successful and not long afterwards, in 1964, I was back in Africa. But it was a new Africa, for Kenya, Uganda and Tanganyika had all attained independence in the interim. There was as yet little change to be seen from former days and soon I was driving a second-hand Land Rover bought in Nairobi to one of the jewels in the crown of East Africa's national parks: the magnificent Queen Elizabeth National Park in western Uganda. Here, for almost the next three years, I was to have the privilege of carrying out research into the life history of a large antelope called the waterbuck, during what has since been termed 'the golden days' of African wild life, before the infamous Idi Amin mirrored what has happened to so many other countries in Africa and tore the country apart.

Golden days they may have been, but it had not been easy getting there, joining what was then only a privileged handful of researchers. The irony was that most people thought one came out with the proverbial silver spoon in one's mouth, to swan around like some 18th-century gentleman naturalist on a vast salary. It had not been like that at all, and at the age of thirty-one I had the princely sum of five hundred pounds a year to live on.

Notes

1. Shirley Williams was the Labour education minister who destroyed the educational system by abolishing grammar schools.

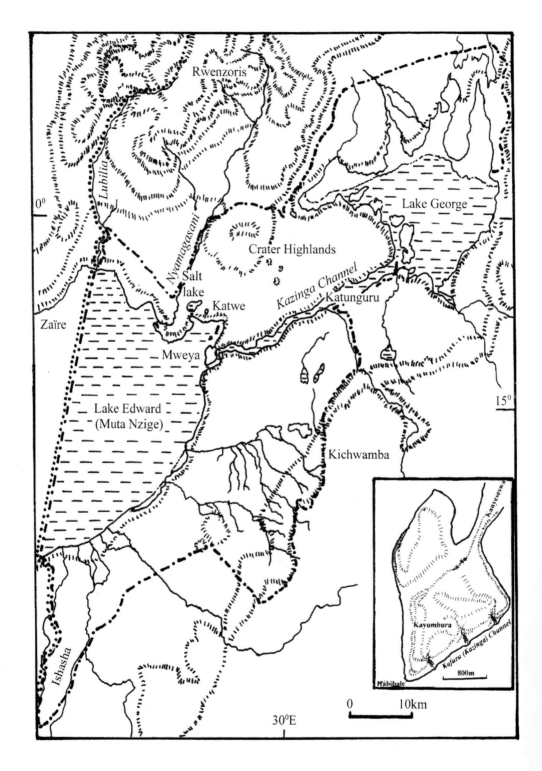

The Queen Elizabeth National Park, Uganda
(with Mweya Peninsula inset).

Chapter 2

The Golden Days

research in Uganda's national parks

Nattily attired in peaked cap with flap hanging down at the back to protect his neck from the sun, Henry Morton Stanley, accompanied by four other Europeans and some 1,500 Africans, was on his way home from the Emin Pasha Relief Expedition when he visited the present-day Queen Elizabeth National Park for the second time. Later to become a 750 square mile wild life gem, this area of rolling hills in western Uganda at the southern end of the Rwenzori Mountains – the Mountains of the Moon of the ancients – descends to flat, grassy plains straddling the Kazinga Channel; a 20 mile long, half-mile wide sluggish waterway joining two large, tranquil lakes, Lakes Edward and George, as Stanley was to name them.

The former *New York Herald* reporter did not think it such an attractive place when he arrived at the village of Katwe on June 17, 1889. Travelling from the Nyamagasani River "The grass of the plain grieved us sorely while travelling through it. The stalks grew to a height of three feet, and its spikelets pierced through the thickest clothing, and clung to every garment as we passed by, and became very irritating and troublesome." The plain was "remarkable for its growth of euphorbia, which have been planted by generations of Wasongora to form zeribas to protect their herds from beasts of prey and for defence against the archers and spearmen of the predatory tribes . . . Many of these euphorbia, that stood in circles round the clustered huts, were venerable patriarchs, quite five centuries old . . . "[1]

Stanley sailed from Katwe across Lake Edward, then known as Muta Nzige, "the killer of locusts" to Habibale, at the southern tip of Mweya

Peninsula. He could see nothing from there but a "formless void", an indication the dense smoke haze from the dry season country-wide burning was just as prevalent then as now.

Leaving Katwe, one of Stanley's party, Jephson, wrote " . . . everything was dried up and sere, and nothing in the shape of trees except euphorbias were to be seen, the whole plain had a peculiarly desolate and dead look."[2] Mweya Peninsula, where seventy-four years later I was to conduct the major part of my study, had eighty-one huts and was "rich in sheep and goats"; while Katwe, centred on the historically important Katwe salt lake sited just outside the present day Park, was estimated to hold two thousand inhabitants. Needless to say, with all this human presence there was no mention of game, except for Stanley's dubious claim that he saw a "great black leopard" leaving the lakeside.

About 1871, the Warasura, Waganda warrior hordes of Buganda's cruel King Mtesa, swept through the area leaving only one man unconquered in the onslaught. This was Kaiyura, chief of Mweya Peninsula. Kakuri, chief of Katwe, fled to the small islands in Katwe Bay, where he lived until his death in 1903. The raiders despoiled "immense herds" of Wasongora cattle, driving off all they were able. Stanley recorded signs of many cattle when he arrived, but the Warasura had driven them into hiding at his approach and the area appeared quiet and almost deserted.

He had passed nearby only eleven years previously, completing Livingstone's explorations by tracing the course of the Lualaba (Zaïre) River. Then, one of the former raiders recounted to him how, on their return journey "as we drove their cattle towards Gambaragara, the earth shook, springs of mud leaped up, and water in the plain was very bitter, and killed many Waganda; it left a white thing around its borders like salt."[3]

Stanley now dismissed this story " . . . nothing of all the horrors expected have we seen except perhaps a dreary monotony of level and uniformity of surface features, grass fallen into the sere through drought, and tufts of rigid euphorbia, so characteristic of poor soil."

Two years after Stanley's second visit, Frederick Lugard, later Lord Lugard, camped for the night on Mweya Peninsula, finding it deserted. Of the plain between Kichwamba and the Kazinga Channel he wrote: "The great plain spread out before us must have swarmed at one time with elephant and buffalo, for their tracks were everywhere; but the former had left and the latter were dead. Shukri bagged two waterbuck and I got an *nsunu* [Uganda kob] but game was very scarce."[4] Lugard, acting for the British East Africa Company, arrived there in July 1891, crossing the Kazinga Channel on the 15th. This was just after the great rinderpest plague had passed through, killing most of the buffalo. The King of Bunyoro, Kabarega, had overthrown the King of Toro, Kasagama, and Lugard's task was to subjugate Kabarega (he was eventually exiled to the Seychelles), and replace Kasagama as King.

"Marched for thirteen miles across the big lacustrine plain . . . Kagolo now informed me that it was the Unyoro custom to fight at night, and they would probably attack us tonight. So I had out a piquet (also a piquet of Waganda) which I visited at 1.30 am . . . Slept in my boots and clothes and had the Maxim laid on the probable point of attack . . . . Everything ready, and if we get five or ten minutes' warning we can make our camp like the mouth of Hell . . . No attack but I slept very light."

Things were a little quieter when I got there!

Lugard built a fort (Fort George) on the ridge between Lake George and the salt lake. "I look on this place as an Eldorado, to be secured at all costs, and I shall strongly recommend in my report that good boats be placed on this lake to collect ivory. It is a very healthy place – no swamp, a light, dry soil and rock, a constant breeze, as healthy a spot as there is in Africa, I should think."

The fort was staffed with Sudanese, from Emin Pasha's abandoned garrison farther north, who promptly plundered the locals, but "Lugard sited it well in the first instance, and to that it owed its safety when attacked by the Batetelas [rebel Manyema], mutineers from Baron Dhanis's column. These ferocious soldiers, well led and armed, attacked this isolated little outpost of the Empire again and again, with the utmost fury, but were beaten off each time. The Sudanese officer in charge showed us, with no little pride, the bullet marks on the walls, and the perforations in doors and shutters, and told us in graphic terms the whole story of the fight."[5]

Later the fort was abandoned, but its former position was still marked in 1967 by a plaque on the side of the road.

Stanley's treaties gave Great Britain control of Uganda, and the boundary with King Leopold's Congo was placed along the 30o meridian, passing through a village called Katunguru. This meant the whole of the area north of the Kazinga Channel formed part of the Belgian Congo. The Colonial Office then discovered a "mistake" had been made. The meridian was in the wrong place and should have run west of Katwe. The explorer Duke Adolphus Frederick of Mecklenberg was later to caustically describe this as "nothing more than a British trick", for the British had discovered the commercial importance of Katwe's salt lake. (The meridian actually lies 5.1 miles west of Katunguru and 25.6 miles *east* of Katwe).

After Lugard's fort was abandoned, in 1904 a party of Belgian officers established themselves at Katwe with an armed force and placed a guard on the salt lake in spite of the chief's (Kimbugwe) protests. No one was allowed to take salt from the lake except those in Belgian employ. But Kimbugwe, loyal to the British, kept a record of all the loads taken out, and awaited the arrival of a British officer. The Belgian party demanded submission of the locals and rumoured they were preparing to meet the British force.

One afternoon it was reported a British officer with a detachment of armed police was within a few miles. That night a lantern was seen moving along the Nyamgasani River – the next morning the Belgian camp was deserted.

In 1907, by mutual agreement the boundary was placed at the Lubilia River, to Britain's advantage.

An animal paradise.

The Queen Elizabeth National Park was gazetted in the area in April 1952, and contrary to Stanley's bleak impression, it was by then at any rate an idyllic place of tranquil lakes surrounded by hills and plains of rolling short grassland, sprinkled with stately candelabra euphorbia trees and clumps of thorny *Capparis* bush, which become a mass of delicate, snowy white, heavily scented flowers in February and March. To the eye of an ecologist the area had all the signs of being degraded by elephants, for only the euphorbias and the

Capparis remain after elephants have removed the more palatable trees and shrubs. But the accounts of Stanley and Lugard show the habitat had not really changed in appearance for the past hundred years. After these early visitors the area was ravaged by a great sleeping sickness epidemic, and those who did not succumb to this dread disease were moved out of the area by the Government for their own safety, leaving it to become an animal paradise.

"Huge hippopotamuses waddling to water"

I had first visited the park in 1956, to be entranced by the great panoramas of game: huge hippopotamuses waddling on land back to water in the early morning after their nightly inland feeding forays, herds of docile elephants blocked the road, and it was one of the rare places in Africa where buffalo stood around in the daytime gazing curiously at one and ruminating like herds of contented cows.

I had entertained no previous thoughts about the species I was to study, the waterbuck, a large, shaggy-looking animal, with long, elegantly ridged, forward-curving horns. But it was the quintessential territorial antelope, the bulls defending a patch of territory against all comers. Territoriality was a type of behaviour rapidly attracting a wider attention, but had yet to be popularized by the American playwright Robert Ardrey in his book *The Territorial Imperative*.

My main study area was the Mweya Peninsula where Kaiyura had been chief in 1889, an inverted triangle of land 1.7 square miles in extent jutting out into Lake Edward, connected to the mainland by a narrow ridge of land known by the tongue-twisting name of Kanyeseswa.

Strangely enough there were no crocodiles in the lakes – no one knows why the Nile crocodile, whose fossils have been found, disappeared from here in the geologically distant past. Yet in recent times, from the 1980s, people have reported a number of sightings around Lake Edward. What could have kept them away for 1.5 million years is one of Nature's great puzzles.

I was not long getting to know the waterbuck in this tranquil place, and had I wished could have established close contact with them. Within two weeks of starting my visits an inquisitive calf approached the Land Rover and I cautiously extended my hand through the window towards it. Advancing hesitantly, suddenly it plonked its moist, black patent-leather nose against the back of my hand in a clumsy bovine kiss, and jumped back with a surprised snort at the unpleasant smell. An old doe, grazing peacefully nearby, looked up, studied me for a few seconds, and then continued grazing. The calf walked away.

Observing waterbuck was a somewhat bucolic existence, especially when on rare days one had not only the impressive backdrop of the distant misty blue Mitumba Mountains rearing up in the Congo behind the silver sheet of Lake Edward, but also the awe-inspiring glacier-capped Rwenzoris looming above the Crater Highlands to the north. Covered as the rain-sodden slopes usually are in dense cloud, only on one or two days a year in April are the mighty peaks to be seen. Stanley walked right past them unaware of their existence and later refused to believe it.

I soon came to recognize the bucks from their size, colour, and horns. The hornless does were more difficult, although they also had their characteristics. Apart from their colour, which ranged from rufous to grey, some were long-legged, others were short. One or two had narrow faces with slanting eyes, which I dubbed 'the houris'. Many I gave names to, but I could not really be sure of most of them unless I marked them in some way. So a programme of darting was introduced, which brought an element of excitement into the study but had the disadvantage of destroying their trust in me.

Darting, or immobilization, at that time was a new technique. It consisted of immobilizing an animal by firing a kind of hypodermic syringe into it, subsequently shown so many times on television that almost every TV addict in Britain and America knew how to do it blindfold. In practice it is not so easy.

The anaesthetic was a powerful new experimental morphine drug, dramatically named M99, one thousand times more potent than morphine itself. A pharmacist concerned in its development placed a single crystal on his tongue and was out cold for forty-eight hours. But despite the fact the minutest trace will kill a man, an elephant requires four thousandths of a gram to anaesthetize it, and a waterbuck, weighing a tenth an elephant does, the same amount!

I shudder now to think of handling such a lethal drug, preparing darts in the laboratory at Mweya. I was well aware of the danger, but there was no antidote perfected. If anything went wrong I knew I had less than two minutes to say my prayers. And something did go wrong! But fortunately when it did I was using a different drug.

The morphine drug was not a success with waterbuck, serving to excite them because we were using too small a dose, not realizing they required as much as an elephant, and then we had to wrestle with them to get them down and rope them. This was difficult enough with four hundred pounds of struggling doe thrashing her legs armed with steel-tipped stiletto-like hooves. Clearly we could not wrestle with a five hundred pound buck, the equivalent of more than two angry Mike Tysons, wielding its needle-pointed horns like rapiers into the bargain. So we decided to fall back on a well-tried drug known as scoline.

Scoline is a paralyzing drug, a muscle relaxant widely used in human surgery. Its disadvantage is that it has no antidote, and an overdose means death by paralyzing the respiratory muscles. The weight of the animal therefore had to be estimated to within ten per cent; a mistake meant certain death. Despite accounts to the effect that it causes pain in humans, nothing was found to indicate this in the waterbuck and it worked smoothly. An animal's subsequent reactions depended upon the circumstances immediately prior to darting. If a suspicious animal had to be chased persistently beforehand in order to approach close enough to dart it, then it would be twice as wild after the event. But an old buck, which always took no notice of me, stood still and did not even flinch when the dart struck his rump with ninety pounds of crossbow pull behind it. He stood there unconcerned until he dropped on the spot and was afterwards none the worse for his experience, getting up and carrying on feeding as if nothing had happened, continuing to ignore my presence.

When an animal went down, with Iain the warden, and my Ugandan assistant, Omal, we would move in, blindfold the animal to calm it, measure it, fix a numbered tag and a coloured plastic ribbon in its ear, and then I would take an impression of its teeth in warmed plasticine. Later I would make a plaster cast of the impression to enable me to assess the animal's age from the amount of wear on its teeth.

Research on waterbuck, Iain steadies a recovering animal.

To try to improve the trajectory of the dart I experimented by replacing the wooden dart shaft with an aluminium one. The result was that, when I released the crossbow trigger, the shaft was pushed into the barrel of the dart and forced the drug out backwards – in a fine spray straight into my one open eye sighted down the crossbow. Fortunately I was not using the morphine drug and, unlike it, scoline must be injected into the bloodstream to exercise its paralyzing properties, so it had no effect on me.

But it was customary to add another drug, making a 'cocktail'. This was hyoscine, which was said to have a tranquillizing effect, but which also has the property of dilating the pupil of the eye. Well I had literally got an eyeful, and for the next forty-eight hours I went around with one pupil completely dilated, so that in the bright sunlight everything had a glittering, silvery edge to it. Then I realized why the waterbuck always hid for forty-eight hours after darting, not from fear but because they could not see properly, and I never used hyoscine again.

Sometimes an animal would recover before I was quite finished with it. On one occasion a large buck went down in a narrow gulley so that we were surrounded on three sides with steep cliffs, not the best of places if he turned around when he recovered, before we had time to clear out. And sure enough he did recover before I had finished, suddenly leaping up without warning. I and my assistants also tried to leap – up the almost vertical sides of the gulley. When I looked back I saw the buck had rushed straight forward and then up the side of the gulley in a flash, taking its sheer walls in his stride while we were still scrabbling ineffectually for footholds.

And the gentle-looking doe could be a fearsome creature when roused.

Early one morning I came across a doe with a newborn calf, the calf lying wet and immobile by her side. I stopped the Land Rover at a respectful distance lest she run off and abandon her offspring. Although I needed to tag the young one with a small marker in its ear, I wanted to be sure the maternal bond had developed before catching it so the mother would return to it. The mother cleaned her calf solicitously, carefully licking it all over, and after some twenty minutes the calf got to its feet unsteadily. The mother then stood up, and after a few unsuccessful attempts, accompanied by falling over, the calf found her teats and began to suckle. When the mother had cleaned up everything, removing all traces which might attract predators to the spot, and the calf had suckled once more and was now lying contentedly by her side, I thought it time to move in and tag it.

I began to edge the Land Rover closer. The doe, which had taken not the slightest notice of me until then, suddenly looked alarmed. She leapt to her feet, advanced to within some two feet of the vehicle and snorted menacingly with hair raised on end, making herself look a good foot taller and presenting such an aggressive aspect I thought it prudent to desist from getting out of the vehicle before her. She then turned and ran with the calf following behind stumblingly for about a hundred yards, when I managed to separate the two in a patch of bush. Seeing the calf standing suddenly bewildered, I jumped out of the Land Rover with Omal, and in a second we had seized the tiny calf and clipped a tag in its ear.

As the tagging pliers pierced the cartilage, the calf gave a little squeak of protest. Instantly the furious mother came charging back through the bushes at us. We leapt ignominiously into the Land Rover and I drove off, but the angry mother gave chase! Galloping behind, she kept lowering her head, trying to butt the tailboard. For a good seventy-five yards she kept this up through the bush, snorting her indignation, but I was careful to keep just beyond her reach lest she hurt herself in her fury. Attacked by a doe waterbuck? Nobody would ever believe it!

People sometimes ask why we subjected these innocent creatures to such indignities as darting and tagging. The reason was that virtually nothing was known of their life histories, and yet it was realized with the growing pressures on land, national parks and game reserves would eventually have to be managed. To manage successfully would require sound knowledge of the life histories of the animals, and we were trying to provide that basis for any possible future use.

Darting waterbuck certainly livened up the research routine, but the real excitement came with darting elephants. It was while a Cambridge veterinarian was at Mweya looking for an elephant on heat that a French TV crew obtained permission to film the immobilization of an elephant, and it was agreed to provide a demonstration. There was a well-known cow elephant called 'Handlebar' of which the left tusk grew around in a half-circle back into the side of her face. This would be a good opportunity to provide a little surgery, removing the tusk to put her out of her misery.

I was an apprentice darter at the time and Roger the vet did the darting while I accompanied him. Handlebar was soon found in some scattered bush feeding peacefully with her group, and Roger, shooting from the open hatch in the top of a Station Wagon Land Rover, sent a dart into her without trouble. She took not the slightest notice, and five minutes later, after some customary swaying, collapsed on the ground.

The TV team were in position nearby but unfortunately the herd was all around the fallen animal, unaware and unconcerned of the reason for her recumbency. Iain was at the wheel, and now drove straight at the herd to chase them off, while we all banged on the sides and shouted. The herd took fright and charged off through the bushes with the accompaniment of much trumpeting and shrieking. But a young calf boldly stayed behind – refusing to abandon what was clearly its mother. Frightened by the Land Rover, it squealed in alarm and the herd wheeled around instantly as if under command, to come crashing back towards us, shoulder to shoulder in an awe-inspiring giant phalanx of fury. Then ensued a hair-raising sequence of chase and be chased among the bushes as we drove straight at the charging herd, crashing through the undergrowth like the elephants themselves, making as much noise as we could.

The herd broke and fled in choking clouds of dust, trumpeting and screaming, only to repeatedly wheel around and come back again as still the obstinate calf would not leave its mother.

Back and forth we crashed through the bushes, now in a dense cloud of dust stirred up by the elephants' feet as they charged about on all sides of us. Once, twice, the calf ran off with them a short way, only to turn and run back to its mother again.

My tongue dry in my mouth, I began to have doubts about the advisability of continuing this exercise, TV team or no TV team, as the elephants became angrier and angrier and more and more determined, trumpeting their fury and pounding the ground with their huge feet, smashing the bushes to smithereens in their wake. They could smash the Land Rover to pieces if one would only pluck up courage enough.

Surely next time that big angry cow, the epitome of fury, ears outstretched like sails, screaming defiance at us, would not stop in her furious charge at the fragile vehicle? Time and again in this frightening manner, huge elephants charged right up to us, only to funk it at the last moment.

Suddenly, amid all this pandemonium, the calf's nerve gave way and it finally fled to the herd, which waited no longer but beat a hasty retreat into the distance.

Somewhat breathless we disgorged from the Land Rover at the motionless cow. There was work to be done and Roger was soon plying a hacksaw through the base of the tusk, sweating in the heat, for ivory is one of the hardest of substances to cut. In the midst of this exertion a TV man thrust a microphone in Roger's face and asked if the operation was dangerous. The question was repeated several times with the camera at a different angle and Roger began to get somewhat exasperated, absorbed in his task and uncomprehending as to why they kept on asking the same question.

But soon the tusk was removed, the wound caused by the tusk pressing into the skin, treated; and a marking collar placed around the elephant's neck. Roger injected the antidote, and we stood back, well pleased with our exertions. The TV team had certainly got value for money.

Suddenly I noticed the lions. At about sixty yards distance three lionesses were stalking towards the inert elephant in the tense, characteristic manner of hunting lions. They gave us humans not so much as a glance. Hastily we scrambled back into the Land Rover and drove straight at them, shouting and banging as we had done with the elephants. But this was a different kettle of fish. Lions were used to noisy tourists, and as far as they were concerned we did not exist, so intent were they upon their prey.

The leading lioness continued her determined stalk, eyes fixed unwaveringly on the motionless elephant. The distance between her and her prey had narrowed to about twenty yards.

"I'll try a thunderflash," said Iain.

Now a thunderflash, as any one who has been an army cadet knows, is a kind of outsize firework used by the army to simulate grenades. If it goes off in your grasp, it will blow your hand off.

Iain threw one down in the path of the lioness and it lay on the ground fizzing loudly. The lioness thought it looked interesting making that funny noise, so she approached and sniffed it as it fizzed away. There was a sudden silence in the Land Rover as we all held our breath, perhaps it hadn't been such a good idea after all, we didn't want an injured lioness on our hands. She thrust her nose right on the thunderflash just as it exploded with a resounding bang!

I swear that lioness didn't even blink!

But a fizzy thing suddenly disappearing in a bang was beyond the lioness's ken, so she simply behaved as if nothing whatsoever had happened and continued her careful stalk towards the elephant.

From Dark Heart To Kalahari

Now all three lionesses were about ten yards away, watching intently. There was nothing more we could do except sit back and watch. Clearly thunderflashes were of no use.

The antidote should take only about two minutes to show its effect, but this was taking much longer. We had given up all hope of the elephant cow not being attacked when suddenly she gave a slight twitch. Instantly the lions lost interest. The intent watchfulness in their eyes vanished like the proverbial scales falling from them, and they looked from side to side with a bored air. The elephant cow started to move in earnest and rocked herself in the manner lying elephants do when trying to stand. Then she was on her feet and walking off a little unsteadily, completely oblivious to all that had happened.

We soon saw her again in the Park, now sporting her marking collar. But the film? Well when, after a long delay, I eventually saw a copy of the final version as shown on television, there was nothing of the mad elephant chase, nor of the lion stalk and the thunderflash exploding. There was only Roger replying exasperatedly in stilted French:

"Non monsieur, ce n'est pas dangereux."

* * *

Not long after this we tried marking another elephant cow. We selected one well out in the open and once more darted it without trouble. She soon went down on her side and the rest of the herd continued on its way unaware. But, horror of horrors, once more a calf remained behind, a bigger one this time, getting on for two years old. Probably thinking its mother had taken an impromptu nap it remained quietly by her side, showing no alarm until we approached in the Land Rover. We had waited until the herd was well away, too far for the calf to call for assistance, but it was also too far for the calf to run after it.

As we came close the calf vainly tried to wake its mother, kicking her with its forefoot and butting with its head. This being to no avail, it gallantly stood its ground, threatening us with ears out, but keeping the mountainous body of its mother between it and us.

I was given the task of painting one of the cow's ears white. We were a bit unsophisticated in those days and had no more collars available. Paint pot in one hand, and brush in the other, I approached the elephant and began to apply paint vigorously to her left ear. At first the calf backed away at my approach, but then decided it wasn't going to have that, and, ears out, charged around from behind its maternal refuge.

An incongruous chase then ensued as I took to my heels running round and round the recumbent elephant, paint pot in hand, slopping paint all over the place and occasionally stopping to slosh a few quick brush strokes on the ear before the calf got too close for comfort.

The bold elephant calf defending its anaesthetized mother.

What the hell were the others doing? Where had they all gone? The elephant calf could do a serious injury if it caught up with me. It's no joke to be battered about by six hundred pounds of angry baby elephant, even if it is only two years old. Out of the corner of my eye I noticed the others had all returned to the Land Rover and occupied with other matters no-one had noticed my plight. When it looked as if the furious calf was almost about to get me I shouted for assistance, and with a battery of humans menacingly confronting the calf I was able to finish painting its mother's ear without further disturbance.

And then it happened again! I looked up from my handiwork and there, draped over a termite mound on the skyline, were the three selfsame lionesses expressing intense interest in the proceedings. Antidote was injected and we retreated to the Land Rover, ready to try and defend calf and mother once more. But our anxiety this time was short-lived, for the cow responded to the antidote, got up and ambled off, her no doubt greatly relieved but indignant calf, hurrying along beside. What a tale it must have tried to tell her!

It was some time before I saw this particular cow again, only to find my painting efforts had been in vain. The first thing she had done had been to cover every inch of the white paint with a good layer of mud, and now you could only tell the ear was different at very close examination.

* * *

Darting hippos was to prove even more exciting than darting elephants. Chris, one of the researchers, was studying the feeding habits of hippos and had a half-grown tame hippo kept in its own swimming pool, which he used to let out in the evenings and follow around, cheek by massive jowl as it grazed, noting down every species of grass that vanished into its cavernous maw.

This was a very friendly hippo and someone had discovered,

goodness knows how, that if you forced your fingers under its thick horny upper lip when it was resting its head on the side of its swimming pool with that dreamy look on its face so characteristic of hippos, then it would open its mouth as only a hippo can, and hold it open in full yawn while you obligingly scratched its palate. When it tired of this it would very slowly close its mouth giving you time to remove your hand without losing it.

To me this strange performance is one of the puzzles of evolution. What possible selection force could produce an erotic zone in the palate of a hippopotamus? Undoubted pleasure that it was, it was something the average hippo was never likely to experience.

It had been a long time before Chris had started his study because he was afraid that when he let the hippo out it would make a bolt for it, straight back into its watery habitat. In fact it just grazed for two or three hours and then ambled contentedly back to its pen and its concrete swimming pool. Yet all the time it was getting thinner and thinner, until one evening, when closely shepherded by Chris with his pencil and notebook, it simply lay down on its side with a grunt and expired. As Roger had now returned to Cambridge I was chief darter, and asked to supply another hippo.

It was more exciting than darting elephants because it had to be done at night when the hippos were well inland grazing, and was only possible on bright, moonlit nights. It was exhilarating standing up in the Land Rover looking out of the hatch in the cool, night air. Dark, menacing shapes abounded everywhere, only to turn out to be nothing more than harmless clumps of *Capparis* bush. When any hippos were spotted their usual reaction was to run for it, and a hippo can move fast, so it was futile to try and chase them.

Our first night's work was unsuccessful. The next night we tried again, and it was some time before I spotted a suitably-sized calf trotting along behind its mother, a huge, fat beast which looked the size of a double-decker bus in the moonlight, and weighed about one-and-a-half tons. Dick, Director of the research institute, was at the wheel, and having got the pair in his sights carefully pursued them. In and out of the silvery clumps of *Capparis* they weaved at a sharp trot, the mother not wishing to keep too quick a pace for her calf. Then suddenly they had eluded us, or at least the driver, for Dick pulled up in the darkness, a cloud having obscured the moon. Looking around from my vantage point in the hatch I spotted the couple about sixty yards away to our right, standing motionless.

As I watched the huge cow hippo suddenly started to charge towards us, a dim hulk, black and threatening in the dark. But there was enough moonlight for me to be able to see she was coming at us at a good clip. I swallowed, and inclining my head through the hatch tried to sound nonchalant:

"She's coming," I said.

There was no answer. Nobody moved a muscle.

"Well, they're a pretty cool lot," I thought, "I mustn't show that I'm scared stiff!"

I stood watching nervously, my hands sweaty on the crossbow, as the huge menacing black hulk of the hippo bore down upon us, bent upon certain destruction like Captain Ahab's monstrous revengeful leviathan.[6]

"I suppose they think it's just a mock charge. She won't follow through, she'll just swerve aside at the last moment, she'll . . . " I thought nervously to myself.

It certainly didn't *look* as if she was going to either stop or swerve aside. Now she was only a few yards away, huge jaws menacingly agape, the moonlight glinting on her massive curved white teeth, hurtling straight at us at a good thirty miles an hour.

Once more I inclined my head through the hatch and tried to sound unconcerned:

"She's on us," I said, in a funny weak, quavery sort of voice.

No one answered, cool as cucumbers!

A fraction of a second later there was an almighty crash as the offside of the Land Rover rose about two feet into the air.

The angry hippo had rammed the front offside with her chin, and then her huge, open jaws, had slid up and across the driver's window, leaving two muddy streaks across it as if she had affectionately kissed it with mud lipstick. Dick had turned his head at the impact to find his face no more than three inches from the hippo's monstrous open jaws, its great white canine teeth gleaming in the moonlight, separated from his face only by the window-glass.

There have been cases in the Park of hippos biting cyclists completely in two, bicycle and all.

We went home. The normally imperturbable Dick was still as white as a sheet when we got out of the Land Rover. It transpired that his and the others immobility had not been due to sangfroid; they, unable to see the hippo, thought I was simply commenting on its activities in the distance.

* * *

It was some three months later before we had an opportunity to try again. Dick prudently decided to give it a rest and Iain took over. Finding hippos seemed to get harder and harder, but at last we were in pursuit of a herd legging it for the water. There was a calf with the herd, which looked a bit small for our purposes, but patience was running thin. As we followed I suddenly saw that the calf had run into a bush and was lying completely doggo.

I called to Iain to stop and reverse back to the bush. The calf lay there, flat against the ground, hoping to avoid detection.

Iain was discussing with Chris whether it was big enough. They seemed undecided and so to cut short further discussion I loosed a dart into it.

"He's darted it!" exclaimed Iain.

"Of course I've darted it!" I replied. I wasn't going to pass up this chance with the hippo lying there waiting to be darted.

It was small and I didn't want to lose it, so as soon as it looked a bit groggy we piled out and I said I wanted to give it the antidote as soon as we had a rope on it.

Phil, the Park engineer, was with us, and he put a rope around its neck and declared it was small enough to hold. I injected the antidote into its rump and within a couple of minutes it had recovered, as was evinced by it suddenly charging off into the night dragging Phil behind it, desperately hanging on to the rope. Seeing Phil rapidly vanishing into the darkness with what looked like an outsize dog on the end of a lead, the rest of us legged it after him to help.

In spite of the hippo's small size I soon found I had made an error of judgement in giving it the antidote quite so soon. Under the influence of M99 the hippo exudes a thick, slimy, mucus-like sweat. In addition it has no angles. Its body is all rounded so you cannot get a rope to hold on to it. Handling a greased pig has nothing on trying to truss up a sweating hippo – even a small one weighing a mere three to four hundred pounds.

It was Phil who devised some knots that eventually secured it, and we bore it back in triumph to release in its private swimming pool.

* * *

Not long after I myself had arrived at Mweya a new warden had taken over. This was Iain, a young man in his first appointment as park warden, accompanied by his attractive blonde wife, Sarah. Brought up with a wild life background, Sarah had an inordinate love of animals and promptly reared an abandoned buffalo calf, which she christened 'Little Moo'. As can be imagined, this quickly became a damned nuisance, reaching a weight of several hundred pounds within a matter of months.

Like the hippo, this creature also had a strange erotic zone. If you brushed its spine with a stiff broom, it would become absolutely rigid, its eyes would glaze, and it would topple over on to the ground, all four legs held out stiffly!

Pigs, including warthogs, will react in a similar manner if you scratch their sides, but then they huddle close together, so such a sensation could be seen to have some purpose. Not so an erotic zone on a buffalo's back.

A warthog was the next pet Sarah reared, and like the buffalo before it, it also soon became a damned nuisance. Fed on nothing but the richest of foods, amongst which chicken featured prominently, it also grew apace. Following Sarah everywhere she went, if a door was closed in its face it would simply squeal at the top of its voice until the door was opened. One of its favourite pastimes was to remove the stuffing from cushions. But despite these shortcomings, Sarah would hear nothing against her pet.

* * *

One day we had a Royal Visit. Her Royal Highness Princess Margaret and Lord Snowdon came to spend part of their honeymoon at Mweya. As the date of their arrival drew near and 'royal fever' mounted, old-timers recalled the last royal visit, when the Queen Mother had officially opened the Park in 1952. Favourite among the stories was that of the cantankerous old recluse who lived in a tumbledown shack high up in the Rwenzori foothills. He had held a position of note in his younger days and the powers that be decided he should be among those presented to the Queen Mother. Somebody was detailed to go and size him up for a new suit for it was guessed he had no suitable attire for the occasion. Neither would he be persuaded to buy one, nor permit himself to be measured. The only thing was to present him with one and hope he would then agree to wear it to meet the Queen Mother.

When the day came the officials were on tenterhooks. Would he turn up? And if he did, would he be wearing the new suit?

He did turn up. And not only that, he was wearing the smart new, navy blue pinstripe suit. With the trousers rolled up to his calves, no socks and a pair of dirty gym shoes that had seen better days!

On the present occasion it was arranged by Iain the researchers should meet the royal couple when they arrived and we duly held ourselves in readiness in our ordinary workaday dress, but with no appearance of eccentricity.

The royal couple arrived early in order to avoid presentations such as had been arranged, but Iain was dogged and persisted with effecting them.

Her Royal Highness and Lord Snowdon stood side by side on the verandah of their specially-constructed honeymoon bungalow as we were paraded somewhat self-consciously before them. HRH stared stonily ahead, drawing on a cigarette. Lord Snowdon stared dreamily into the distance of Lake Edward. Neither spoke nor deigned to look at us as we stood in line faces upturned like supplicants, staring up at them.

We began to shuffle our feet. After a long silence had passed, Phil the engineer decided it was time somebody said something. He grinned chummily at Lord Snowdon:

"S'pose you'll be taking lots of photographs?" he queried in a matey tone of voice.

Awakened from his contemplation of the far distance, Lord Snowdon's eyebrows crawled in slow motion up his forehead like two furry caterpillars arching themselves. His eyes slightly changed their angle of perception to where, looking downwards guided by his nose, they encountered Phil's matey grin. A bemused expression appeared over his face.

"Yeees, I suppose I might," he drawled.

And that was all they did say.

We shuffled our feet in embarrassment, and gradually edged ourselves away in a disordered shambles, which would have caused a sergeant major to have a fit.

After the royal couple had rested they decided to go on a game drive. It had always been the custom in the Park, in order to provide good viewing and stop tourists from driving off the tracks, to shoot a buffalo from time to time and drag it near to a track for the lions to feed on. So accustomed had the lions become to this practice that it was necessary only to fire a gun into the air and wait awhile for a pride to come looking for its dinner.

There was always the exception.

In order that the royal visitors would not be disappointed Iain had duly shot a buffalo and dragged it to a suitable vantage point the day before. No lions appeared. The next morning there were still no lions to be seen.

Informed that the royal couple would go for their drive after lunch, Iain asked us all to search the Park and let him know where the lions were. We knew the area pretty thoroughly and scattered in all directions in our search, visiting all the likely lion spots. They were still nowhere to be seen.

Oh well, that was the luck of the game. Iain informed Her Royal Highness the lions could not be found, but she dismissed it as nothing to worry about.

Iain drove the royal couple out, past the dead buffalo. A pride of lions with several small cubs was tucking into it hungrily! I am sure Her Highness must have regarded Iain's announcement that the lions could not be found as showmanship! Later the Deputy Permanent Secretary to the Prime Minister's Office, who accompanied the tour, reported: "A 'lion kill' had been conveniently prepared."[7] Well almost not quite!

When the party came upon a family of warthogs running across the ground, tails erect in the air, the Princess jumped up and down in her seat with excitement, "Chase them! Chase them!" she cried.

I somehow think Iain would never have lasted long in Elizabethan times without losing his head.

He turned and looked at Her Highness:

"But it's a National Park," he protested.

"I don't care! I don't care! Chase them!" she cried.

Iain thought better of it than to question the Royal Command a second time and so gave chase, much to the delight of the Princess.

* * *

While all this was going on, I was driving some of the royal entourage around in another vehicle. We came upon one of the huge old bull buffaloes standing blocking the middle of the road. I drew up to within a few feet of him. He turned his head and glowered balefully at us. Then he calmly began to urinate, splashing a generous puddle into the middle of the road. Having thus expressed his contempt of us, he finished off with a little wriggle of his pizzle.

"That's one for Lord Snowdon," a voice behind me in the royal entourage remarked.

With a toss of its head the buffalo ambled off disdainfully into the bush.

* * *

In the evening Iain and Sarah were invited to dine with the royal couple at the hotel lodge. Poor Sarah was so nervous we had to fill her up with whisky first, but no doubt her royal hostess would have approved of the measure. They reported their hostess was charming at dinner, but it seems that, whether at the Princess's request or not we do not know, a young interfering royal aide had changed the seating arrangements nearly precipitating a diplomatic incident, a Ugandan government minister being highly offended at losing his place at table next to the Princess.

* * *

More darting adventures were to follow when in July 1965 I received a radio message requesting me to fly to the extreme north-west of Uganda to dart a rare white rhinoceros which had been found with a wire snare around one of its forelegs. There were only sixty or so of this species left in Uganda, in a remote area of woodland across the Nile known as Ajai's Island. Since it was a cow, and believed to be pregnant, it was important to try to save her. At that time little was known of the drug dosages for rhinos, and even a white rhino's weight I could only hazard a guess at, but I agreed to have a try at saving the animal.

A Uganda Police light aircraft flew in and picked me up to take me to a remote airstrip in the north, where Robin the Game Warden was waiting for me.

Robin was a person with a death wish. A hero in the Korean War, he had lead outrageous assaults on enemy positions under heavy fire. Later he was employed on the early schemes to reduce the numbers of hippo in the Queen Elizabeth Park. This comprised shooting out groups of bull hippos inhabiting inland wallows or ponds. Just to put zest into the exercise, Robin's method was to wade out into the wallows and induce the hippos to charge him. A hippo charges through the water at an amazing speed in a great roar of foam, huge mouth agape, a sight frightening enough to cause the stoutest of hearts to quail. But Robin stood his ground and calmly shot them as if he were on a clay pigeon shoot.

"But aren't you scared? Don't you want to turn and run when they charge you?" someone asked.

"Of course," was Robin's laconic reply, "but how the hell can you when you're stuck in mud up to your knees?"

Now he had nothing quite as exciting to do and so had a reputation for seldom being sober. But he was sober enough when I arrived, and I was impressed with his concern for the white rhinos. There was still a fairly long trip ahead in his battered old Land Rover, and over the Nile by ferry boat, where a wily Ugandan incongruously tried to entice passengers to part with their wealth with the three-card trick.

The next day we went on foot into the area and met a game guard who had been keeping watch on the animal. She was still there, not far away, now hardly moving because of the snare that had cut deep into her right foreleg. Left alone gangrene would set in and she would soon weaken and die.

I prepared a dart with M99 and loaded the crossbow. Robin said I should go forward with the game guard who would keep me covered with his rifle. The white rhino is said to be a relatively docile creature, unlike the cantankerous black rhino, which more often than not charges first and thinks afterwards, if it thinks at all. But under circumstances like these who knew what the animal might do, suffering as it was the agonies of a snare biting into its leg.

The game guard stalked carefully through the woodland before me, and we had not gone far when he pointed ahead. There, in the shadows of the bush, was an enormous brown backside. I had not realized white rhinos were so huge (and they are, of course, brown not white); it was more like an elephant than a rhino. Fortunately it was facing directly away from us, so I approached a little closer to make sure of hitting the target in the right spot. I decided to sit cross-legged, rather than risk a standing shot.

Slowly I began to sink down. A dry leaf crackled slightly under my leg as I positioned myself on the ground.

The rhino charged off as if it had been shot. It certainly wasn't taking any chances.

We took up the trail again. Obviously I would have to be absolutely silent if I were to get a shot at her. Stalking, and trying not to rustle a single dry leaf when the ground is covered with them, is a fatiguing business. And it was hot work too, but at least she couldn't go far in her lame condition.

Yes, there she was. The game guard indicated her again. Still facing directly away from us. It would have been much more difficult if she had turned towards us to see whether she was being followed.

I repeated the process of sinking down, and this time achieved it noiselessly. The huge bulk remained motionless in front of me as I took careful aim.

Thwack! The dart went into her rump exactly where I wanted it to, and again she charged off.

We called up Robin and I decided to give her about five minutes. It was all guesswork and I was besieged with doubts. Was the dosage enough for such a huge beast? I had estimated one-and-a-half tons, she looked much more. Would she go down?

I waited in a fever of impatience for the five minutes to pass and then signalled the advance. Once more we stalked forward trying not to make a sound, but we need not have worried – she was already down and on her side. Nevertheless I approached cautiously and clapped my hands, for darted animals have a nasty habit of suddenly mustering all of their resources and leaping up when you think they are out cold. Not so this one. She lay there oblivious.

We quickly had the snare cut free from the bone and cleaned the ugly wound, covered it with penicillin grease and powder, and then bandaged it. Not that the bandage would last for long, but it might give the wound a head start in healing and I had no antibiotic injections that I could give her.

The job was soon accomplished and I was ready to give the antidote. That done I waited in vain for it to take effect. As with other species it should take about two minutes, but the peacefully sleeping rhino, breathing a little rapidly, showed no sign of waking up.

Robin banged a tin can near her ear. We sloshed cold water over her head. She twitched her ears and kept her tail tightly curled up like a pig's, but that was all.

I administered more antidote, but all it elicited was more ear-twitching. I couldn't give any more after that because it could have reversed the process and acted like the drug itself.

Rolling the anaesthetized white rhinoceros onto its brisket.

Things began to look gloomy. I must have greatly overdosed her in her weakened state. She had been reported as hardly moving and had probably eaten almost nothing for the past few days. I was aware a number of deaths had occurred with darted black rhinos in Kenya caused by leaving them lying for too long on their sides, their great weight paralyzing the shoulder nerve so they were unable to stand again. The white rhino is much heavier than the black and I was already worried about the length of time she had been on her side.

Robin had about twenty workers standing by so I had them build a heap of brushwood alongside the rhino. We then rolled her against it so she was lying on her brisket, propped against the pile of brushwood. But she only had to start to struggle and she would roll over again. She showed no signs of doing so, continuing to lie there breathing stertorously.

We waited until dark. There was nothing further I could do except ask Robin to post a guard nearby to chase off any hyaenas that might come around.

In some gloom we went off to the nearby cabin. After a brief meal I went to bed, nagged with doubts about the rhino.

Robin and I were up sharp at dawn and went off before breakfast to see what had happened. As we approached the spot some vultures flopped up lazily from the treetops. Robin looked at me:

"It looks as if we've been unlucky," he said.

I nodded dumbly, sadly disappointed at my failure.

We came up to the guard. Robin spoke to him. His face brightened:

"She's fine," he said, "she got up not long ago and wandered off feeding."

We pressed forward, and sure enough there was the great hulk in the distance, hungrily munching grass much to the chagrin of the vultures, which had been attracted hopefully to the trampled ground and her motionless form.

I wanted to cry from pleasure and relief. It was all I could do to blink back the tears. It was the first time such a thing had been achieved.

Three months later she had a calf.

But all was in vain. All of the white rhinos in northern Uganda have since been wiped out by poachers, and now only less than a couple of dozen of this rare animal maintain a tenuous existence in Northen Zaïre.

* * *

After some months at Mweya, Iain the warden was posted to the Kidepo National Park in the extreme north-east corner of Uganda on the border with the Sudan. He had been there with Sarah about six months when I visited them for Christmas.

Kidepo was entirely different from the Queen Elizabeth Park, for it was an almost waterless, desert-like country, home of the picturesque Karamojong who still scorned the use of clothing. Just across the border in the Sudan were the fierce Didinga who sported special man-killing spears with small stabbing heads, and carried little rectangular shields used for parrying spear thrusts in hand-to-hand fighting. Their favourite pastime was to come over the border, cross the Park's dusty 30 miles, and raid the Karamojong's cattle. Anyone who got in the way was killed. The Karamojong couldn't do much about it because the Uganda Government wouldn't let them carry spears any longer, and the police didn't fancy doing anything about it either. So Government created a no man's land – the Kidepo National Park – and left it to the park guards to do something. Which they did courageously.

Now what could be better entertainment for a Christmas morning than to steal a couple of hundred cattle and blood a few spears? And that was precisely what the Didinga did on Christmas morning 1966.

We were looking forward to a lazy day when the report came in. Immediately Iain got together a patrol and sent it off in the direction the raiders had taken across the Park. He then took off in his four-seater Cessna light aircraft to look for them. Sarah went with him, and A., a friend who with his wife was also spending Christmas there. I declined to go aloft as I find flying in light aircraft does not agree with my stomach if the weather is hot and turbulent.

Half an hour later Iain returned. The raiding party located, he wanted to send some instructions to the ground patrol by means of a vehicle. This done he was ready to take off again. Sarah was full of excitement at the chase, but offered her seat to me. I demurred but it sounded ungracious, so reluctantly I took her place and strapped myself in the rear right hand seat behind A.

A quick taxi down the bush airstrip and we were in the air. Soon we were over the raiders hustling the cattle flat out towards the north, but still with a long day's journey to reach the border. In order to slow them down and give the ground patrol a chance to catch up, Iain decided to try diving at the herd to make it scatter and put the aircraft into a steep descent.

The running figures of the raiders checked their headlong flight and stood looking up at the aircraft. Diving down towards them with the ground rushing towards us at two hundred miles an hour I was beginning to feel for my stomach and wish my feet were on the ground, when there was a loud CRACK! A. gave a little groan and Iain looked at him sharply, pulling the plane out of the dive.

Seated behind as I was I thought something had given way in the plane with the force of the descent, but as we levelled out I saw with consternation a rapidly widening pool of blood at my feet. Something was seriously wrong with A.

"We had better get back to camp quickly," I said to Iain, in as calm a voice as I could muster.

But Iain had seen what had happened and was already turning the aircraft towards camp. I have heard it said it is impossible to hit an aircraft in flight with an ordinary firearm, but one of the raiders had succeeded in doing just that; simply pointing his rifle at the aircraft and pulling the trigger. And this with probably nothing more than a battered old First World War Lee Enfield .303; for this was in the days before such raiders had the sophisticated military automatic assault rifles that are now commonplace.

The bullet had entered the fuselage on the right hand side, passing into the cockpit and hitting A. on the point of the jaw to lodge under his left ear, blowing his left lower jaw through the side of his face. Had the bullet been three inches to the right it would have hit the engine, and the aircraft may never have come out of that dive.

In his haste Iain made a rather bumpy landing, which A. later stated was the most painful part of the whole experience. I stayed in the aircraft with him while Iain dashed off to find the First Aid box and a lady doctor who we knew was holidaying at the park campsite.

I waited anxiously with the smell of blood in my nostrils, the temperature in the cockpit rising unbearably in the hot sun.

What could be keeping Iain?

It turned out he couldn't find the key of the First Aid box and the doctor was out on a game drive. Meanwhile A. was lying quietly, slowly bleeding to death. Never losing consciousness, he later confided it felt as if the whole top of his head had been blown off. In hindsight I should have tried to stem the flow of blood, but all the time I was expecting the First Aid box to be brought.

Eventually the doctor was found and the First Aid box forced open. She stitched the wound, stemming the flow of blood, and said he must get proper attention without delay. Iain made ready to fly him to Kampala, about three hours' flight away. The doctor would go with him. Moments later they were in the air, and with Sarah and A.'s wife I was left to sit around glum and silent, Christmas lunch forgotten.

Halfway to Kampala the doctor said A.'s pulse was fading and they must do something immediately. A. tried to protest he could make it to Kampala, but Iain decided to turn off to the mission hospital at Moroto, headquarters of the Karamoja District.

The airstrip at which they landed was some distance from the small township and the only vehicle there was a Land Rover used as a fire engine. A furious altercation ensued between Iain and the driver who refused to allow the vehicle to be misused for carrying a dying man to hospital. Resistance was eventually overcome and off they drove into town. It was now four in the afternoon and as they drove up to the hospital, which for some sinister reason was staffed entirely by Russians, the sister was just locking the door prior to going home. The doctor had already left but she said she would get him without delay. Soon he had given A. a blood transfusion and a message had been radioed to Kampala for a Police aircraft to come and collect him.

It was dark when the aircraft landed using only the lights of the fire engine Land Rover to guide it, and moments later A. was whisked away to Kampala, still fully conscious. Later, after he had grown a beard, it was impossible to tell what had happened to him.

But it had been a close run thing.

An American tourist proclaimed loudly in the hotel bar at Mweya it had taken him ten years to pluck up enough courage to holiday in Africa. He had now been there for ten hours and no one had thrown a spear at him. Worse things could happen!

* * *

The Murchison Falls National Park was Uganda's second national park, also gazetted in 1952. It lay in the north of Uganda where the rapacious chief KabaRega roamed in Stanley's time. An area of almost 1,500 square miles it straddles the Victoria Nile of which the forested banks with their huge, somnolent crocodiles, gave it a far more savage look than Lake Edward's placid shores.

In March 1864, Samuel Baker with his wife Florence, were exploring Lake Albert searching for the source of the Nile when he noted that the Nile cabbage were gently eddying in one direction " . . . as

I lay upon my back, on my angarep, I amused myself before I woke my men by watching the fog slowly lifting from the river. While thus employed I was struck by the fact, that the little green water-plants, like floating cabbages… were certainly, although very slowly, moving to the west. I immediately jumped up, and watched them most attentively; there was no doubt about it; they were travelling towards the Albert lake. We were now about eighteen miles in a direct line from Magungo, and there was a current in the river, which, however slight, was nevertheless perceptible."[8]

Baker followed the direction the Nile cabbage seemed to be coming from, and so discovered the Victoria Nile and its mighty falls where the Nile plunges an awesome 141 feet through a narrow cleft in the rocks. He named them Murchison Falls after the President of the Royal Geographic Society. The huge crocodiles that waited beneath in hundreds for stunned victims swept over in the torrent were still there when I first saw the Falls, but they are largely gone today, victim of the poacher's greed, although General Amin is said to have provided plenty of food for them in the shape of prisoners thrown over the Falls.

In 1967 there were 14,500 elephants in the Park, so many in fact they had destroyed vast areas of woodland by ring-barking the trees, creating stark skeleton forests of dead trees reminiscent of a shell-blasted First World War landscape in Flanders. In 1991 only 530 elephants remained. There is no longer any need for the signs which proclaimed "Elephants Have Right of Way".

It was in 1967 I paid a visit to the young warden and his wife known respectively as 'Ant' and 'Flea', at Chobe, in the east of the park. On the second day of my visit General Amin, yet to become the notorious tyrant of Uganda, paid the area a call.

He flew into the Park airstrip in his private twin-engine aircraft piloted by an Israeli, having first been game spotting from the air. At the airstrip he was met by some of his soldiers in a Land Rover. They drove off to where he had spotted the game and came back in the evening with the vehicle piled high with carcases of Uganda kob shot in the adjacent game reserve. Satisfied with his exercise, Amin went off to the hotel bar to get drunk.

Later I went into the bar with Ant for a drink, to see by chance Amin, who by the expedient of leaning against it, appeared to be trying to prevent a wall from falling over. He looked at us unseeingly with glazed, bloodshot eyes. I didn't even realise who it was as I passed him.

Ant and I were in the middle of a drink when Amin's personal Israeli pilot approached Ant and said he would need help in taking off, for probably about ten o'clock Amin would suddenly order the return to Kampala. The pilot did not like the idea of taking off from an unlighted bush airstrip in the dark, but he assured us he could do it if necessary. Ant agreed to help and rounded up all the hurricane lamps he could find – it didn't amount to many – and these we placed along the sides of the airstrip for as far as we could. But their feeble, flickering lights were hardly visible, so at the pilot's request it was agreed Ant and I would drive down the airstrip in our Land Rovers as fast as we could in front of the aircraft as it was taking off. This would illuminate the pilot's path and also drive off any animals that might be in the way.

True to form, at about ten o'clock the now very drunk Amin ordered the return to Kampala. Ant and I lined up our Land Rovers side by side in front of the aircraft. The aircraft's engines were started up. We gave it a few minutes to warm up and then began to race neck and neck down the airstrip.

Well, race was hardly the right word to use, for a Land Rover is a very sluggish vehicle. It has no acceleration. A twin-engine aircraft, on the other hand, has considerable acceleration, so the contest was rather uneven.

We were less than halfway down the strip and had reached about sixty miles an hour or less, when there was suddenly a deafening roar.

Ant and I heard it simultaneously and yanked our vehicles left and right off the strip, as the aircraft just skimmed over us and vanished into the darkness.

We both needed another drink after that!

* * *

Just before my time came to leave Mweya I decided to pay a quick visit to Zaïre, the former Belgian Congo, since we were right on the border of the famous Albert National Park. Things had been quiet there now for a while after its former long years of murderous turmoil and it seemed safe to enter. I thought it would be an adventure.

There was no reply from Kampala to my request for a visa, so I packed a few things into my Land Rover and set off. Passing the Uganda frontier post was no problem, but I began to feel a little nervous when I drew up at the Zaïrois barrier.

After paying a vehicle tax, I came to the immigration official: a young man, blinking smilingly at me from behind oversize spectacles. He took my passport and gave me a little tattered slip of paper. I began to remonstrate and he carelessly flung my passport onto a table. I wasn't going to get it back.

Now I remembered the story a well known wild life photographer had told me concerning his attempt to enter Zaïre a couple of years before. When the immigration official took the party's passports, he laid the official out with a straight right to the jaw, grabbed the passports back, jumped into his vehicle and drove off. The problem was the vehicle was facing into Zaïre! So he drove hell-for-leather to another border post about sixty miles distant, praying there was no radio communication between them. There wasn't, and he managed to drive out innocently. It must have been one of the shortest visits on record!

Well I wasn't going to try anything like that.

But before I could drive off I was pounced upon by two Laurel and Hardy-like characters, one very large, one very small, in ragged soldiers' dress, who proclaimed themselves to be 'currency officers'. They took me into a little tin sentry's hut by the side of the road and drawing a filthy piece of old curtain across the entrance, asked to see my wallet.

I thought, "This is it".

Before I had left Mweya, the hotel manager had advised me to take US dollar bills, a currency in demand everywhere. He had plenty since tourists sometimes asked him to change them and so my wallet was stacked with the green dollar bills.

When I opened it the currency officers' eyes nearly popped out of their heads. They took the wallet, examined it, and then handed it back to me. I pocketed it thankfully. They then explained in French they were hungry. I pretended not to understand, and they pointed to their mouths. Procrastinating for as long as I dared, when it began to look as if they were beginning to turn nasty, I drew out a single dollar bill and gave it to them. It was nothing to me, but worth about three times its face value in Zaïre.

The currency officers were delighted, and beaming with pleasure insisted on escorting me to my vehicle. I thought I had got off lightly, but I was still worried about my passport.

I drove along the red earth road into the Congo. No work had been done on it for at least seven years and there were huge depressions in it. There were surprised stares from the few Africans I passed. Amazingly I came across a wayside petrol station with petrol for sale. The attendant had never seen a dollar bill before and initially refused them, but another African urged him to accept.

My first destination was the old Albert National Park headquarters at Rumangabo on the slopes of the Virunga volcanoes, which I reached by about midday. It was situated at the edge of the forest approached by a steep, winding track. As I was driving up the track a jeep crowded with

Congolese soldiers came round a blind curve at speed on the wrong side of the road. We narrowly escaped collision and I thought there would be trouble, but they all roared with laughter and sped on their way.

The Rumangabo headquarters was like a time capsule, exactly as it was seven years before when Jacques Verschuren, warden of the Albert National Park, had fled for his life. The guards were delighted to have a visitor and took me on a guided tour of their mausoleum.

Verschuren's office was just as he had left it: carefully cleaned and dusted every day and with fresh flowers placed in a vase. But the papers he had left on the desk were yellow with age, like the rolls of maps in the corner and the row of books on the bookshelf. It was like entering a museum, but to the Africans it was a shrine. They were simply awaiting the day when Jacques Verschuren would return and take up where he had so abruptly left off.

I was shown to my room. There were clean sheets on the bed, but the mattress and pillow were hard as iron. The plumbing had long since rusted away.

My intention had been to visit the active volcano of Nyamalagira, but the guards informed me it was forty miles walk away through the forest. No, I could not drive any closer but they could arrange porters for me. I wasn't prepared for such an expedition, and the little slip of paper that the immigration officer had given me allowed me only four days' visit. I had to call it off.

I decided I would retrace my steps northwards and visit the Rutshuru area, the Zaïre equivalent of the Queen Elizabeth Park, equally famed for its hippos, elephants and buffalo. The guards were disappointed but agreed there was much more to see there. I bundled my few things back into the Land Rover and set off once more along the road I had just travelled.

Two hours later I arrived at Rwindi Camp and was pleasantly surprised to find the hotel was working, managed by a pleasant Zaïrois.

There were even visitors, Belgian military families from Kinshasha. There was a restaurant, which served a passable meal (but also a glass of water which gave me diarrhoea for two weeks), and a camp of *rondavels*, round thatched huts.

I was shown my room. Again the pillow and mattress were rock hard, but I slept a bit better that night than I had thought I was going to several hours before.

The next two days I spent game viewing. The habitat was little different from that of the Queen Elizabeth Park, but there was less to see after seven years of disorder.

Soon it was time to return to the border and I was filled with apprehension about my passport.

My friends the currency officers were the first to meet me and I gave them another dollar bill. The big one put his arm around my shoulders and delightedly they escorted me to the immigration office.

The young immigration officer came out, blinking behind his oversize spectacles. The moment of truth had arrived. He beamed:

"Hello Mister Clive," he said, and handed my passport to me.

I'm glad I hadn't been tempted to punch him on the jaw.

* * *

At Mweya all the unmarried men, which comprised everybody except the Director, lived in the 'bachelors' mess', served by an old cook called Erisa. Erisa once remarked to Chris he had carried 'Johnson' over a river. Chris ridiculed the idea thinking he meant Johnston (Sir Harry Johnston) who had been there at the beginning of the century. Some years later, browsing in a second hand bookshop in Bloomsbury, I came across a copy of a book published in 1908 called *Tramps Round the Mountains of the Moon* by the Reverend Broadwood Johnson. Opening the book, there, staring out at me from a faded photograph was Erisa as a boy of twelve years old!

Johnson wrote: "He was only a little chap, but more thoughtful than most of them, and wasn't often wrong." He had been brought to him at Mengo " . . . [he] had never served a European before and seemed so young to take away from his home (being only about eleven years old), that I demurred. However, on his coming back again and pressing it, I agreed, telling him that if he didn't feel happy out there [Kabarole in Toro] he must come back home. This was Erisa . . . ."

As to carrying him across the water, Johnson wrote: "For a European to wade through up to his waste in the icy water of the glacier stream, with a blazing sun overhead, would almost certainly lead to a dose of fever, and your porters prefer to save you the risk by giving you a lift on their shoulders." He illustrated this thoughtfulness on the part of his porters with a photograph of the operation in his book.

The Reverend Broadwood Johnson not getting his feet wet.

I always regretted not being able to show Erisa, already very old when I left Uganda, his photograph in Johnson's book. But Johnson's days, Erisa's days, and my days, in Uganda, have gone forever. Amin's bloody reign of terror saw to that.

The Hippo

Silhouettes against a million stars
The boughs of mighty succulents clutch the sky
Like unlit candelabras in some vast Hadean hall.
Far below, the moon's wan shaft
Makes water's ripples tinsel on an oily calm.
Then, great Behemoth's grunt booms out,
No idle play, but threatening challenge this.
And, unafraid, an answering roar
Echoes in the Stygian dark.

Splash! Splash! Splash! A dreadful battle sounds,
Which I, unseeing, visualize,
As challenger and challenged surge and sway,
Each mighty maw agape,
Each seeking seizure with eburnean vicious teeth.
Then, suddenly, as all began, they sink, abruptly,
And the foam subsides.
And quiet darkness reigns once more.

Then, far below, I see the hippo clamber onto land,
The moon sheen oil upon his massive hulk,
As pond'rously he plods his way along
Anfractuous paths that wind into the night.

From Dark Heart To Kalahari

Here, man's incubus of dark,
makes his transcendence of the beasts into a lesser role,
And shadows of the sylvan murk,
turn erstwhile' frighted beasts into contemptuous despots of the wild,
Usurping weak and fearful man, cowering in some fortified abode.

But dawn once more reverses all,
And man arises, as new born, to seek revenge for
night's tempestuous fear,
And in the Pandean display of day
no unseen terrors now hold sway.

Great Behemoth returns to his aquatic home,
Hurrying to beat the sun's harsh ray,
Immerses in the water's balm,
A rotund pink and shiny beast,
To start his gurgles, grunts and giant farts,
That send up stinking bubbles to the surface scum,
A grotesque, comic object now,
With bristly snout and red-rimmed eye,
Covering bizarre obesity,
Waiting night's cloak of darkness for respectability.

Notes

1. H. M. Stanley 1890 *In Darkest Africa.*
2. D. Middleton ed. 1969 *The Diary of A. J. Mounteney Jephson.*
3. H. M. Stanley 1878 *Through the Dark Continent.*
4. M. Perham 1959 ed. *The Diaries of Lord Lugard.*
5. A. R. Cook 1945 *Uganda Memories (1897-1940).*
6. H. Melville *Moby Dick.*
7. Douglas & Marcelle Brown 1996 *Looking Back at the Uganda Protectorate. Recollections of District Officers.*
8. S. W. Baker 1866 *The Albert N'yanza, Great Basin of the Nile.*

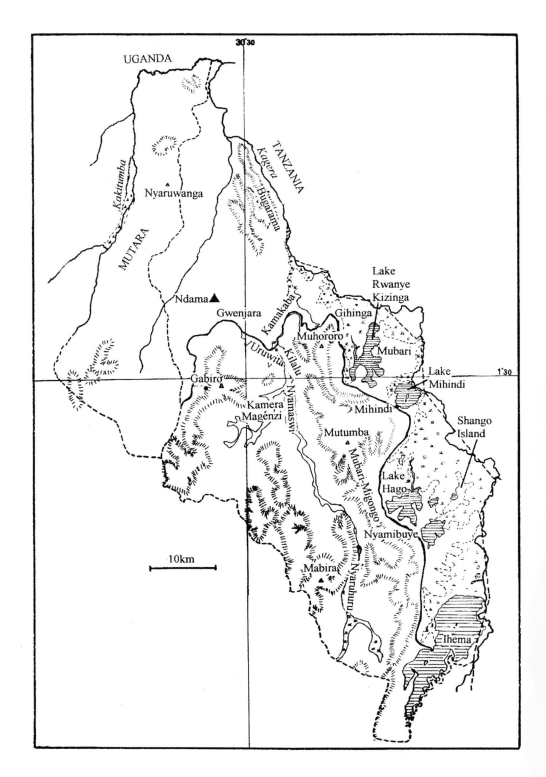

The Akagera National Park, Rwanda.

Chapter 3

The Imitation Pearl

Rwanda's plains and mountains

I heard that the British Government, through its Ministry of Overseas Development, was looking for an ecologist to conduct a survey of the Akagera National Park in Rwanda, the country the old German colonists had called 'the pearl of Africa' before it came under Belgian control. That was how, after my return to England from Uganda, I found myself in the building known as 'Eland House, Stag Place', next to London's Victoria Station. Clearly the person who named that building wasn't much of a zoologist.

I was being interviewed by a stout, middle-aged, florid-faced man.

"We want you to do a little spying for us," he was saying, pressing his fingertips together and regarding me intently.

Gulp! Shades of Graham Greene! Already in my mind's eye I was visualizing myself in some exotic capital leaving messages on the top of the cistern in the gents' public convenience.

"You see," he continued, "we don't know very much about the place."

Such ignorance was explained by the fact the Ministry of Overseas Development had recently taken over responsibility for the country from the Foreign Office in some government reshuffle, and of course the FO was not going to give any information away. But with my 'controller's' arrangement the next day I made my way to the FO.

I sat in a bleak corridor on an ancient, worn, leather-covered sofa, which had horsehair sprouting out all over it. A modern Mata Hari noisily clip-clopped the whole length of the long marble-tiled corridor in her high-heeled shoes. Everyone behind their closed doors must have heard her. I suppose that was the intention.

Eventually my contact came out from behind one of the doors and I rose and shook hands. I made as if to enter the office from which he had emerged. No, that was not allowed. Visitors had to be interviewed on the old horsehair sofa in the corridor. I felt like pointing out that was rather a case of shutting the stable door after the horse had bolted in view of Philby's defection, but I seated myself again without demur. I wondered how many other spies had been interviewed on the old sofa.

All the urbane young man could or would tell me about Rwanda was that you drove along the road, passed a handful of tin huts, and suddenly realised you had passed through the capital, Kigali. So you then had to turn around and drive back.

It wasn't, of course, quite like that. In fact the first thing that happens is you find a tollgate blocking the road and are obliged to pay an extortionately high fee in order to proceed to Kigali on the only three miles of tarmac which the country boasted.

In Kigali I found an excellent little booklet for sale on Rwanda, providing full details of its economy, agriculture, and anything else that a spy might want to know. So I bought a copy and sent it to the florid-faced man in Eland House in fulfilment of my spying assignment.

It was produced in England.

But that was to come later, and first I drove into Rwanda from Uganda to arrive one evening at Gabiro, entrance to the Akagera National Park. Gazetted by the Belgians in 1934 this was one of the earliest national parks in Africa. The explorer Speke can claim to have been the first European to have seen the Akagera Park, or Kagera as it used to be called, when in November 1861 he reached Lake Mujunju in Tanganyika, which he promptly named Lake Windermere. He never got further than looking at the area of the park from a distance, and the first white man to actually visit it was our old friend Stanley. This was in March 1876, accompanied by 2,300 natives supplied as escort by King Mtesa of Buganda. His three European companions were all dead by this time.

Now sporting a pith helmet in place of his peaked cap, Stanley boated a few miles up and down the Kagera River in the southern part of the present park, and also around Lake Ihema, spending a night on the then inhabited island in the lake. When he tried to land on the western shore near a small village: "the natives snarled like so many spiteful dogs, and drew their bows, which compelled us . . .to sheer off and leave them to their ferocious exclusiveness". Ihema means a tent, and the island and lake may have got their name from Stanley's visit, for it was probably the first time the inhabitants had seen such an object.

It was to be 32 years later before a European gave a brief description of the hinterland of the park. This was the Duke of Mecklenberg, who in July 1907 entered Rwanda from the north via Merama Hill and worked his way down east of the Kakitumba River, accompanied by eight other Europeans, 35 askaris or policemen, and numberless servants, cooks and porters. He reported the country east of the Kakitumba River deserted, and venturing as far eastwards as Ndama Hill, a bare three miles inside the present park, he described the area as steppe, sparsely covered with acacia scrub, dwindling to tree-less open steppe.

It hadn't changed when I got there.

North of Mount Ndama, which rises only 1000 feet above the plain and hardly qualifies for the title 'Mount', the Duke attempted a day's excursion to the Kagcra River, but failed to make it, a round trip of about twenty miles: "The farther we proceeded eastwards the more hilly and picturesque the country became with its herds of elands, jimara (lyre antelopes) [topi], and zebras. The steppe is chiefly covered with the umbrella palm, which grows in shady clumps. At one of these latter, on a slope near the summit, we saw a troop of equine antelopes [roan antelope] browsing."[1]

After this the Duke reported his position was particularly critical. One of his officers wrote: "Our people's stock of vegetable food had been entirely consumed, and we had already subsisted for two days entirely on meat. As far as the eye could see no habitation could be descried . . . As it was impossible to hold out any longer under such conditions, we decided with the greatest reluctance, to abandon our interesting labours and to proceed to the next village."

Thus we never got any further information on the park.

The Germans, hearing stories of the giant Watutsi warrior race and their immense herds of cattle, had called Rwanda 'the pearl of Africa' and 'the cradle of the Nile'. But they soon became disabused of the idea of some earthly paradise when they found it was overpopulated and overgrazed. The eastern part, which the Duke found so empty, was devoid of habitation because of a great sleeping sickness epidemic, which had wiped out both man and cattle at the turn of the century.

I was more fortunate than the Duke in that when I came to the area in 1968 there was a small hotel at the entrance to the Park, called the Gabiro Guest House. It was a simple enough place, half a dozen papyrus thatched-roof chalets, the usual iron-hard mattress and pillows, and a restaurant, which served a barely passable meal.

There was nothing to do there, the bar not being a very inviting place, and at this, my first visit, the electricity generator was not working. So there was nothing for it but an early night, going to bed in the dark.

About nine o'clock I was aroused from the deep sleep into which I had fallen by a banging on the door. Reluctantly I got out of bed, stumbled in the dark across to the door and opened it.

Without a word an African servant thrust a candle into my hand and disappeared. So I had a candle, but no matches.

I went back to bed.

It seemed I had just dropped off once more when I was re-awakened yet again by a banging on the door. Again I stumbled across and opened it. Again without a word an African servant thrust a pail of water into my hand and disappeared. I placed it on the floor next to the non-functional washbowl and went back to bed. There were no more disturbances and I slept soundly.

In the morning there was a pool of water on the floor and the bucket was empty. It had a hole in the bottom.

The next night the electricity supply was still not functional and it was early to bed once more. Towards ten o'clock I was roused once again from my slumbers. Some damn fool shouting his head off was driving a vehicle round and round the building at high speed in low gear, engine whining in protest.

Drunken revellers from the bar, I thought. My god! Was it going to be like this every night?

I had only a smattering of French, barely remembered from my schooldays, but it was sufficient for what he was shouting to gradually permeate my somnolent brain.

"*Gardez le feu! Gardez le feu!*"

"Gardez le feu," I repeated sleepily to myself. "What did that mean? *Gardez le feu . . . gardez le feu . . .* !" I leapt out of bed and pulling on my boots ran outside in my pyjama trousers. For the building had a thatched roof.

Well, the building wasn't on fire, and after his exhortation "Beware of the fire!" shouted from his Land Rover instead of simply knocking at the door, the manager was standing, together with a small group, watching a grass fire which was at some distance but gradually moving in our direction. It didn't look serious enough to keep me out of bed and I retired. They seemed to think it very amusing that I was in my pyjama trousers.

* * *

The Akagera Park was a long strip of land bordering the Kagera River, about twenty-five miles at its widest and sixty-six miles long, covering a total area of about 1,046 square miles, for the most part patchy grassland and acacia woodland, with a high ridge of land running parallel to the river. The Kagera River, which flows into Lake Victoria and is thus the southernmost source of the Nile, hence the other German name for the country of 'cradle of the Nile', consists here of a series of lakes and papyrus swamps before becoming a narrow channel in the north of the park.

It was pleasant country with herds of zebra, topi, eland, impala and buffalo, but no elephant (although some were subsequently introduced), and had been administered with military precision by the Belgians, until tragedy struck.

Towards the end of 1959 trouble flared up in Rwanda when the formerly vassal Bahutu turned on their Watutsi overlords. Massacres followed and a band of Watutsi fled northwards to Uganda. Their route led them past Gabiro and the house of the Belgian park warden. They attacked at night, shooting the warden through a window as he sat calmly reading. Then they tried to enter and take the body for ritual mutilation, but the warden's wife seized a gun and drove the attackers off. The Belgians reacted to the murder by completely abandoning the park, and although a Rwandan warden was appointed it remained without any attention being paid to it for seven years.

That I was there was due to a bird-loving British High Commissioner who thought something ought to be done about the abandoned park. He pulled the necessary strings to get the British Government to finance a study and make recommendations for its development – although Rwanda was not a Commonwealth country. An initial study was conducted by Bruce Kinloch, the former Uganda Chief Game Warden, who recommended an in-depth ecological study. Alarm bells were soon ringing in Belgium, and within days of my arrival a Belgian adviser on national parks was appointed to the Rwandan government. Within two weeks a young Belgian husband and wife couple had been appointed as ecologists in the south of the park.

My first task was to visit the young Rwandan park warden, or *Conservateur* as they are known in francophone Africa. In Belgian colonial times this was a very prestigious appointment, and the Belgians built their wardens huge palatial houses, more like those of British colonial governors than those one would associate with a park warden. This one was no exception, sited on the summit of a small hill and approached by a steep winding track. In front of the great doorway was a large, semicircular, tiled patio, reached by a broad flight of steps.

I drove up and got out of my Land Rover.

The *Conservateur* was standing in the middle of the patio, ebony black and naked except for a pair of brilliant azure blue swimming trunks. In his hands he held a pair of knitting needles with which he clicked away industriously, while at his feet a large coloured ball of wool bounced about on the ground as he yanked it into purl and plain. The slightest of smiles flickered over his face as I mounted the steps and greeted him.

I explained my mission in my elementary French.

The knitting stopped. His face screwed up into an exaggerated frown:

"But I don't want the place turned into a zoological garden."

(What he really meant was "I don't want to have any work to do.")

This was a time for quick thinking.

"Of course you don't. But your government wants to make money from tourism from the area, and it can't do that without developing it."

His face broke into a smile.

"Yes," he said, "all right."

And he went back to his knitting. The interview was over.

* * *

Whereas their English counterparts were lucky if they even had a tent to go on patrol with, Belgian wardens never believed in roughing it, and in the east of the park were three substantial, small stone chalets, complete with flush toilets, showers and kitchen ranges. These they used as bases to patrol from. Of course the plumbing had long ago ceased to work, but with a bit of effort I could soon turn one of these into a comfortable base. So I decided to install myself in the central one, which overlooked an almost circular lake with a small island in the centre – Lake Mihindi. After seven years' abandonment the small house was in a bit of a mess, but the bats were soon chased out of the roof, the bees' nest disposed of, and a sort of water system got working once more.

People were amazed at my bravery in living alone at this remote spot, fearful it seems that the ghosts of seven years past would come and haunt me.

I did find a box of human bones complete with skull in the house, and this I did place outside so that my dreams would not be disturbed. One of the guards told me the bones had been found in a cave, high up on the side of a bluff called Muhororo. In pre-colonial times robbers used to inhabit the cave as it overlooked a main footpath where they could pounce on travellers. Perhaps one such bandit was wounded and went back to the cave to die, or perhaps it was the body of a victim. Anyway, it made a good story.

Later I managed to drive onto the top of Muhororo, something never previously done. The top was as flat as a billiard table, covered with a short, green, lawn-like sward, over which one could drive at seventy miles an hour – as long as you didn't hit a warthog hole. From the top one had a wonderful panoramic view of the Kagera, stretching into the misty blue of Tanzania's Karagwe. The guard told me he had walked over the plateau with the former warden:

"And what did you see?" I asked.

The guard thought for a moment.

"I saw that he was tired," was the reply.

* * *

My work was to carry out an ecological survey of the Park and its adjacent hunting reserve, the Mutara Reserve, in order to make recommendations for tourism development. This involved counting samples of animals for two weeks in every month, conducting vegetation surveys, identifying the types and frequency of different trees, bushes and grasses, exploring routes and possible development sites, and a host of other activities. Often it meant leaving the house before dawn and returning again after dark. Usually I would forego breakfast and just munch something hurriedly at midday while continuing to work. It was not unusual to have to mend at least two punctures during the day, for the two-inch long acacia thorns went through the tyres with the ease of nails.

Prior to my departure from England I had met a young lady helping a colleague study roe deer. I asked her if she would like to help me in Africa for a season, as I knew the difficulties of working on one's own in the bush. It was a wise request because after seven years of doing nothing the park guards were not accustomed to the hours I insisted upon. The park driver I was assigned had never driven off the road, and became so confused at driving through the bushes that one day he suddenly drove straight at a large bush, stopping abruptly at the last minute just when I thought we were about to crash into it.

"What did you do that for?" me, irritated.

"I don't know," was the reply.

Yes, I certainly needed some help.

* * *

On our monthly supply run to Kigali I saw an African standing by the road holding up for sale a baby grey duiker, one of the smallest of antelopes. I hoped that F., the young lady who had joined me, had not seen it but she had. The result was a foregone conclusion. I said I would stop and let her buy it if she promised not to become too fond of it, knowing full well these creatures seldom survive long in captivity. The promise was easily given with of course no intention of upholding it, an extortionate price was paid without argument and F. became the happy possessor of the charming baby buck.

I called it Diddums, but F. thought the Hutu name of *Isha* a more dignified cognomen.

Isha thrived on the care lavished upon him and showed no inclination to try and leave the house, spending his nights (for it was indeed a 'he'), sleeping on F.'s bed.

I planted a small apology of a vegetable garden in front of the verandah, but the soils were so poor it barely yielded one crop. The tomatoes however were not doing too badly, but just as they were turning red a spurfowl, a bird like a partridge, came into the garden and polished off the lot. But I still had the cabbages.

It was not long before Isha wandered about outside the house on his own during the day and it also wasn't long before he discovered the vegetable patch. Hopping over the wire netting he started to help himself to the cabbages. Seeing his misdemeanour I went out, seized him firmly and plonked him down roughly on the other side of the wire. He stood a moment, shook his head irritably, and walked away. I went back inside the house.

Fifteen minutes later Isha was back feeding on the cabbages again. I repeated my actions, a little more roughly this time. Isha reacted in the same manner as before, shaking his head and then walking off as if he couldn't care less about a few cabbages.

Shortly afterwards he was back yet a third time. I ran out and seized him, chiding him angrily. Isha then proceeded to let out a very loud, angry bleat, like a goat being slaughtered.

"What are you doing to him?" cried out F., alarmed.

I replied shortly that I wasn't doing anything to him.

Diddums.

Bellowing lustily as if to give lie to my answer, he then puffed out his cheeks in indignation, and when I plonked him on the ground stood there blowing out his cheeks like an angry child in an extraordinary display of petulance, before stiffly stalking off.

This time he didn't go back. Even duikers can learn.

The evening after F.'s return departure to England, when Isha was about six months old and sporting a pair of short, spiky horns, instead of just resting as was his wont with F. around, he padded endlessly back and forth around the verandah, which was wired in with mosquito netting. By eight o'clock, when I was ready to turn in after a long day, he still hadn't stopped, his small hooves keeping up an incessant clicking on the smooth cement floor.

I decided there was only one thing for it. Let him out into the night. He was old enough now to look after himself.

Three months went by after that and I never caught a glimpse of little Isha. I thought with remorse he must have perhaps been taken by a python. Poor little Isha, we had even taken him on trips to Uganda, for everywhere that F. went the buck was sure to go. Smuggling him across the border in a cardboard box, the Uganda customs guard had insisted on looking inside. Isha just looked out at him inquiringly and the guard closed the box with a smile. On another occasion F. tried to smuggle him through in a rucksack, until heavy panting sounds and struggling indicated he was close to being suffocated.

It was now August, the burning season, the time every year when most of Africa goes up in smoke and fierce grass fires consume all of the dry, six-foot high grass. Such a fire swept around the house, leaving a smouldering, blackened wilderness in its wake. But at least one could see! After six months of being hemmed in on all sides by a seemingly impenetrable forest of grass one can appreciate why the African wants to burn it, wiping out the hidden terror of stalking carnivores.

The ashes were barely cool when the cook called to me to come out to the back of the house. There was little Isha standing just outside the kitchen door, shoulders hunched and head hanging, an absolute picture of dejection!

The cook thought it a huge joke.

"Now his house has burnt down he's come back to ours," he laughed.

I stroked him and he waggled his tail. I gave him some tit-bits to eat and he then wandered off, looking a bit less dejected. After that I always saw him near the house in the evenings, and if I walked towards him he would come up to me and stand while I stroked him. This, I felt, was how it should be with a wild animal, free to do as it pleased, but yet in harmony with one: like the evening when a noisy troop of vervet monkeys came by foraging in front of the house. Vervet monkeys are small and mischievous and they came leaping and chattering, now running on the ground, now swinging in the bushes. Every so often one would stand on its hind legs and stare around, looking for danger.

Then Isha came along, and as the monkeys jumped and danced around, he began to have a great game charging at them. First he went for one, then another, racing back and forth and getting more and more excited. Was it territorial defence? To me it just looked as if he was having a great game.

Laughing, I went out to him. The monkeys who had joined in the game beat a retreat, and after a last parting charge at them, Isha turned and came charging at me. Stopping just in front of my legs he stood there quivering all over with excitement, and oh! So pleased with himself as I bent and stroked him.

I have always wondered how Isha fared after I left. I do hope the guards didn't put him in their stew pot.

* * *

An astonishing sight, migrating catfish in the Akagera Park.

One day an astonishing sight met my eyes when crossing the Kamakaba, a watercourse of only a few feet in width, for it was a seething mass of migrating catfish, a solid wriggling mass of huge fish all fighting their way upstream and throwing themselves at the causeway like leaping salmon. When they could advance no farther they would make their way into the surrounding floodplain pools to spawn as soon as it rained enough to fill them. I took some back to camp to eat, but when I saw the large spindly nematode worms that riddled the flesh I was put off for life from eating catfish!

The park was not an area where one was likely to have much in the way of adventures with big game. For some reason there were no elephants there, the last one recorded being a solitary visitor from Tanganyika which died of old age in the park in 1946. But the name of a place in the extreme north-west of the Mutara Hunting Reserve, Kijojo, means 'huge elephant' suggesting perhaps once a giant tusker was killed there. I thought it might serve as a tourist draw if some elephants were introduced and made some tentative inquiries about the possibility of catching some in the Queen Elizabeth Park and bringing them here. Somehow this got translated into an intent by a diplomat who mentioned to a Ugandan official that it was going to happen. This caused a near diplomatic incident and I was told by the Director of the Ugandan National Parks that we would have to forget about it for the time being. In my report to the British Government, which was communicated to the Rwandan government, I recommended introducing 6 young cows and 4 young bulls. Later, in 1975, at the Presidents' request a group of 25 young elephants was translocated from the south of Rwanda where the country's last remaining savanna herd was being exterminated. Some 25 years later these had increased to 60.

In 1958 six black rhinos were introduced from Tanganyika and I sometimes came across their droppings, as well as having one run across in front of me on one occasion. There were numbers of hippos in the Kagera River and its lakes in the more inaccessible places hidden from view by papyrus swamps, and a few large crocodiles. There were plenty of buffalo, but not as numerous as I had experienced in Uganda. One could have trouble with lions if one spent much time on foot, and I often came across prides, including a lioness with a wire snare around her neck. The most numerous animals were impala antelope along the lakeshores, while inland were large herds of topi on the open plains, a good number of zebra, and about five hundred and fifty eland usually in one large herd. The rarest of the big game was the roan antelope, which existed only in small numbers. Of lesser game, most common was the oribi, a small antelope, the male with short, upright horns. The park was allegedly notable for its population of sitatunga, a shy marsh-living antelope with specially adapted splayed hooves to allow it to live in swamps. Well I never saw a single one, and only slight signs of their probable existence from the air; but a study twenty years later claimed the swamps were overrun with them, about nine thousand to be exact. It appears a rise in water level causing loss of habitat and easy approach by poachers had caused their disappearance in my time.

An early map-maker had diligently filled in all of the old local names of places on a map of the park, some of which I was able to have translated. Travelling from Gabiro, the 'place where things are distributed' (e.g. money, possibly a reference to paying labourers in colonial times), one passed on the way to Mihindi such places as Kanyonza, 'place of thorny bushes'; Gwenjara, the 'place of hunger', on to Kilalu plain, literally 'plain of madness', although what the significance of that name was I never discovered. Far to the left of this route was a hill, called Nyngo, 'tobacco pipe'; and farther still the fearful-sounding Kamera Mgenzi, or 'engulfer of strangers', a deep swamp. The name Mihindi may have referred to the growing of maize, while farther south between Lake Kishanju, 'hippo lake', and Lake Hago, 'those yonder', perhaps referring to people from the other side of the water, was Karugaju, 'place of the brown bull', a reference to earlier times when cattle were kept in the area. In the Mutara Reserve was the awesome-sounding Lutambabalenzi, 'place of sacrifice of the boys'.

The 116 square mile Mutara Hunting Reserve was adjacent to the Akagera Park on its north-west side, looked after by a cheerful rogue of a game warden called Mazumbuko. He confided to me he wanted to get into 'teewee', but it took me some time to understand what he was getting at. There was not much game in the Mutara because it was partly settled, and the only interesting thing I found there was a human skull with a neat bullet hole in the cranium: a grim reminder of the uprising.

The warden of the Mutara Hunting Reserve with a fine buffalo head.

In 1990 the Watutsi who had fled to Uganda in 1959 made a comeback. It was reported the leader of the insurgents had declared he was going to wipe out all the animals in the Park and settle himself and his men in it. Fortunately this never came to pass as such.

* * *

Apart from studying the Akagera Park, I was charged also with looking at the Volcano National Park, Rwanda's second park, which covered the extinct volcanoes of Karisimbi, Visoke, Sabinyo, Mgahinga and Muhavura, with Mikeno on the other side of the border in the Congo. It was here Dian Fossey became a household name from habituating the rare mountain gorilla.

Dian was very jealous of her gorillas, and apart from waging a single-handed war with the Batwa poachers in the mountain forests, she also waged it at that time against any visitors who might wish to penetrate her forest domain. Having fled from the Congo side, when I made my first visit in December 1968 she had only been at Visoke a year, and had yet to get to the stage of shaking hands with gorillas, which was to make her so famous.

I had always wanted to photograph this great monarch of the mountain forests since I had first tracked them in 1957 in the dense forests of Mount Muhavura on the Uganda side, but they were much too timid in those days to wait to have their photos taken. I had then written to Dian when I was in Uganda and she was in the Congo. She received the letter about a year later, dutifully forwarded to her in Rwanda by the Zaïrean authorities, although she had been forced to flee for her life from them.

Now that I was in Rwanda I wrote to her again, and permission was granted for myself and F. to visit her camp, provided I did not bring a camera!

Well I wasn't a photographer but an ecologist supposed to be doing a job of work, and whether or not I took photographs was at that time not a consideration, so I bowed to her instruction. At the end of the visit, before leaving I told Dian that in my report I would have to recommend the gorillas be open to visits by tourists, as there could be no future for the area simply as a private research domain.

"Over my dead body," she replied.

Tragically murdered, she did give her life for the gorillas, but not in a war against tourists. Not long after my visit she acquiesced in the opening-up of part of the area to tourism as probably the only way of saving the gorillas by focusing public attention upon their plight. And that is what was done, with considerable success.

Intensive settlement reaches high up into the foothills of the volcanoes, and after you leave these precarious fields angled at almost forty-five degrees, it is a very stiff climb, almost ladder-like in its ascent, up a very muddy, slippery, footpath. It almost always drizzles with rain. But for those who make this arduous climb, emerging from the dense bamboo and coming out onto the level ground in the *Hagenia* woodland, it is like entering a Disney fairyland. Here the undergrowth is short and green, in a forest of gnarled and twisted trees that look a thousand years old, with their rugged branches draped in grey masses of old man's beard lichen. At any moment you expect to see the seven dwarves hi-hoing along. The gorillas are usually on the steeper slopes above this fairytale woodland, where their favourite food the giant celery is to be found.

After the descent from the mountains, wet, cold, and covered in mud, I decided to stay the night at a hotel in the little township of Ruhengeri at the foot of the volcanoes. This hotel went under the misnomer, as I was to discover, of "Weekend Relax".

Although the nights at this altitude were freezing cold, the fireplaces in the hotel rooms had not seen a fire for many years. Nothing but ice-cold water came out of the bath 'hot' tap. It was impossible to wash properly, and impossible to dry one's wet clothes.

The lavatories had no paper.

In the morning we were anxious to get away from such hardship as quickly as possible, but we had not reckoned with the habits of the Belgian proprietor. He did not rise until ten o'clock, and until then we could not pay our bill.

Hotels were always a surprise in Rwanda, usually an unpleasant one. I had occasion to spend a night at a well-known Swiss-owned hotel, named of course the Edelweiss, near the northern end of Lake Kivu. Notices in each bedroom warned the occupant companions were not allowed in the rooms, and nobody was likely to argue the point once they had met the formidable proprietress, an extremely large, stout, typically Swiss woman, hair piled high on the top of her head like one of the ugly sisters in a Cinderella pantomime.

The food in this establishment had a reputation for excellence and one diner, so the story goes, ordered the speciality. After a long wait it was served.

"I can't eat all that!" the man exclaimed, eyeing his laden plate.

"Vat!" the proprietress thundered, "I cook for you my best dish, and you say you vill not eat it! You vill eat it all!"

And she stood over the luckless diner, arms akimbo, until he had consumed every morsel on his plate.

* * *

Later I made another trip to the volcanoes with a party from Kigali to climb to Visoke Lake, a crater lake of great beauty high on the summit of Visoke.

One of the group was an American missionary, of what sect I never inquired, but he was certainly paid well enough to spread the gospel and had all the latest and most expensive Hasselblad photographic equipment, and the best of camping paraphernalia. Among the latter was an ingenious pop-up tent, which folded down to something no larger than a sun umbrella.

On the way to Ruhengeri we passed a lorry, which had crashed into the bank at the side of the road. Two dead bodies were still sitting gruesomely upright in the cab. The preacher leapt out when we halted and excitedly began to photograph the macabre scene from a multitude of angles. As he walked back to our vehicle he must have noticed our somewhat incredulous expressions:

"Death is never very pleasant, is it?" he murmured, stowing away his camera.

* * *

We had engaged a guide and porters for the climb, but as afternoon drew on we were clearly still well away from our objective of spending the night at the lake. The leader who had organized the trip said we should leave the footpath and strike straight upwards to the summit. I had been in this type of forest before, and demurred. But he was adamant the guide was taking us the long way around, and so we left the path, which itself was only a narrow, slippery animal trail, and struck straight upwards through the forest.

It was of course a mistake.

The forest floor soon gave way to sharp, angular boulders, wet and slippery, on which one risked twisting an ankle at almost every step. At the same time the mountainside became steeper and steeper. The boulders were covered with sodden moss on which we slipped and stumbled, hauling ourselves through the thick vegetation, pulling aside sodden branches and thoroughly soaking ourselves. How I cursed the leader's impetuosity! It was obvious we would not make it now before nightfall. When indeed night fell we were still on a slope of forty-five degrees in dense, cold, wet undergrowth.

There was nothing for it but to bed down where we were and hope for the best.

I shared the small one-man tent of the expedition's organizer. Pitched at a crazy angle on the slope, I was only prevented from rolling downhill by the tent wall and an uncomfortable rock that stuck into my side. It had started to drizzle long ago and we were all thoroughly wet through, but I was more worried about the African porters than I was about myself. For I had read the Duke of Mecklenberg's book.

The Africans sat in a huddle in the drizzle under a barely adequate piece of canvas they had stretched above them as a sorry token protection against the rain, unable to light a fire in the wet. When the African gets cold he loses heart. I told them they should try and make themselves a bit more comfortable but they took no notice. After all, there was in fact very little they could do, and they knew as well as I how bitterly cold it would get at this altitude before the night was over.

In 1907 one of the Duke of Mecklenberg's party, Kirchstein, was the first European to climb Visoke. But before this he climbed Karisimbi, its sister volcano: "As we had to return by the southern side of the mountain on account of it being an easier descent, I selected the shorter cut right across the Branca crater . . . [ah! that shorter route] We had safely traversed the first half of the moor when we were assailed by an extraordinarily violent shower of hail which came down from an almost bright sky, whilst dense fog gathered at the same time. The temperature sank to zero, and then a snowstorm of such fury set in that, if I had not myself been a witness of it, I should have deemed it impossible in equatorial Africa. My carriers had scarcely perceived the snow when they threw away their loads, lay down on the ground, and with wails declared that they must die. It was quite in vain that I urged them to pursue the march . . . All my persuasion, insistence and even threats brought no result. *Amri ya mungu* (It is the decree of the gods, we must die) was the only reply that I could elicit . . . Summing up all my remaining strength of will I fought my way, wading up to my knees in icy cold water, accompanied by my two Askari and a very few followers, through the storm and snow straight to the edge of the crater. Arrived there we contrived to erect a temporary camp in the shelter of the trees and made a fire. Time after time, accompanied only by the two Askari, I penetrated the pathless swamp, and so brought one hapless native after the other to the warm camp fire . . .But even our own strength failed at last. 'Master, if we have to go out again, we shall never return alive; we can do no more!' declared the Askari, and their looks corroborated only too well the truth of their words. These brave fellows had really done all that it was possible for human power to do. They had come to the end of their strength. The closing darkness, too, made any further attempt at rescue hopeless . . .Absolutely drenched through, without any tent, limbs shivering from emotion and cold, and wrapped in a blanket only – that is how we spent the sleepless night round the camp fire, only to have to resume our work of exhumation again in the first grey light of morning. *Exhumation*, not rescue, for what remained to be rescued was heartrendingly little. Very few of the luckless ones . . .showed any trace of life. All the rest, twenty in number, and nearly half my caravan, lay corpses in the snow. Frozen under a tropical sun! Faces horribly distorted by the death agony, fingers scraping deeply into the snow, so they lay! A terrible spectacle for us who had arrived too late to save them."

I could not forget Kirchstein's terrible experience during my sleepless night cramped in the tiny tent, albeit a bit warmer than the night he had passed. But what of the porters? Anxiously, at first light I checked. It was a relief to find they were not corpses in the snow, or more correctly, corpses in the rain.

After a cold breakfast we continued the climb, reaching the crater lake with its surroundings of weird giant groundsel and senecios after about another hour of hard going.

* * *

The fateful crater of Mount Karisimbi.

In 1968 I was in Kigali for the annual Independence Day celebrations. Arriving at the stadium at the stated time on the official invitation of 10 a.m., I found the place completely empty! It was a good hour later before anyone else began to drift in. After the President finally took his place two hours behind schedule, we were treated to a twenty-one-gun salute. This was carried out with one small gun, which produced a dense cloud of smoke each time the blank shell was fired. As the cloud of smoke grew thicker and thicker, the Belgian officer firing the gun appeared to be uncertain whether to keep to his timing or to let the smoke clear a bit. He decided to keep to his timing while the audience choked in the fog of smoke.

Watutsi dancers at Independence Day celebrations in Kigali, July 1968.

Afterwards we adjourned to the President's garden for the reception. This consisted of a sort of self-service of crates of bottled beer scattered on the grass to which the guests helped themselves. No glasses being provided the ambassadors and other distinguished dignitaries were obliged to swig it from the bottle.

* * *

When it was finally time to leave Rwanda, I had to make my way via Nairobi to get my plant samples identified at the East African Herbarium. Peter Greenway, who had started his career as a gardener at Kew Gardens, was East Africa's most famous botanist. A short, dumpy man in his seventies, he was usually attired in colonial-type baggy shorts, and wore old-fashioned, thin-rimmed 'grandfather' spectacles. He is alleged to have stated that my plant collection, which was an 'ecological' one and not for classification purposes, was the worst plant collection he had ever seen. And that must have been saying something since he had started his botanical career in pre-war Tanganyika! But I was comforted by the fact that I had heard an amusing story about him related by a horticulturist. The said horticulturist was himself taking up an appointment in Kenya. On board ship, the customary mode of travel until the mid-sixties, he fell to talking to a charming old lady who, when he told her that he was an horticulturist, replied that her little boy Peter simply *loved* collecting wild flowers. The horticulturist, being a kindly fellow, said that in that case, he would collect some and send them to her son. He was assured her little boy would be delighted. True to his word, after taking up his appointment, the horticulturist collected some specimens together and sent them to Master Peter Greenway, with a short letter:

"Dear Peter,

Your mummy told me that you love collecting wild flowers so I am sending you some for your collection."

Not long afterwards the writer of the letter discovered "little

Peter" (OBE, D.Sc., FLS) was one of the most distinguished botanists in Africa.

* * *

In 1997 the Akagera Park was reduced in size by almost 62.5% from its 1,046 square miles to 393 square miles, leaving only a strip of land comprising the eastern slopes of the Mubari-Migongo Hills, most of the remaining area being lakes and swamp. The eland, topi and roan antelope habitat has gone. The adjacent Mutara Hunting Reserve was done away with altogether. Although the remaining habitat is suitable for buffalo and impala, the poaching pressures on this narrow strip of land will mean their rapid demise. Since my time in the Park in 1969 the declines in 2002 were estimated at buffalo 93%, eland 83%, impala 70%, topi 55% and zebra 62%. From 1998 numbers had fallen by 78% for buffalo, impala 67%, topi 65%, waterbuck 54% and zebra 79%.

Adieu Akagera!

Notes

1. Adolphus Frederick Duke of Mecklenberg 1910 *In the Heart of Africa.*

Chapter 4

Beneath the Snows
of Kilimanjaro

Trips and troubles in Tanzania

On Africa's highest mountain, high above the town of Moshi in northern Tanzania, lies the College of African Wildlife Management. Nestling 4000 feet up on the slopes of Mount Kilimanjaro, on a clear day in December it is framed by the awe-inspiring backdrop of Kilimanjaro's glacier-clad summit looming overpoweringly above it for yet another breathtaking fifteen thousand feet. When the missionary Rebmann reported in May 1848 he had seen a snow-capped mountain on the equator he was ridiculed by Britain's armchair geographers.

It was not until 1861 the German Baron von der Decken visited Moshi, headquarters of the rapacious Wachagga Chief Mandara, a child at the time. And it was October 1889 before anyone climbed to Kilimanjaro's snows, when Hans Meyer, Professor of Geology at Leipzig University, together with Ludwig Purtscheller, and the Chagga guide Yohani Lauwo, allegedly still alive in 1989 aged 118, reached the summit.

An instructor at the College of African Wildlife Management at Mweka was my next African assignment after Rwanda. The College had been set up in 1963 to teach the Africans who would take over the running of the game departments, national parks and game reserves in independent Africa. It was sited in what had originally been Tanganyika's German school, and one elderly German resident could still remember the days before the First World War when the wall at the rear of the main hall was decorated with a huge swastika emblem. Now this same wall was adorned with the mounted heads of game animals and magnificent pairs of elephant tusks. There was also a record rhinoceros horn, which disappeared after a graduation ceremony.

Tony, the Principal and a former Tanganyikan game warden, one day flew me over the top of Mount Kilimanjaro in the College's little two-seater Piper Cub aircraft. Although I have never liked flying in light aircraft this was an unforgettably exhilarating experience. I had climbed the mountain on foot in 1956 with two friends and wrote home at the time: "Two girls joined our party and the first day we set off in pouring rain for a ten mile walk through sodden forest with nothing but mud and water underfoot. This was from 4,500 to 10,000 feet where we spent the night in a hut. The next day we walked for another ten miles out of the forest and onto the moorland to another hut at 12,500 feet. By now it was pretty cold and most of the time we were covered in cloud . . .From here the next day we walked another ten miles getting our first glimpse of the mountain peak . . .About the last five miles was a trek across an arid desert with a bitterly icy wind blowing . . .and on two occasions I felt sick from the altitude as we had now reached 15,000 feet. We had to cover our faces with vaseline to prevent chapping and sunburn. All these treks started about nine a.m. and finished about four p.m. At two a.m. on the fourth day we had to get up for the final ascent. Its cold anywhere at this time in the morning and at this altitude it was bitterly cold with the incessant wind blowing. We set off in a line in the dark following the guide in front who had a lantern. When dawn broke and the sun came up we found that we were on the scree . . .This was the hardest of all and when we got to about 17,000 or 18,000 feet the effects of the altitude told and one could only stagger about ten paces and then flop down for fifteen minutes or more rest. We never seemed to get any closer to the top. The girls had dropped out by this time. We finally got to a point called Gillman's Point at eleven-thirty, it having taken us eight and a half hours to climb 3,600 feet, which is not much more than half a mile although it was actually about four miles as we didn't go straight up. This point is about 18,600 feet and although it is not the highest, which is 19,300 feet, we decided we had had enough and didn't go any further. At this altitude I felt as if I had a terrific hangover with my head spinning every time I stood up and I had no desire to take any pictures, though I did take some . . .All I wanted to do was to go to sleep, as did the others . . . "

The pinnacles of Mawenzi with Mount Kilimanjaro's Kibo Peak behind.

Now, seated in an aircraft, I was doing it in much more comfortable style. We climbed gradually on the eastern side of the twin peak of Mawenzi, which rises to a breathtaking 16,893 feet, peering down at its incredible spires of crumbly lava rearing vertically for thousands of feet. It is one of the hardest and most dangerous climbs in the world, and few people have attempted it, let alone visited Mawenzi's precipitous eastern slopes where in many of its steep forested valleys no human foot has ever trod. The brown, jagged lava rocks, look like the most unfriendly place in the world, and as we were climbing towards them I saw the glint of aircraft wreckage scattered on the steep mountainside far, far, below; all that remained of a twin-engine aircraft which had flown into the mountainside in the fifties, killing all on board.

With this grim reminder to cheer me, I returned to gazing at the mountain's hostile crags, and then, finally we were flying across the saddle, a bleak almost bare, boulder-strewn plain, towards the great ice-clad dome of the mighty Kilimanjaro itself.To clear its 19,365 feet we had to get to a good 20,000 feet; a height which under normal circumstances was well beyond oxygen limits. Because of the upward air currents one can still manage this without oxygen masks, but it leaves one gasping for breath at the slightest exertion.

As we neared the glacier-clad summit I could not but help feeling we were taking a bit of a risk. All Tony ever carried in the aircraft was a bottle of whisky, there were no blankets or warm clothing, and we were dressed only in light shirts and shorts. If we came down up here we would be frozen to death before we had even managed to finish the bottle of whisky.

Labouring in the thin air at this altitude, the aircraft engine clanked away like an old banger with the big end gone. Slowly we had risen above the crater rim and were flying across the centre of the crater itself so that I could look directly down into its layered, sulphurous-coloured lava bowl. Then we were making for the sheer vertical wall of ice to Kaiser Wilhelm Point, the highest part of the rim, and the highest point in the whole of Africa (now renamed Uhuru [freedom] Point).

The engine clanked and rattled away and I sat gasping for breath in the back seat having simply leaned forward to take some photographs. Tony sat impassively, staring at the wall of ice before us and urging the tiny craft upward. We could never turn if the engine didn't have power enough to rise above it in time.

Closer and closer it loomed, frightening in its awesome whiteness, great building blocks of ice piled one on top of the other like a giant's wall for hundreds of feet vertically before us. The wheezing, rattling aircraft couldn't possibly make it in time.

And then suddenly we were high enough, sailing over the point seemingly without effort while two lonely climbers standing below, tiny figures in a background of white snow, waved excitedly to us.

The next moment we were in space; the crater's rim dropping almost sheer below us for thousands of feet. I felt like a vulture must do when it hangs floating in air over a cliff face. And we were no bigger than a small bird, suspended in this immensity of space. And suspended we were, for we were so high it took the aircraft almost two hours to glide down to earth again.

Yes, that was certainly a flight to remember.

* * *

One of the advantages of teaching at Mweka was that we visited many of the East African national parks and reserves with the students. And I spent much of the rest of my African career bumping into former students who had become wardens scattered throughout the length and breadth of Africa, in countries as far apart as Nigeria and Botswana.

There were frequent visits to Kenya's Tsavo National Park, and I recall the excitement on one occasion we were camped there. It was our first morning in camp and I was washing in the canvas washbasin at the entrance to my tent, when one of the students came streaking out of the adjoining bushes holding up his trousers with both hands! The next moment he was followed by an elephant in hot pursuit. As we laughed uproariously, out came a whole herd of elephants, which charged between the rows of tents. That stopped us laughing pretty quickly. But they went straight through without checking their flight and disappeared into the bush on the other side.

Pat Hemingway, a fellow instructor, thought the plight of the distressed student was almost as funny as that of a white hunter he had seen chased by a rhino. Always a fount of stories, Pat recalled the hunter in question was very short and sported an immense, floppy-brimmed bush hat. He described how the hunter had come legging it out of the bushes, holding on to his hat with one hand and his rifle with the other, while hard on his heels was a furious rhino. Pat could do nothing but laugh helplessly at the sight. The hunter (or the hunted) then turned in his undignified flight, pointed his rifle in the general direction of the rhino, and pulled the trigger while holding the gun with one hand and his hat on his head with the other, killing the rhino outright. That was in the days when there were plenty of rhinos.

If that was a lucky shot then it was surpassed by one of our students, a buxom Ghanaian girl called Vivian. Every student had to shoot a buffalo as part of the training, and one of the instructors had, together with Vivian, approached an old bull standing quietly in the bushes. Vivian was given the signal to shoot, and pulled the trigger of the heavy calibre rifle. The bullet went wide and the buffalo charged off. At the same time there was an almighty crash in the bushes behind and another buffalo, unseen, dropped dead with Vivian's bullet through its heart!

Pat, son of Ernest Hemingway who had made Kilimanjaro famous through his book *The Snows of Kilimanjaro*, was one of the best-known personalities at the College, having given up professional hunting to teach there. His penetrating and almost incessant loud laugh always betrayed his presence. A person who never stood on ceremony he always pleased himself what he did.

Such was the occasion when the College was paid a visit by the Queen of Denmark. It was arranged that Her Majesty would take tea in the staff common room and she had insisted upon complete informality.

While others appeared jacketless in open-necked shirts, to me informal dress meant appearing in a suit with collar and tie, and like Mr Turveydrop in Dickens's *Bleak House* of whom the Prince of Wales once asked who he was because he was so smartly dressed, the Queen asked the Principal if I was a reporter. Flattering for reporters I suppose.

While the Queen sat at one end of the small room sipping tea with the Principal, most of us stood at the other end trying to appear to be chatting informally. Pat suddenly breezed in, late as usual, and since there was no formal presentation, turned towards us and started talking. I drily remarked to him that although dress was supposed to be informal, it was taking things a bit too far to come in with one's flies undone.

Pat hastily turned his back on the Queen while he zipped up his gaping front. It was perhaps fortunate there had been no formal full-frontal presentation!

* * *

An interest of mine was relocating the sites of photographic scenes in old books to see how the habitat had changed with the passage of time. In pursuit of this I went with Pat to the eastern Serengeti to rediscover the site of a scene taken in 1931 by Hans Reck, discoverer of Olduvai Gorge, famous for its early human fossils. I showed a copy of the photograph to Pat. It depicted a cairn of stones on the Serengeti plains with the title 'Maasai grave'. Pat was his usual iconoclastic self:

"Rubbish!" he shouted (Pat always expressed himself in tones several volumes higher than others).

"Rubbish! The Maasai never bury their dead. Grave indeed!"

It was not long, by reference to the horizon, before I had located the very same cairn, unchanged in appearance after a span of forty-three years. Unchanged that is except for one remarkable fact. That very previous night a jackal had dug into the base of the cairn and there, lying on the surface, was a human skull! The chances of such an event occurring are incalculable. There is a greater probability of winning the lottery or swimming the Atlantic. What strange stroke of fate had caused the jackal to dig out this skull, which was probably at least one hundred years old, the very night before our visit? The skull was dry and fragile from age, and it rained the next night. Had we come several days later it would have been no more than dust.

I had never known Pat so silent!

The cairn on the Serengeti with the skull.

When I examined the skull closely I found evidence of knife cuts at the base of the cranium, suggesting perhaps a hole had been cut to remove the brains as in some process of mummification. Tanzanians pale if you mention *mumyani* – the evil spirit, which comes at night to suck out your brains. Is the word related to the ancient Egyptian word *mummy* as some suppose? And did these early inhabitants of the Serengeti have Ancient Egyptian traditions still remembered in Tanzanian folklore?

Anthropological research has shown they were not Maasai but a tribe called the Datoga, who now live near Singida to the south but who formerly lived all over the Ngorongoro Highlands, until ousted sometime between 1836 and 1851 by the Maasai after a great battle in the Ngorongoro Crater. The cairns in which they traditionally buried their dead were called *bunged*.

Pat was right about the Maasai though.

* * *

To the west of Arusha, in northern Tanzania before you get to the great wall of the Rift Valley, lies a remote and arid area dominated by East Africa's only recently active volcano – Lengai, the Mountain of God, which last erupted in 1967. I arranged to climb it with a German colleague from the College and a visiting friend of his, and one weekend found us on our way to this barren area of Maasailand, an area at that time visited by few Europeans. The track climbs a steep range of hills, so rough that my Land Rover wheels just spun ineffectually on the rocks and I was forced to unload the trailer I was pulling. This delayed us and we had to spend the night there.

The next morning we descended into the Rift Valley and drove south towards Lengai's distant peak. There was no clear track and eventually we came upon a group of Maasai elders sitting a little way apart from their *manyatta*, the cluster of round-domed huts made of cow dung mixed with earth. Speaking in Kiswahili, we asked them the way to the distant mountain. One of them jumped up and insisted he would accompany us, he had been there before and only he could find the way.

Without further ado he opened the offside door of the Land Rover, and attired simply in his ochre-coloured blanket knotted over his left shoulder, jumped in and perched himself on top of my cook's lap. Now Hakulini, my cook, was an Mchagga from Kilimanjaro, with an age-old terror of the Maasai reaching back into history. Hakulini's face expressed utter astonishment at this liberty.

"You can't do that!" he spluttered at the Maasai sitting on his lap.

But our self-appointed guide simply chuckled and waved me on.

It was straightforward going at first, although slow grinding through the soft volcanic dust, which we soon drove into. But as we got closer to the volcano so we came to the recent lava flows and our progress became more and more hair-raising.

These fan-shaped flows stretched towards us in thin fingers, smooth on the top like tarmac, but they had become dissected by weathering. The result was one would find oneself driving comfortably up a smooth incline, but as it got higher and higher so the flow got narrower and narrower, until there was barely space for the vehicle to pass, with a sheer drop of several feet on either side!

Hakulini's eyes were starting out of his head,

"But we can't go there!" he would shout at the Maasai, "This is a motor car, not a donkey!"

The Maasai would look at him in surprise, then dismiss his protests with a gesture and urge me forward. Always, just when it seemed the width of the flow had run out on us, and the Land Rover was about to be left straddled on its axles, it would broaden out and descend again.

It was the same with the rivulets of sterile soda water that flowed in some depressions. My guide would gaily wave me forward, Hakulini would shout protests, but in this case I would get out and have a look first. I didn't want to get bogged down to the axles in soft ooze. But always the guide was right, and the depressions had hard lava bottoms covered with water only a few inches deep.

We got as far as the grassy hillocks at the base of the volcano when it was time to make camp for the night. Our guide urged us on but we thought better of it. We would walk from here at first light. So we camped on this barren spur, passing an uneventful night, our guide simply sleeping on the ground rolled in his flimsy blanket.

Preparing camp on Lengai, December 1972.

In the morning he said we should make our way around to the other side of the volcano where there was a route to the summit. My German companion dismissed the idea with contempt. The volcano's peak loomed above us, its smooth sides covered with grass until near the summit. We would simply walk straight up – the shortest way. Such confidence had a familiar ring and I should have known better than to let myself be swayed by it and ignore the Maasai guide's advice. It was argued the other way would be too far and we did not have time enough for attempting it.

So we aimed straight up the mountainside. As we advanced, so the side got steeper and steeper, as volcanoes do. I soon found myself left behind by my younger companions.

From a distance it looked like a smooth, grassy slope, changing to bare volcanic lava near the summit. But as one got higher so one found progress was continually impeded by sheer-sided ravines dropping down vertically for hundreds of feet: ravines which sliced through the crumbly, jagged lava at all angles, invisible from the surface. One was obliged to continually retrace one's steps downwards to find a way around, only to then find oneself confronted by another such obstacle higher up. The guide had certainly known what he was talking about when he had told us that this was not the side to climb.

Eventually, for the first time in my life, I had to give up. Age was beginning to take its toll and I sat down gasping and puffing on the dry, forty-five-degree grassy slope, the summit still far, far, above me.

It was a good view anyway – if you can call a panorama of a bleak, arid wilderness of sere grass with not a sign of life as far as the eye could see, a good view! Not even a bird broke the monotony of this desolation.

High above me on the mountainside, the Maasai, now a tiny speck of red in his blanket, came to a halt and sat down. He had accepted the overruling of his advice in good part and attacked the sheer mountainside with enthusiasm. A funny thing, because the Maasai don't usually like what they consider pointless physical exertion, and also call most volcanoes *shaitan* or 'devil', fearing to go near them. This volcano was called the opposite – 'Mountain of God', but still one would have thought a Maasai would be reluctant to venture up it.

His voice piped out distantly over the stillness:

"*Mimi na chokaaaaaa . . . !*" "I am tirrrrred!" he shouted.

I was too.

112

My companions were by now out of sight somewhere so I made my way back slowly to camp. The Maasai followed suit, and not long afterwards my colleagues turned up, having also admitted defeat.

Clearly the summit could not be reached from this side, but we did not have time to try again by the correct route and were obliged to pack up camp and depart.

When we came to the Maasai's *manyatta* we found a remarkable thing had happened. Out of an almost cloudless sky it had rained during the night and the ground was already a carpet of green. Our guide was both amazed and delighted, for green grass means healthy cattle and cattle are the Maasai's most treasured possession. He must have put it down to some spiritual intervention– his reward for guiding the white men to the Mountain of God.

At least I like to think he did.

* * *

The Maasai were one of the anachronisms of changing Africa, always surprising one with an obstinate clinging to their traditional lifestyle on the one hand, and their knowledge of the modern world on the other.

One day I was in the Longido Maasai area to the west of Mount Kilimanjaro, where, assisted by Pat we had just shot a Grant's gazelle in connection with a research project I was conducting. The research necessitated the animal be weighed and samples taken from it without delay. So as soon as the animal dropped I raced up to it in my Land Rover, hurriedly lifted the carcase into the back and drove off at speed to find the nearest suitable thorn tree from which I could suspend a weighing machine. A tree with a convenient branch was soon found, the weighing machine rigged, and the carcase suspended from it.

When the shot had been fired there had been two Maasai walking in the far distance, dressed as usual simply in their blankets tied with a knot over one shoulder, and carrying their traditional spears with three-foot-long blades. Now they came running towards us, loping swiftly over the ground in long strides. I thought that due to our haste they probably thought we were poachers and were coming to investigate. They arrived breathless, blankets flapping around their naked thighs, spears gripped in their hands.

One came forward and leaning on his spear craned his neck, peering at the weighing machine.

"He's never seen one before," I thought.

"Fifty kilogrammes," he announced, turning and grinning at me.

It was indeed.

* * *

Not far from the College, about halfway to the town of Arusha, lived a colourful character the self-styled 'Doctor' Von N., a Hungarian who after some twenty years in Tanzania spoke the local language, Kiswahili, fluently, but could hardly understand or speak a word of English. He sported typical Hungarian side whiskers and ran a guesthouse constructed in Bavarian hunting-lodge fashion. Adjoining it he had a small zoological garden with a number of animals kept in somewhat inadequate conditions. Not everyone would keep fully grown lions in a pen fenced only with chicken wire! The result of this inadequacy was that from time to time an animal found its way out.

Such an event happened to the leopard and I was called in to recapture it.

When I arrived the leopard was crouching in a space between a wire pen and a palisade fence, waiting for nightfall before venturing further. To my astonishment the zoo was still open and visitors with children were walking about, although excluded from the immediate area of the leopard. But that didn't amount to much if it had tried to make a break for it.

Darting was the only suitable way of recapturing it, but an angry leopard is a very dangerous animal and my concern was what would it do when I shot a dart into it? Would it explode into a ball of fury, turning on me helpless with no more than the darting gun to defend myself with? Or would it rush into the gardens and attack the nearest passer-by?

Well whatever it did, those were chances we would have to take.

I was about to prepare to dart it when Von N. indicated I should wait a few minutes, and he departed to his quarters. He returned shortly afterwards attired in Tyrolean hunting cape and Tyrolean hat replete with feather in it! It was obviously important to be properly dressed on such occasions.

When all was ready I took up a position with the darting rifle. I found I had a gap of about three inches between the wooden palisades through which I had to shoot the dart to hit the leopard's rump. I didn't want to get too close otherwise the impact of the dart would be too great, causing injury to the animal. On the other hand, the farther away, the less likely I was to hit the target. The dart bore only a tuft of wool at the end like a fairground airgun dart, and was thus not very accurate. One could only aim and hope for the best.

With Von N. in his Tyrolean hunting attire guarding me at one side, I took a deep breath and pulled the trigger. The gun, which fired a type of .22 cartridge went off with quite a loud report. With a *thwack!* the dart stuck in the wooden palisade about one inch to the side of the gap. The leopard didn't stir. I cursed under my breath and reloaded.

I fired again, and now there was a dart stuck in the palisade on the other side of the gap.

The leopard didn't move a muscle.

There was now only one dart left.

I reloaded and fired again. The dart sailed through the two-inch gap striking the leopard fair and square in the middle of the haunch. Just where it was supposed to.

The leopard never budged an inch.

After that it was all plain sailing. Within ten minutes the leopard was comatose and we hauled it out. Von N. took a photograph of myself and various helpers who appeared, all standing around the inert body, and then it was carried away and put into its cage.

As a special honour I was then invited into Von N.'s holy of holies – his private apartments done out in the grand manner of a hunting lodge. Huge elephant tusks greeted one either side of the lounge entrance, and a veritable herd of mounted buffalo heads leered down with sightless glass eyes from the dark panelled walls.

But what particularly caught my eye was a small oil painting of a lion and lioness which had pride of place over the chimney piece. I remarked upon it.

"Zat iss very much worth. Two tousand pounds."

Von N. confided it was by the Hungarian animal painter G. Vastagh (1866-1919). To me it was remarkable because I had a print of the selfsame painting hanging in pride of place above my chimney piece at home in Oxfordshire!

* * *

Von N.'s leopard-hunting attire brought to mind memories of another hat in incongruous surroundings. I took leave while at the College to visit Mombasa to buy a Zanzibar chest, fine wooden chests in Arab style studded with ornamental brass and brass nails, but no longer made in Zanzibar since the revolution there. Down a narrow street in the old Arab quarter of the city I found a shop that boasted 'Zanzibari' antiques.

The fat, bow-legged Indian merchant looked like Peter Ustinov, or like Peter Ustinov playing the part of a fat, bow-legged Indian merchant. The shop was quite empty inside but the proprietor said he could provide me with what I wanted if I took him to another address. Whereupon he placed a tweed trilby on his head, of which the hatband was gaily adorned with trout flies redolent of Scottish becks or southern English chalk streams.

I followed his waddling figure out into the hot Mombasa street where Panamas were more appropriate than Scottish tweeds and trout flies.

As we drove through the city he explained he had a very fine chest, not exactly antique, but the wood was antique. Driftwood, I supposed. He had loaned the chest to an Indian friend for a display of his wedding gifts, but, he assured me, he hadn't given it to the friend and now the wedding was over he would borrow it back, and let him have another later.

We stopped before a block of flats in Mombasa's main street and mounted the two flights of stairs. He knocked on a door, which was opened by a young Indian woman. He spoke to her, she protested volubly, but he brushed her protests aside, pushed in and beckoned me to follow him.

He indicated the chest. I agreed it would suit me and so we seized the handles and carried it out, the Indian woman complaining bitterly. The merchant ignored her and we sweated down the two flights of stairs with the chest and heaved it into my vehicle.

On reflection I don't know which was the more incongruous: my fat friend's fly fisherman's hat under the tropical sun, or the method of obtaining a Zanzibar chest!

* * *

Another character who lived not far from the College was Desmond Vesey-Fitzgerald, then an ecologist in the Arusha National Park. Vesey, as he was universally called, was one of a tiny privileged band who had been employed as overseas ecologists by the British Government in the 1930s by what Evelyn Waugh described as 'that last . . . survivor of the "Fairy Godmother Departments"', the Empire Marketing Board. As such Vesey had led an immensely interesting life, pursuing ecology in such far-flung places as South America, the Seychelles and East Africa; in days when both the places and the word 'ecologist' were almost unknown.

A short, dumpy man, with the same grandfather spectacles, he might have passed for the brother of Peter Greenway. He always sported a bush jacket, shorts and calf-length despatch rider's boots. Now past retirement age he still showed an unflagging enthusiasm for ecology and worked harder than many a young graduate.

Few people knew he was appointed as the first biologist to the Kenya Game Department in 1947. About to begin a vegetation survey of the Tsavo National Park in 1949 he was abruptly sent on temporary secondment to the International Red Locust Control Service in Northern Rhodesia. His three-month temporary assignment lasted fifteen years, and it was to be almost thirty years before a vegetation survey was finally conducted in Tsavo by another botanist.

Vesey was always one for a good story and he told me how, while working for the Game Department, he had glued together two very long rhino horns as an exhibit for the annual Nairobi Royal Agricultural Show. The idea was not to try to deceive anybody, but simply to draw attention to the Game Department's stand. Several years later a Chief Game Warden found the discarded and long-forgotten exhibit in a store and measured it with astonishment. Vesey alleged it then for many years graced the pages of Rowland Ward's *Records of Big Game* – the nimrod's bible - as a world record trophy.

It was to surface again in 1991 when it appeared in a photograph illustrating a World Wide Fund for Nature campaign report and had been specially selected for retention by the Game Department as an outstanding example of an exceptionally long rhino horn. After I drew attention to Vesey's story, the horn, or more correctly horns, were burnt.

His best story perhaps was when he was with his boss, an entomologist named Myers, working in British Guiana in 1933. They were out on the pampas when Evelyn Waugh came along. Vesey remembered him as a shiny pink, round-faced youth, quite out of place in the rough environment of the pampas.

As is custom with travellers in remote places, they invited Waugh to share their lunch. Now the standard food of people in those parts was a slab of dried meat, *tasso*, carried under the saddle on the horse's back so that it became softened with the horse's sweat. While Myers was preparing the campfire, Vesey went over to his horse and, lifting a corner of the saddle, started to saw off strips of meat from the slab with his pocketknife. Waugh's eyes popped in astonishment and his pink face started to turn an unhealthy shade of green. Nervously he suggested the two join *him* for lunch, and somewhat tired of their endless diet of *tasso* they readily agreed. Thereupon Waugh produced a Fortnum and Mason's hamper and they partook of a sumptuous banquet out on the pampas, dining as they had never dined before! Pâté, caviar, it was all there!

The upshot was, according to Vesey, that in his book *Ninety-two Days*, Waugh related how he had come across two mad entomologists who had tried to eat one of their horse's saddles. The reality, as recorded in Waugh's diary, was somewhat more prosaic. His entry for 16 January 1933 noted that he came up with a rancher named Major Weller "and two entomologists named Myers and Fitzgerald. Myers dysentery. They had killed a bush turkey; gave them rum; lunched with them. Myers employed by Empire Marketing Board."[1]

In *Ninety-two Days*, Waugh's reference is equally brief:"A meeting on the trail with three Englishmen . . . the other two naturalists . . . The three were coming down together on foot. One had dysentery and looked deathly; the other two by contrast abnormally robust. They had just shot a 'bush turkey'. We stewed it and ate it together and then parted company, though not before one of the naturalists had caught a peculiar fly in the nostril of my horse."

Six miles beyond where they met up Waugh arrived at a rest camp, so they were not so far out in the blue. On 14 January he had listed his stores, purchased in Georgetown. They comprised two tins of herrings, nine tins of corned beef, four tins of salmon, three tins of sausage, two tins of tongue, four tins of meat and veg, six of tomato soup, jam, milk, etc. There was no Fortnum and Mason's hamper, no pâté, no caviar.

But old men forget, and it was a good story anyway.

* * *

We often took the trainees to the Arusha National Park, a jewel of a park only 45 miles distant from the College. As you approached the perfect little volcanic crater of Ngurdoto, with its steep, thickly forested sides, there was a signboard proclaiming a syrupy American text:

"Let no one say, to your shame, that all was beauty, until you came."

Everytime he passed this admonition Pat would exclaim:

"I can't help being ugly!"

From the forested rim one looked down onto the grassy floor of the crater, its lawnlike quality swarming with game – an Ngorongoro in miniature. In 1974 there were 70 buffalo, numbers of warthog, giraffe and rhinos. With the trainees we did a sweep of the crater floor to collect the skulls of animals that had died naturally in the crater in order to work out their ages. It was rather a hair-raising exercise, with the buffalo thundering excitedly to and fro – one came straight at the advancing line of trainees, to sheer off at the last moment. A rhino crashed off somewhere in the undergrowth . . .

Examination of the collection of buffalo skulls showed they were not old animals when they had died. The crater was not some tranquil forest retreat where old buffaloes went to spend their last days as romantic imagination would like to have it, rather animals were probably dying in the prime of life competing for space in the area. So much for the romantic image.

When I went back seven years later in 1982, the crater floor was empty.

"Where are the animals?" I asked the park guide.

"Animals?" he queried. "There aren't any animals here."

Ngurdoto, this former jewel in the crown of the Tanzania National Parks, had become something that now unknowing tourists just came to look at for its scenic beauty. The animals had all gone.

Adjoining stands the extinct volcano of Mount Meru rising to 14,977 feet, whose forested slopes were like a fairytale wonderland. A picturesque waterfall, giant forest trees in mysterious, shady ravines; green fairy lawns, and the bleak, cinder crater at the summit. Vesey had cut a motor track to the crater using elephant paths, at one point passing right through the middle of a huge fig-tree, which straddled the track.

One day he found a long and very valuable mountaineer's rope suspended from the rim's highest point and dangling into the crater. A park guard recovered it with great difficulty. No one ever claimed it. Who was this mysterious climber, and what happened to him? Do his bones lie forgotten somewhere among the crater's jumbled volcanic rocks?

The crater has claimed at least two deaths, when a too-daring light aircraft flew into it and couldn't get enough lift to get out again, flying into the sheer side of the crater wall where the scar of its impact remains to this day.

Once Vesey found a sacrificed black goat in a glade – propitiation to a rain god, evidence witchcraft still flourished in secret in its forest depths. In the crater was a place called Njeku, which means an old woman who has the power to make rain. Here the rainmaking priestess used to, and probably still does, make sacrifices in the hollow of a sacred juniper tree.

Alas, on my return in 1982 this wonderland was no longer accessible. The stream from the waterfall had cut the ford at the base and, well, it had been too much effort to repair it. Probably the forest had already closed in on Vesey's remarkable track.

Not far from here Hardy Kruger, who starred with John Wayne in the film *Hatari*, had set up a little safari lodge, called Momella. That now had all the signs of neglect and decay to which I had become accustomed. But there was still a cook, sitting on the doorstep as if hoping someone might pass by. If so, his wish was granted and he eagerly rustled up a simple meal of boiled chicken served in the large, bleak, and almost totally bare, dining hall. Momella had seen better days than this.

In the 1930s Joyce Boyd came to live in a house which her husband built for her on the western side of the present park, describing her life in this tranquil spot in her book *My Farm in Lion Country*. The ruins of her house were still there, the corner pillars rearing erect and forlorn in the forest like ancient Roman columns of some mysterious lost city. We used to camp by a pool just below them standing stark and gaunt above us on the skyline. Decay had followed decay.

* * *

On August 21 1899, one of the first big game photographers, the German C. G. Schillings, visited an area in northern Tanzania a few miles south of Mweka. In his book *In Wildest Africa* he reproduced a sketch map of the route he took and a list of the animals seen. I repeated the walk in this area, the Masimani Hills area, with a group of students on August 8 1971, almost exactly seventy-two years later.

We recorded: baboons; a pair of ostriches; 4 dikdik; 4 warthog; a kori bustard; baboons; 2-3 week old elephant tracks; a hyrax on Masimani Hill; 12 guinea fowl, 5 yellowneck spurfowl and one young male gerenuk.

Schillings recorded: waterbuck; 150 zebra; herd of impala; 2 reedbuck; baboons; about 40 waterbuck; 15-20 Grant's gazelles; guinea fowls; bustard; 2 secretary birds; 3 gerenuk; herd of oryx; 2 rhino; 2 rhino; 8-12 giraffe; 5 ostrich; giraffes; zebra with waterbucks; waterbucks and Grant's gazelles; Grant's gazelles; herd of impala; 2 warthog; lion tracks; one jackal; elephant track.

The local people reported giraffe, zebra and lion in the area, as well as hippos and crocs in the river; but the difference between my observations and Schillings's bore grim testimony, if any was needed, to the changing state of Africa.

* * *

The reason for establishing Mweka College had been fear that after Independence there would be no trained Africans to take the place of the departing expatriate wardens. But whereas in colonial times having been an army officer was usually seen as the best qualification for the job, the development of game management as a science, a necessity in view of the development pressures surging across Africa; and the American influence, where in fact a quite different situation prevailed concerning park management, meant that training had to be more formalized. Africans had to be taught skills that their colonial predecessors never knew, and indeed, never had need for.

Generally I found the students amenable and interested in their work. Only one was troublesome – a large stout Nigerian, named after a well-known brand of washing powder.

There was a new instructor at the college, a young Indian girl, a former student who had distinguished herself by having a rhino which she had tried to photograph at close quarters, trample over her legs as she threw herself sideways to avoid its indignant charge. She was reading out a list of the students who were to depart on a field trip. When she came to the end of the list, the Nigerian raised his hand.

"I am not on the list," he stated.

I could see the young girl was flustered; she had read out one of his several names and didn't know what more to say. It was my job to back her up so I thought I had better put the student down before he became impossible for her to handle.

"Well, if you've come here under a false name, we will have to hand you over to the secret police," I announced.

Fifty-nine students exploded into a roar of laughter. The Nigerian glowered sullenly.

The class was eventually dismissed, still laughing at the joke, and I went to my office. The Nigerian put on his Ton-ton Macoute dark glasses and followed me with purposeful tread.

"What did you mean?" he asked me, coming into my office.

"Nothing," I replied.

"So you have nothing further to say?"

"Nothing."

He walked out.

Then began the great battle of wills between him and myself.

Being older than the other students, it was the loss of face from being laughed at that had upset him, and he now began to wage a campaign against me. The upshot was he made such a nuisance of himself the Principal, now a Tanzanian, announced he would be expelled. Shortly after this announcement I was in the administrator's office when the Nigerian came in. Seeing me he burst out:

"Help me, sir! Help me!"

I regarded him sternly.

"Look at me, sir! Look at me!" he cried, pointing to his face with a forefinger, whereupon a large tear oozed out of his right eye and rolled slowly down his cheek.

I don't know how he did it, but I was unmoved.

He then sank to his knees, and heaving his vast form about like some cumbrous hippopotamus, bowing his head he seized my boots as if to kiss them.

The Tanzanian administrator was acutely embarrassed.

"Now, now," he remonstrated.

I was of the opinion a different approach was necessary.

"Get up and stop making a fool of yourself!" I snapped.

He leapt up with agility as if he had been stung, and stood staring impassively in front. There was not a sign of a tear on his face.

I walked out.

This approach having failed, he voiced his complaint loudly everywhere and to anybody, and someone, an outsider, suggested he take it to the political party, TANU, the Tanganyika African National Union. The next thing we knew was that the political heavies had descended on the College, eager to make an example, as they thought, of a racist white man.

All the instructors were told there would be a meeting in the staff common room, which we would have to attend. While waiting for the appointed hour Pat came into my office and talked nonsense in a loud voice. This was for the benefit of the plain-clothes policeman who was casually standing outside of my open office window listening to our conversation, a place where no-one would normally stand by himself. He didn't have a mackintosh and trilby, but he did wear a Chairman Mao flat cap, souvenir of his Chinese training.

Eventually we were all called in to sit around the coffee tables ranged down the centre of the room.

The Principal sat at the head, we were seated down one side, and a row of grim inquisitors faced us on the other. A stout lady, a political

125

commissar perhaps? Always the most vindictive. Two nondescript men. They were out for blood! They wanted a scapegoat to show the party they were active in rooting out any vestiges of white colonialism that might be lingering on in their socialist paradise.

One of the nondescript men screwed up his face into a stage frown of concentration:

"Who are these secret police?" he asked me. "There are no such people in Tanzania."

I replied it was just a joke, but he didn't want to hear. The stout female commissar made a note on a scrap of paper and passed it to him. He studied it with prolonged attention, and then ostentatiously placed it into his mouth, carefully chewed it up and swallowed it. There were no secret police in Tanzania!

Discussion ranged endlessly. I was accused (I learnt afterwards) of being too proud because I didn't say anything. Pat was accused of having too much to say. It was difficult to satisfy them. They were rather in a quandary because they found all the instructors, most of whom were Tanzanian, were united in my defence. Whereas they wanted a scapegoat to show they were upholding their socialist commitments and weeding out the imperialist bullies, crushing the last remnants of colonial oppression.

Finally they turned to the Nigerian himself. He was called in. I began by asking him how we had got on together before the event in question,

"Oh, excellent," was the reply. The inquisitors were thrown into disarray. This wasn't the sort of reply they had expected, nor wanted to hear.

He then created further confusion by turning his attack on the Principal. After that he lost his case. The inquisitors left without coming to any conclusion.

A week later I was shopping in Moshi at ten o'clock one morning when I saw the 'secret policeman' standing on the main street pavement in his pyjamas. Rather than trying to merge into the background, a little difficult it must be admitted when standing in the street in one's night attire, he greeted me like a long-lost friend with a cheery wave and a beaming smile, his stern, paper-swallowing episode forgotten. It turned out the pyjamas were not some sort of disguise, he pointed out he lived in an adjacent flat and hadn't got dressed yet.

Well, that's Africa all over.

Notes

1. M. Davie ed. 1976 *The Diaries of Evelyn Waugh*.

Chapter 5

In the Dark Heart

the Central African Republic and Emperor Bokassa

When in Africa there is plenty of time to sit and think. I was doing just that, sitting in my Land Rover flapping ineffectually at the persistent attentions of myriads of sweat bees, my hams clammy and uncomfortable on the plastic seat as I perspired steadily in the heat like a saucepan coming slowly to the boil. Ahead of me the band of workers, black bodies shining through holes in their tattered shirts like black plums dotting a suet pudding, hacked at the vegetation, cutting the semblance of a track before me into the green-blue haze of the endless bush. We were deep in the Bamingui-Bangoran National Park, three days distant from the nearest handful of seedy mud huts dignified by the name of village. Blighted, yes, that was the word. Everything here was blighted. It was not the fault of the peasants. They had suffered too long under too many despots to have the will to do better any more. It was, as one cynical Frenchman described it, *"un pays sans espoir"* (a land without hope).

The workers were singing now as they chopped away, a catching onomatopoeic melody in which they took turns to imitate the sound of musical instruments. The twanging of the *koundi*, a type of guitar; the tinkling melody of the *balafon*, a hand-held xylophone; and the ch-ch-ch of the *keke*, castanets made from the dried shells of a fruit half-filled with small stones. I wished idly I had a tape recorder with me. Later I bought one, but they never sang the song again. Their gaiety came and went like so many soap bubbles.

Heat, flies, sweat. Mile after mile of endless bush. Four thousand three hundred square miles to be precise. If this wasn't wildest Africa

129

then what was? And I was one man with one clapped-out Land Rover charged with studying, planning and developing this vast trackless area more than half the size of Wales.

But let's start with Bangui (pronounced bong-gee as in 'bongos') the capital of the even now little-known former French colony of Oubangui-Chari, the country I now found myself in.

In 1939 the only hotel Bangui boasted was known as the *Hôtel Pain*, of which the American author Negley Farson wrote the English word was more appropriate than the French. It was famous for having a bidet in the dining room, not used, we hope, by the lady diners. Negley Farson found most of its guests were drunk by nine-thirty in the morning. The Governor of the colony informed him with satisfaction that of the twenty men he had come out with, seventeen were already dead. Little wonder: the drinking parties, which started at breakfast, were still going on at lunchtime, and perhaps little wonder also the participants did not survive for long.

In the evening the colonial officials, looking like naval officers in white drill uniforms bearing gold-striped epaulettes, sat drinking on the terrace. They spent their time dreaming of retirement in France. The dress may have changed, but the dreams haven't. Neither has Negley Farson's description of the "depressing heaviness of Bangui", and the Oubangui River, originally the Mubangi, which "ran malevolently past."[1]

Oubangui-Chari was later to become known as the Central African Republic, as that is where it is, its arbitrarily-drawn boundaries placing it right in the centre of the continent, the dark heart of Africa; leading to the wry French sarcasm that the country doesn't even have a proper name.

The earliest explorers who bypassed it were perhaps luckier than they knew. Doctor Gustav Nacthigal, a German medical doctor-explorer, nearly reached it in 1873 from the north, but had to turn back at the flood plains of the Salamat, near present-day Am Timam in Chad. Some vague hint of the existence of the Oubangui River seems to have reached Italian or Portuguese explorers in the latter seventeenth century, but Bangui was first reached on the river in February 1885 by the English Baptist missionary George Grenfell, exploring from his base at Stanley Pool. Just beyond Bangui a series of rapids makes the river impassable to large boats. Here Grenfell found the natives hostile. Men, women and children took refuge in "crows' nests" built in the forks of large trees, reached by rope ladders which they hauled up after them. Thus ensconced they proceeded to shoot poisoned arrows at the boat. In view of this unfriendly reception Grenfell did not attempt to establish a station. But this pugnacity of the inhabitants did not deter the French, who established the station of Bangui four years later.

Ninety years later the world was shocked to hear of the predilection for human flesh of the deposed tyrant ruler of the country, Emperor Bokassa. But this came as no surprise to many expatriates who lived there. According to Karamojo Bell, "the greatest elephant hunter of them all" who hunted the Oubangui River from Bangui between 1912 and 1914, there was a "fairly heavy traffic in female slaves from the Belgian Congo side. The trade medium was chiefly cartridges and percussion caps and gunpowder. The girls were brought overfat and sold either as wives or for the table".[2]

Marcus Daly, an American elephant hunter who hunted there in the 1920s, claimed although cannibalism was then rife, it was not so prior to 1914: "All my carriers were cannibals . . . my line of carriers would suddenly drop loads, draw their spears and rush headlong into the bush. Soon I would hear screams and shouting, and in a few minutes they would return, each with a limb or part of some unfortunate victim – child, man or woman . . . That night, if I strolled past the cooking-pots, all those pieces would be there rolling round and about in the boiling water".[3]

The second French administrator of the colony, Doctor Adolphe Cureau, who as well as being an administrator was also an anthropologist, wrote in 1915 that "for a long time" the commandants of the Bangui Station were obliged to post armed sentries on the cemetery to protect newly interred bodies from being exhumed and eaten.[4] The track to the first house I lived in during my séjour in the country took a right hand turn opposite this selfsame cemetery gate, and on the corner where it branched off was a mud hut in which lived three old crones who could well have passed for the three witches in Macbeth. These three old hags eyeing me malevolently from beneath grim lowered black brows, sullen and unsmiling, sent shivers up my spine as I passed each day. I wondered if their former husband, for I supposed they were widows, had not built his hut at that strategic point for some particular gruesome purpose, and now his old widows bemoaned the passing of better days.

From this point the track passed through what had once been an experimental farm until Bokassa expelled the Frenchmen running it, and so on to my house, the former French farm manager's. It was situated on the summit of a small hill providing a pleasant prospect, but quite isolated and reached by a causeway backing up a dam. Water for the house was provided by one of those remarkable machines called a ram, the only thing that could still be made to work. Before the causeway was a shed, stacked with large packing cases containing the machinery for a model dairy. During my time there I was to see these packing cases slowly disintegrate under the ravages of termites, and a stout tree grow up between one of the pieces of machinery.

The causeway became undermined bit by bit in the rains, and cut off from the other side I was obliged to lay two planks across the chasm which formed – over which precarious structure I drove my vehicle, a feat I accomplished one night after having imbibed more than was wise. But with further rain the gap soon became too wide for the length of the planks and I was forced to park next to the rotting packing cases and climb back and forth across the ravine on foot.

The few farm employees laboured dilatorily, for like all low-grade workers at the time they had not been paid for two years, but if they quit then they knew they never would be.

* * *

The Central African Republic, or C A R as it is known for short, had one great attraction in its early days – its elephants, enticing all the famous names in elephant hunting. This was not because of the size of the ivory, although that was of the best and remained so until the elephant massacres of the late 1970s and early 1980s, but because it was the only country which issued a 'commercial' elephant-hunting permit, allowing an unlimited number to be shot. This continued until 1932, and the CAR was also the last country on the continent to stop (officially) ivory collection. This it did in 1979, only to reopen it again in 1981, finally closing it again (officially) in 1989.

Elephant hunting had been encouraged in the east from the end of the 19th century, most recognized of the first hunters being a Frenchman Fredon who had been thrown out of the administration for having killed a guard. Another of the early ones was an American named Cherry who had been a former mechanic on a Congo Free State steamboat. Later the Scotsman 'Karamojo' Bell hunted here and on the Aouk River in the north in 1912. But it was the south-eastern corner of the country, the so-called 'lost triangle' of the Upper Mbomou River, which was to become the main area of attraction in the Twenties and Thirties.

There were only ten or so of this elite company of adventurers, the first to go there another Scotsman, James Sutherland, who had already written a book about his elephant-hunting exploits in southern and eastern Africa. He was poisoned by his cook in 1929, when the Azande inhabitants decided to wipe out all Europeans. The cook laced his tea with poison but Sutherland realized this and vomited it up. Nevertheless he became paralysed in one leg and blind in one eye but lived on for another three years, still slaughtering a few more elephants.

* * *

This, then, was the country I had now come to. Although many tourists still arrive by the route Negley Farson took, from Zaïre, crossing the Oubangui River at Bangassou and driving to Bangui, this was now mainly confined to converted army Bedford trucks full of very dirty-looking young Britishers, young men with scruffy beards and young girls in short shorts and brown legs, all needing a good wash.

I arrived by the more conventional way on an Air Afrique Boeing 747, landing just after midnight at Bangui-Mpoko airport. When you step out of the aircraft onto the tarmac, even at one o'clock in the morning the humid heat suffocates you like a blanket thrown over one's head. It was not without some trepidation I ventured forth from the apparent comfortable security of the aircraft, for this was Bokassa's country. He had not yet declared himself emperor, that was to come later, but his megalomania and erratic behaviour had already established him as one of the less predictable of Africa's petty dictators. Hardly surprising behaviour for a man whose father, Chief Mindogon, was flogged to death when Bokassa was six years old (1927) because he had not supplied enough wild rubber collectors for a French commercial company. (The French pretend he was flogged for cannibalism).

You drove into the centre of the town along a street across which hung an illuminated sign, later smashed during one of the riots, stating Bangui was the "*Coquette Ville de Paris*". It certainly didn't feel like it, and Negley Farson's "depressing heaviness" hung everywhere. Like him I installed myself at the Rock Hotel as the *Hôtel Pain* was now called. It had been reopened only a day or so before my arrival. Bokassa had brought a party to dine there one evening and was so enraged at the total of the bill he had ordered immediate closure of the hotel and the deportation of its manager. It was rather unfortunate for the guests who woke up one morning to find their hotel had closed!

An attempted coup was still fresh in the minds of many, although they knew better than to speak too loudly of it. A grenade had been thrown at Bokassa when he stepped from his plane at the airport one day, but in typical CAR fashion it had failed to explode. Mass arrests had followed with a show trial in the indoor sports stadium. Ten of those alleged to have been involved were sentenced to death, ten to 10 years' imprisonment and ten to 20 years'. One of the ringleaders sentenced to death, Obrou by name, was married to one of the Martines.

The Martine farce was as if out of a Gilbert and Sullivan opera. It related to an illegitimate daughter of Bokassa begot of a Vietnamese woman when he was serving in the French army in Vietnam. One day Bokassa suddenly decided he wanted to find his daughter and a woman claiming to be her was brought to Bangui and handsomely received by Bokassa. All went well until a second Martine turned up claiming to be the real daughter. With a judgement worthy of Solomon, Bokassa adopted the first Martine, so they became known as the "False Martine" and the "True Martine". He then married them off to two of his senior army officers, one being Obrou who was now condemned to death, Bokassa reproaching him for his action in attempting his assassination after he had been so generous as to give him one of his daughters to marry.

One of the Martines, whether true or false I know not, ran a Vietnamese restaurant in Bangui. A French lawyer resident in Bangui was dining there and relieved himself against the wall at the back. Toilets were scarce in Bangui. He was spotted and Martine complained to Bokassa she had been insulted. Later, gendarmes surrounded his house and he was unable to leave fearing arrest and incarceration in the notorious Ngaragba prison, known as the House of Deaths or the Devil's Hole, where sodomy by the *godobé*, the low-life criminals, and official torture, eventually followed by death, were likely to be one's fate. The guards were said to be trained in torture techniques by a one-time Czechoslovakian director of the prison named Otto Sacher, a colonial settler in the country. Eventually the lawyer was saved from this grim fate by being deported.

Shortly after arrival in this somewhat tense atmosphere I went to make myself known to the Honorary British Consul. He was a Frenchman, unable to speak a word of English. I was an Englishman almost unable to speak a word of French. His secretary could manage a little better than either of us and acted as interpreter. At that time I was a rarity in the CAR; you could count the number of Britishers on the fingers of one hand (I couldn't because I didn't know of any others). Few of the French would speak in English to one, even if they knew how. Just as the British overseas are more British than the British, so are the French more French than the French and maintain a strict Gallic antipathy.

After I had been there a number of years, I was sitting on the terrace of the Rock Hotel, which overlooks the Oubangui River as it did in Negley Farson's day, when a man introduced himself to me. Not only was he an Englishman, but he owned a great part of Bangui as well, being married to the daughter of one of the early Governors!

My Central African counterpart, Latakpi, was a huge African who looked like Idi Amin. He appeared gentle enough, although he did subsequently get a ninety-five per cent pass mark in judo at a college in Canada. He also, appropriately enough, got a ninety per cent pass mark for acting. He went to Canada to study wild life management, and I never did discover what judo and acting had to do with it.

My office was a shabby wooden building with a corrugated iron roof that had seen better days, and provided all the accomplishments of an oven. Sitting sweltering in the heat was bad enough, but what I disliked most were the armies of rats and cockroaches. There was little I could do to stem the tide of the latter, but I waged constant war with traps and poison against the rats. After all, it is not very nice to have to clean rat droppings and urine off one's desk in the morning before starting work. It may have happened in Pepys's day in London, but here we were in the 1970s!

The wooden steps to the office had fallen into disrepair long ago and one mounted to the doorway on a pile of old car tyres.

This decrepit structure dignified with the name of 'office' was situated in a relict patch of tropical rain forest on a hillside above the town at the end of a very bumpy track, turning off from a road that bore the incongruous name of "*La Route du Grande Corniche*" after a more famous road in the Riviera.

Looking around at the decay, with the tall sombre forest trees pressing in on me, I felt like Joseph Conrad's Marlow surveying the company station in *Heart of Darkness*. There was much here to remind me of Conrad's epic, even the rattle of chains could be heard, caused not by shackled slaves, but by a disconsolate chimpanzee in a cage, chained around the neck for fear he would burst through the thick iron bars of his prison. Once, glancing through the window shutter of the office, I saw a small boy standing looking at the chimpanzee. The boy had a pleasant, but mournful face, the reason for the latter being readily apparent. Dressed only in a pair of trunks he carried around his neck a placard bearing the words "*Un enfant à vendre*" (Child for sale). I turned away quickly. I did not want to look.

The unfortunate chimpanzee was one of the inmates of the Bangui Zoo. This comprised five small cages imprisoning as many miserable animals, which, by a process of rigorous natural selection, had managed to survive.

There was a large lioness in a cage in which she could barely turn around. By all accounts she must have been at least twenty-five years old. She met her demise in a curious manner after I had left the country. The President wanted to make a gift of two lion skins to a visiting dignitary. One wild lion was shot but there was difficulty in obtaining a second one. The Government "veterinarian" therefore garotted the old lioness in her cage by means of pulling her against the bars with a piece of wire around her neck, and the skin of the hapless creature was presented to the visiting dignitary.

Two emaciated leopards had somehow survived despite heavy worm loads; and an old spotted hyaena which had once escaped but came back to its tiny cage the next morning of its own accord, unable to face the outside world any longer. A number of small crocodiles, a peacock, and Dimanche (Sunday), the chimpanzee, completed the dismal menagerie.

Dimanche was an old and powerful male, the delight of hordes of Bangui schoolchildren. Often was my work interrupted by the noise of fifty or more small children chanting rhythmically and clapping hands in front of his cage, breaking off repeatedly into squeals of laughter when Dimanche would oblige with a swaying dance which terminated in a furious jumping up and down on the spot, creating a deafening clatter on the boards of the floor of the cage. Sometimes, wily old Dimanche, who for the most part sat there glowering impassively at his tormentors with expressionless beady brown eyes, would suddenly seize an incautious child's schoolbag, and then laughter turned to howls and tears as Dimanche began methodically to destroy its contents. I hesitate to admit it, but Dimanche fell in love with me. Perhaps my pink face looked like that of a young female chimp, or perhaps it was that I spoke to him occasionally when all was quiet but never teased him. The result of this affection was that one day, when an African assistant of mine got too close to the cage, Dimanche, consumed with jealousy grabbed his arm with lightning speed and gave the shrieking captive a good bite.

Once, when all was quiet, I heard the approach of cautious footsteps, and peering from behind my shutters I saw the Director of Hunting with scowling mien approaching the hyaena cage. Glancing furtively around and satisfied he was apparently unobserved, he quickly stuffed his pockets full with handfuls of hyaena turds he snatched from under the cage, and then hurried away. What devilish purpose he required that for was anyone's guess.

I arrived at my post in this unhappy country shortly before the annual parade in honour of Bokassa, and Latakpi was occupied with making a float to display some of the animals in this 'bread and circuses' charade. The float consisted of three cages constructed of inch-thick iron bars mounted on a massive two-wheeled trolley used for transporting bulldozers. The whole contraption looked like some menagerie straight out of mediaeval Venice.

The hyaena was anaesthetized with a dart gun and placed in the first cage. A leopard, similarly treated, was placed in the third, and the lioness was to take pride of place in the centre. At the last minute Latakpi changed his mind. He didn't want any accidents to happen and, as he well knew, untoward things had a habit of happening in Bangui. So in place of the lioness he put the peacock between the leopard and the hyaena. There was no chance of that hapless bird breaking out through inch-thick iron bars!

The morning of the great day arrived and a small tractor chugged up the hill to tow the float away. Latakpi was proud of his effort; this would really be something to impress the crowds!

The tractor hooked up the float with its patient occupants and moved off. About fifteen yards further on the track descended rather sharply around a bend and the trailer, built to carry bulldozers, tilted up backwards, snatching the tractor high into the air and spinning it upside down before it then rocked forward and crashed the tractor to the ground. I did not witness this interesting manoeuvre myself, but when I arrived for work the next day I found the road blocked by an inverted tractor somewhat the worse for wear, and the three stationary cages. There was a rather surprised-looking hyaena in one, an indignant peacock in the second, and a nonchalant leopard in the third.

Latakpi confided to me afterwards it must have been the tractor driver's fault, "because he wasn't hurt".

* * *

Bangui was always full of surprises – seldom pleasant ones. Imagine walking into the shower, turning on the tap and finding yourself being sprayed with DDT! Two days later the United Nations office issued a warning to all staff not to drink water until further notice. Further notice was never issued. Many rumours circulated as to the cause. One of the more grisly was that the body of the waterworks watchman, who had disappeared for two days, had been found floating in the storage tank, and so they had poured DDT into the water to sterilize it. Another, and probably the most likely, was that they had run out of chlorine and so, conscientiously, had put DDT into the water instead. The long-term effects on those who drank the water have probably now manifested themselves among Bangui's more permanent residents as 'Parkinson's Disease'.

This wasn't the only way one might become poisoned by insecticide. In the Portuguese-owned leading grocery store of Bangui I witnessed an African woman assistant squirting insecticide *on* the fresh fish, which was flown in fortnightly from Paris. No wonder there were no flies on it!

Then there was the Great Petrol Shortage. Petrol suddenly became impossible to obtain in Bangui. All manner of excuses were put forward. All, that is, except the real one, that somebody was pocketing the proceeds from the sales so there was no money to pay for more. At the height of the crisis the diplomatic petrol station, where all the Aid vehicles filled up, was delivered with 20,000 litres of water. Cars and lorries filled their tanks, drove about fifty yards, and came to a spluttering halt.

In preparation for the accommodation of all the visitors he expected would come to his coronation as self-appointed Emperor, Bokassa had a village built of two hundred asbestos prefabs, all imported from South Africa. I was later to move into one of these after the coronation (they were not used, even the hotels were not filled to capacity for the great event), and I drove up to the back door to examine the house. Pulling up in my Land Rover I suddenly found myself slowly sinking into the ground, the Land Rover ending up with its nose pointing into a deep cesspit, poised on the edge with its back wheels in the air! I extricated myself gingerly without the vehicle completing the descent and precipitating me well and truly into the *merde*, as the French would say.

The reason for this mishap was the workmen who had constructed the houses helped themselves to the cement with which to make the cesspit covers, and simply covered the latter over with thin sheets of asbestos (meant for the walls of the houses), disguising them with a layer of earth like an elephant trap. Cement was at a premium in Bangui because of Bokassa's insatiable demand for his grandiose personal construction schemes.

* * *

The first time I saw Bokassa was when he delivered a political speech at the indoor sports stadium known as the Omnisports Stadium. Latakpi hurried into the office one morning and said we had to go *immediately* to the stadium to hear the President speak. Arriving there we sat down in this vast hall with a stage at one end, at the back of which were seated the ministers and members of the diplomatic corps. After an interminable wait, during which time the hall filled with thousands of Africans among whom I could not see another single white face, Bokassa walked in accompanied by his beloved wife Catherine. At least that's the way he liked to describe her. Behind him walked four men: a short, bull-necked Japanese, undoubtedly the karate expert; a thin, young, Italian-looking man with a sneer on his face, the knife expert; a sallow-faced white man who was clearly the marksman and a massive African who was undoubtedly the strangler. They were all killers, Bokassa's private bodyguard. I expect he gave them prisoners to practise on.

Everyone rose when Bokassa came in, and then sat down again after he had seated himself. He then stood to address the crowd and Catherine, half turning, frowned at the ambassadors and with an imperious gesture of her hand signalled them to stand up. Then Bokassa indicated everyone could sit down again and proceeded to speak at great length in Sango, the *lingua franca* of the country. Sango is not all that different to Swahili, but needless to say I could not understand a word.

Afterwards I asked Latakpi what it was all about. Oh, he would tell me later. Obviously it was of no importance after all. Much later I read Bokassa had been announcing a new constitution for the country.

* * *

I had not been long in Bangui before extraordinary rumours began to circulate about Bokassa. I was to learn that in Bangui rumours, however extraordinary, always turned out to be true. The rumours this time were that he was going to declare himself Emperor, and the Central African Republic was to become the Central African Empire, without, however, any conquests of neighbouring territories. People spoke of his crown covered in diamonds and of his golden coronation throne.

Eventually it became public knowledge and all effort was directed towards preparations for the great coronation. Bokassa wanted the Pope to come and crown him but the Pope was unable to, so Bokassa asked the Roman Catholic Archbishop of Bangui to do the honours. With jesuitical diplomacy the Archbishop agreed instead to bless him at the cathedral after he was crowned. A sort of Appian Way was therefore built to the cathedral of several gigantic concrete Corinthian archways along the route from the sports stadium, where he had decided to crown himself. On the day a giant red carpet was laid out covering the whole of the cathedral steps. Instructions were issued on the radio as to how the emperor should be addressed, softly and with respect, and there was much discussion among the French over the gender of the mode of address. In the French language, for some incomprehensible reason the feminine mode of address *Sa Majesté* is used (literally Her Majesty), even if addressing a man, and not the masculine *Son Majesté*.

The great day finally came on the fourth of December 1977 (Napoleon was crowned on the second of December). Like Napoleon, Bokassa crowned himself; although in the former case the would-be emperor snatched the crown out of the Pope's hands. Sceptical of the whole affair I stayed at home as it was announced one could not take photographs. It turned out photography was freely permitted and Bokassa beamed benignly at all the cameras as he was driven in procession to the cathedral for his blessing. However I was invited to the great banquet to be held in the evening at the palace, *Le Palais de la Renaissance*. The expected attendance of thousands of dignitaries from all over the world having failed to materialize, at the last minute the two thousand places at table had to be filled with lesser mortals.

Although earlier a few light drops of rain had fallen, it was fortunately a fine evening as the banquet took place in the open courtyard. Raised on a dais at the far end was one of Bokassa's mounted trophies, which he obviously wanted all the world to see. It was a cow rhinoceros complete with fetus, which had been almost at term, mounted in the attitude of gruesomely running alongside its erstwhile mother. "Naturalised" the French call it, but we call it "stuffed". Bokassa had shot the pregnant rhinoceros in the Bamingui-Bangoran National Park, to "prevent it from attacking him."

The African men, senior government officials and diplomatic staff, were all resplendent in white tie and tails and their ladies in evening dresses with white evening gloves. Many no doubt had purchased these expensive attires especially for the event under dire threat. I made do with the same dinner jacket I had brought to Africa when I first went out to Kenya in 1953. It was a bit tight around the waist twenty years later, but I managed. It was in Kenya, those many years ago when it had somewhat more wear, I noticed one day the lapels were gummed up with a black substance. I looked more closely, scraped the substance with a fingernail, and suddenly realized what it was. Boot polish! The Kikuyu room boy had been giving a shine to the lapels with my black boot-polish brush!

After the display of sartorial elegance was seated, and the usual long delay befitting as he saw it of his status, Bokassa entered wearing a circlet of solid gold laurel leaves on his head in the style of a Roman emperor. Apart from that little extravagance he, like the rest, was dressed in white tie and tails and did not take the Roman connection to the extent of wearing a toga. As he walked in, accompanied by his Empress Catherine, the masses turned and looked at him. Bokassa began to glower and muttered to his Empress. Then someone diplomatically started to clap and it was slowly taken up by the crowd. Bokassa beamed; graciously acknowledging his subjects' adoration he waved the carved ebony stick he always affected which he called his *canne de justice*, used to beat people with, sometimes to death.

While the band of the French Marines in their spotless white uniforms played, the pantomime, designed by a French aristocrat, continued. Pairs of French chefs bore each dish of the banquet before

Bokassa on the kind of stretcher seen in a Bruegel painting. The head chef tasted the dish and then offered it to Bokassa to taste, who gave his gracious approval. That of course was only for the top table. We had to content ourselves with lesser dishes, but good enough, being prepared by the leading French restaurant in Bangui (for which they were never paid, the owners finally fleeing the country).

The fare, trout in aspic, was simple, as it had to be for so many diners; accompanied by pink champagne in specially-labelled Bokassa coronation bottles. After the courses appeared to have finished different waiters were then seen carrying plates with the appearance of some sort of sweet – a chocolate pudding topped with a maraschino cherry. Well, there was room for more. So I took a helping along with others of like mind and found it was not chocolate pudding as I had supposed, but spiced chunks of meat covered with a brown sauce. Strange that such a dish was topped with a maraschino cherry. It was not the sort of dish to follow the *petit fours* we had already partaken of so I left it unfinished.

When later I read of Bokassa's gastronomic fondness for the flesh of his victims I am glad I did so. To serve them up at his coronation banquet with a cherry on top is just the sort of joke that would have appealed to him. Indeed he is reported as having said to the French Minister of Cooperation who was at the high table, "You never noticed, but you ate human flesh!"

Bokassa was widely reported to have once invited the American ambassador to a dinner party at which the soup was stewed, fat caterpillars. The ambassador, not wishing to offend his host, took a small helping and forced himself to consume it. Bokassa asked him if he had enjoyed the soup. The ambassador, with all the diplomacy he could muster, politely replied he had.

"Ha!" Bokassa shouted, knowing full well the ambassador's answer had been given simply out of diplomacy, "he likes it. Give him some more!"

The unfortunate ambassador's plate was then filled at Bokassa's insistence with another generous helping of stewed caterpillars and Bokassa watched the ambassador malignantly until he had emptied his plate.

Bokassa's alleged cannibalism may have been no more than part of a plan of misinformation designed by Paris to discredit him, so that the French would not be criticized for their invasion of the country and removing him from power, although no one disbelieved it at the time. One of my workers asserted Bokassa should be executed and everyone allowed to eat a piece of him (there wouldn't have been enough to go round) because he had eaten his people. He himself wanted to eat a little piece. A strange reasoning but one showing no abhorrence of eating human flesh, only the circumstances of it were objected to. But 'evidence' given at the public trial held later by Phillippe Linguissa, an alleged cook, sounded like something from the Addams Family:

"In 1977, a soldier presented himself at the kitchen of the children's band where I work, and gave me some orders: "Take some dishes filled with salt, spices, onions, and bring some wine". I got into the car and we rode to Berengo [Bokassa's palace], eighty kilometres from Bangui.

"At the Palace, someone put me in a large kitchen. It was in Bokassa's house of wood and corrugated iron. The emperor came:

'Ah grandfather, have you done military service?'

"I showed him my military papers and he replied:

'Right, then you must obey'.

"He went and opened the refrigerator, and took out the body of a man. It had no head, hands or feet.

'You go and prepare that like a stew.'

"Me, I cried. I have said that I can cook a chicken or a sheep. Not a man. Without speaking he took out his revolver. I said to him, kill me.

'No, I wish to eat at eight o'clock.'

"I went to work as if I was cooking a chicken, sewing up the skin with a needle and thread which Bokassa had given me. I sprinkled it with gin and Pernod and placed the whole corpse in a big tank and slid it into a great oven. When I pulled it out to look at the cooking, the body began to move, it fastened itself on to me, pulling my arm. It struggled so much that it dirtied all of the kitchen. I asked its pardon and I was able to place it back in the oven."

When the witness, who appeared to be somewhat drunk, then asked the 'judge' for the money he had been promised by the President, the court could contain its laughter no longer.

Nevertheless, I'm glad I didn't eat the cherry-topped dish.

The day after the banquet there was a colourful parade in Bangui where all the panoply of the coronation was on show. The fifty mounted horsemen dressed in replicas of 19th-century Napoleonic uniforms, silver bands dressed in scarlet, silver bands dressed in blue, drum majorettes specially trained by an imported American drum majorette who, while leading them in the parade dropped her mace (probably because of a hangover from the night before), and tribes in traditional dress, or undress as the case may be. All paraded past the Emperor wearing his gold laurel leaves on his head.

The euphoria did not last for long. Bankrupt before the coronation, the country was in a worse state afterwards with a third of the country's annual budget having been spent on the extravaganza. Murmurings were heard which got louder and louder. Trouble started in the schools and at the university – hardly surprising considering there were 140 Russian 'teachers' in the country. After a strike at the university, which was temporarily settled, it was rumoured that in the event of more trouble there Bokassa had ordered it to be bombed, and his personal French pilot had fled the country in order to avoid being required to carry out the command.

Trouble soon spilled onto the streets. My house at that time was in the United Nations' compound, a group of half a dozen houses situated not far from a crossroads where the demonstrations always began. As is now common in such riots, schoolchildren were placed in the forefront while the instigators and all the main rioters followed behind. Such tactics had little effect here. Troops, comprising Bokassa's private army recruited largely from Zaïre, were sent to confront them and open fire if necessary. They did not restrain themselves for long.

The trouble started at night and I was awakened at some unearthly hour by the sound of an army truck stuck in a ditch. The agonized, penetrating, high-pitched whine of its protesting differential went on for hours as the driver struggled ineffectually to get it out, keeping me awake until I wanted to scream at his stupidity.

News of a likely disturbance had been received early, and we had been instructed to remain at home for the day. Well, that was a good opportunity for me to get some work done on a scientific book I was writing about my former waterbuck studies in Uganda.

In the morning the cries of the mob could be heard demonstrating on the road not far from the house and I was industriously hammering away at my typewriter when the shooting started. Volleys of bullets whistled over my roof – a bit wide of the mark, but to misquote Samuel Johnson (as he is so often misquoted), "the thought of the imminence of death concentrates the mind wonderfully", and I continued to pound away. While doing so a young Frenchman from one of the neighbouring houses poked his head through my open doorway and asked what I was doing.

"Oh, I'm just working on a book," I informed him offhandedly.

Much later I learnt that the other inmates of the compound, all married couples except for one, had gathered together on the small lawn at the back of my house, the women crying and hysterical, the men trying to calm them, the women fearing a second sort of Shaba, the uprising in Zaïre when the European women had been raped. I had typed away merrily oblivious to it all.

In the Dark Heart

It was much later still I learned of the story current in Bangui of the mad Englishman who sat "writing his bloody book" while all hell was being let loose around him.

Not long after that the inevitable coup was effected while Bokassa had gone on a visit to Libya, allegedly taking his crown of diamonds with him.

On the morning of 20 September 1979 I was awoken by the sound of muffled drums playing a funeral march, an eerie, slow but regular, boom! boom! boom! I could hear no shouting or singing, just the regular, muffled beat of the drums, their mournful note depressing, desolate, in the dead hours before dawn, like a presage of doom. A strange way to celebrate the overthrow of a tyrant, but at the time I did not know the cause. All I knew was something was up and a procession was marching into town.

First thing in the morning I went into the United Nations office and a co-worker came in and said he had passed French paratroopers everywhere in town. They had been flown in at night and by morning had taken up pre-arranged positions in buildings at strategic points throughout Bangui. The news had certainly got around quickly to the native population, and by morning the demonstration had turned to looting. Every shop in Bangui, except luckily the main grocery stores, had been completely ransacked. Even the fittings were stolen. The excuse was they were Bokassa's property, but of course the rioters knew this was not so in all cases. All of the Libyan and Lebanese shops in the native quarter were stripped. The entire stock of United Nations food aid disappeared from its store (it was publicly denied by the agency). It was all done too quickly for the French troops to be able to prevent it.

Not long before this, in the United Nations' 'Year of the Child', there had been the infamous child-killing episode in which Bokassa was alleged to have personally assisted in stoning some children to death in Ngaragba prison. These were children who had taken part in one of the demonstrations against him, throwing stones at his car. Some years later I was watching a Terry Wogan television show in which he interviewed the Director of Amnesty International. Wogan opened the interview by asking the Director what it felt like to have the power to overthrow governments, as he had done in the case of Bokassa because of his killing of the children. The Director simply smiled noncommittally in reply. The newspaper reports and Amnesty International's role appear to have been far from the truth.

The account of an eyewitness who was a prisoner in Ngaragba at the time makes no mention of Bokassa being present, which the witness certainly would have done if it had been true, as he owed no favours to Bokassa. All he saw were prison guards stoning the children when they were brought in. Most of the subsequent deaths were from suffocation during the ensuing night, over one hundred being squeezed into a cell designed to hold thirty persons, and thirty to forty in a cell designed for only two. In the hot tropical night at least thirty persons, including some adults, died; and one child was seen beaten to death because he repeatedly shouted for water to drink.[5]

Often represented as such, the overthrow of Bokassa had nothing to do with the child deaths. Countries do not invade other countries simply because a few children have been massacred. The truth was very different. Although the overthrow had apparently been planned by Paris for some time, and it was in the French interest as a part of this plan to discredit Bokassa as much as possible, branding him a cannibal and child killer, the French military pipped an invasion of the Libyans by a mere twenty-four hours. When in the morning they entered a 'school', which the Libyans were building, they found thirty Libyan troops already in hiding there. In the native quarter I saw an old military truck from the Libyan embassy blocking the road with all of its tyres shot out. One Frenchman reported that when he arrived by air on the scheduled flight from Paris the night before, some two dozen large Russians, obvious KGB types, had disembarked at Bangui in preparation for the Libyan takeover.

Rumour had it the Prime Minister, Ange Patassé, in return for assistance in removing Bokassa, had negotiated with the Libyans to provide them with a base in the north of the country, an international-standard airstrip in Bokassa's private hunting reserve adjoining the north of the Bamingui-Bangoran National Park. From there they could attack Chad. So the Libyans had enticed Bokassa out of the country, but the French, aware of what was going on, forestalled the invasion by taking over the country themselves in an operation which they code-named 'Barracuda'. They then reinstalled the former president, David Dacko, whom Bokassa had overthrown thirteen years before; in spite of the fact the country did not want the return of this un-elected president but favoured Ange Patassé.

In October 1982, when President Mitterand refused to give any more handouts to the new military regime under President Kolingba, which had overthrown Dacko, apparently with the latter's connivance because of the increasing hostility towards himself, Kolingba retaliated by inviting the Libyans in. The Libyans supplied one million pounds, sixty-two 'technicians', four T 62 tanks, eight armoured cars and a number of lorries, jeeps and mortars. This was followed by a further two million pounds cash. So one had the anomalous position of French troops side by side with a contingent of enemy Libyan troops, complete with tanks.

Mitterand paid up and the Libyans withdrew, but left their tanks behind. Ready for the next time, which wasn't so long in the coming, in May 2001.

* * *

I worked under six different Ministers of State during my stay, beginning with Ange Patassé who later became Bokassa's Prime

Minister. Forced to flee after Bokassa's overthrow because of his opposition to Dacko's reinstallation as President, Patassé claimed he had engineered the overthrow and was the rightful President. That didn't go down at all well with Dacko's henchmen, so they blew his house up. Patassé fled to the United Nations office where arriving one morning I was surprised to see a very frightened Patassé sitting in the entrance lounge. The UN told him they could not get involved and he fled to an embassy. A survivor, he eventually made President in 1992, in the following ten years with the help of the Libyans weathering six attempts to overthrow him until finally overthrown in late 2002 when out of the country, by a rebel leader General François Bozizé. Bozizé had been a second lieutenant in the early days of Bokassa's regime, promoted instantly to general after he hit a Frenchman who had been disrespectful to the president, and eventually became Patassé's foremost companion-in-arms, until he led a failed coup against him and fled to Chad.

Considered of insufficient importance to be reported in the English-speaking media, beginning in October 2002 military insurgents led by Bozizé stationed in the north-west of the country, assumed control of the north and then descended on Bangui unopposed until they reached the town itself. A tremendous shooting battle was engaged in Bangui of which we know little, most Europeans having fled. Patassé had enlisted a private army of Congolese, but these having been unpaid for some time took to looting the town as well as did the rebels. Only time will tell whether Bozizé, loyal to Bokassa to the end, will prove to be yet another tyrant. Latest indications are that he is.

* * *

Bokassa changed his ministers frequently for fear they might become too influential, and one replacement was a young man who could not have been more than about twenty-two years of age. Shortly after his appointment he excitedly called me into his office, together with his senior officials, to reveal to us a 'secret':

"The Director General believes someone is trying to poison him."

Everyone present, except apparently the Minister, knew the Director General was a drunk and came to work, when he did come to the office at all, almost totally incapable.

The last Minister of my acquaintance was one of the military commanders appointed by General Kolingba's military government, Commandant Evariste-Martial Konzale. He sat behind his desk in full disruptive pattern camouflage combat fatigues and gave 'orders'.

"*C'est un ordre!*" (That's an order!) he would bark.

Receiving a consultant expert whom he was not sure how to deal with, he demonstrated his offhandedness towards the interview by an elaborate display of picking his nose and a vigorous cleaning of his ears; minutely examining the fruits of his labours on the end of his little finger and glancing from time to time at his visitor with feigned disinterest.

* * *

Cooks in Bangui were, as elsewhere, difficult to find, more so those who would accompany one on safari, or those who were not light-fingered. One young man was excellent, an expert at cooking couscous and Italian dishes. Unfortunately he was also a compulsive thief. After the fourth bottle of whisky had disappeared and a number of minor items – but it was the whisky which mattered the most – I was obliged to dispense abruptly with his services. Another came, who was also a capable cook. His reference from his previous employer bore a statement in cryptic French, which I did not understand at the time, to the effect he chose to please himself.

After two weeks had passed I announced I would have guests to dinner on the Saturday night. Saturday evening came and, since he had not turned up at the appointed time, I began to prepare dinner myself. He didn't turn up at all, and I was obliged to cook the meal unaided. A big enough nightmare for any host or hostess having French guests to dinner, but since I was unskilled in the culinary arts it was doubly so for me. In spite of this, apart from the *coq au vin* being somewhat overcooked, the dinner passed off well enough.

Three months later the cook suddenly reappeared and simply said he was back. My rejoinder to that left him looking somewhat puzzled at my unreasonableness as he reluctantly took his leave.

The problem was solved when I found Bernard. Bernard (pronounced Burn-aargh) was an old Mandjia, old meaning he was probably in his late fifties. He had grey hairs and a pleasant wrinkled face, the sort of face that always made missionaries (of whom there were plenty in the country) greet him warmly as *baba* (father) whenever we met them on our travels. Of course he had his faults, too much *douma* (honey wine) from time to time, and a tendency to help himself to small things, which he thought I wouldn't notice.

One trick, which took me some time to catch on to, was exchanging the blades in my razor with his old ones. I often wondered why my razor had suddenly gone blunt. It was the same with the torch: I never could understand why the batteries would suddenly go flat. One day he didn't replace the cap properly, and then I twigged.

Fans of the TV show *To the Manor Born* will recall the great shout of laughter that went up when Penelope Keith appeared dressed in a Union Jack plastic apron. I decided such an apron was just the thing to liven up Bernard's appearance when I was camping in some remote spot, and would serve as a defiant gesture of my English chauvinism, submerged as I was in Francophone attitudes. But one evening I invited Monsieur G. and his wife to dine in Bangui. M G. had been appointed by Bokassa to look after his presidential hunting reserve. It turned out

Top Left: One of the Emperor
Bokassa's Corinthian archways.
Top Right: Bands in scarlet.
Centre Left: Bokassa's cavalry
in Napoleonic uniforms.
Centre Right: Bangui Belle.
Bottom: Bands in blue.

Top: Coronation parade participants in undress. *Centre Left:* Dimanche in the Bangui Zoo. *Centre Right:* A balanced rock on Kaga Pungourou. *Bottom:* An immense hostile wilderness, the Bamingui-Bangoran National Park.

Top Left: Two of the skulls from the tomb. *Top Right:* The natural rock tomb where the skulls were found. *Centre:* On the mysterious kagas. *Bottom:* A view of the mysterious kagas.

Top Left: Bernard in camp, in his apron.
Top Right: Kakumale with a giant poisoned tiger fish.
Centre Left: A scene from "Middle Earth" in the Bamingui-Bangoran National Park.
Centre Right: Bernard, ready for Mass on Christmas Day.
Bottom: The signature of Green's expedition on a baobab, 1858.

Top: Author with pygmies at Bayanga. *Centre:* Hippopotamus in the Saint-Floris Park. *Bottom:* Giant eland.

Top Left: The forlorn chapel. *Top Right:* Maasai, one of the anachronisms of Africa. *Centre:* Over the summit of Mount Kilimanjaro, 1972. *Bottom:* Lengai, the "Mountain of God".

Top: The long grass, Bamingui-Bangoran National Park. *Centre Left:* Karagwe, Tanzania, from Muhororo in the Akagera Park with topi. *Centre Right:* Siapi, the end of the last tall forest in Burkina Faso. *Bottom:* The crater of Karisimbi with its bizarre giant groundsel and senecios.

Top Left: A main road in Botswana. *Top Right:* Chapman's Pool. *Centre:* The Kalahari Desert
Bottom: The shape of things to come? Water supply for game in the Gemsbok National Park

M G. was a Gaullist, and he was so affronted by the faithful Bernard waiting at table in his Union Jack apron that he studiedly ignored me the entire evening, addressing his remarks instead to my other guest, an American, loudly applauding the part of the Americans for winning the war in Europe.

I thought to myself that if ever he came to dinner again I would lay out a Union Jack tablecloth as well.

Having been trained in French colonial times, starting his career as a *marmiton*, a small boy who washes the pots and pans for the cook, Bernard was a first-class bush cook. Everything was prepared on a circular piece of metal cut from the end of a 44-gallon steel drum, placed on three rocks or termite mounds. This makes an excellent hob, and can be used even in the rain. In the ashes of the campfire he baked bread, and always thought it highly amusing when it failed to rise because the yeast had gone off. He would grin and drop the leaden mass with a resounding thump onto the table before me.

The only thing that never failed to put me off of my food was his habit of placing one finger on the side of his nose and with a snort, vigorously showering the contents of his nasal passages everywhere. I often wondered what I was eating, and not without good cause as one incident showed.

I had paid a visit to some French friends who were running the Manovo-Gounda-Saint Floris National Park in the north, Annie-Evelyn and Jean-Luc Temporal. We breakfasted just after dawn the first morning seated in the open at a long rough wooden table at the Manovo camp, one of the finest ways imaginable to have breakfast. I announced I would have coffee, and with Gallic politeness Jean-Luc said he would have English tea since he was breakfasting with an Englishman.

Bernard duly obliged, placing my battered old enamel teapot on the table before Jean-Luc.

Jean-Luc poured himself a cup.

He looked at it.

"*C'est bien ca?*" (Is it all right?)

Ah! Here was Gallic obtuseness, I thought.

He passed the cup to me. I looked at it. It certainly did not seem quite right: very dark, in fact almost black in colour.

I sniffed the proffered cup. It was odourless.

Strange. I took the lid off the teapot and peered inside like some Mad Hatter. The tea was quite black in colour. I sniffed again. No smell at all.

I swilled the tea around. There was something white floating in it. I took a closer look. Yes, it was a bar of washing soap!

"Bernarrrd!"

Bernard came ambling across. The mystery was soon explained. The evening before, as was his wont, he flung everything into his tin bucket: mugs, teapot, soap and all. The soap happened to land inside the teapot. In the morning, half asleep, he seized the teapot, threw in some tea, poured in the hot water, and plonked it on the table without another thought.

That was how we got "*thé au savon*". It took a long time to live down that one with my French friends.

* * *

Not far south of Bangui the dense tropical forest begins – once it included Bangui itself – and here one meets the pygmies. These supposedly primitive and backward people demand more for a day's hire than the official minimum daily industrial wage in Bangui, as I discovered when I wanted to hire some to erect a radio aerial for my office. You can either pay what they ask, or go without. Pygmies don't bargain. In addition to the wage, I was informed, one must provide them at midday with tinned fish (herrings in tomato sauce) and bread (French *baguettes*), otherwise they lose interest. This inducement seemed unnecessary to me; all I wanted them to do was to climb two tall trees, haul up a piece of string to which the radio aerial was attached, and make it fast. Simple.

Pygmies are supposed to be adept at climbing forest trees and one might suppose that one pygmy would be sufficient for the task, but no, they insisted that three were necessary. One to climb, and two to stand and watch.

Climbing about thirty feet up a tree is something I suppose a Royal Marine Commando, or an SAS soldier, could accomplish in about two minutes with the aid of a short length of rope. These pygmies took the whole day, the climbing being done with painstaking slowness. And of course, from midday onwards it got slower and slower, the more and more hungry they became.

"Finish the job," I told them, "then you will get your fish and bread."

Having at long last finished one tree, they then didn't want to do the second, but an aerial only half suspended was not of much use to me. I cajoled and threatened and by four o'clock the job, which had started at nine in the morning, was completed!

I was to experience more of the pygmy's procrastinating ways when I paid a visit to the heart of Bambuti pygmy land, south of Nola in the extreme south-west of the country. Here a long tongue of the CAR stretches down the Sangha River, with the dense tropical forest of Cameroon on one side and that of the Congo on the other.

For my first sorties into the dense forest I based myself at a forestry station run by a Yugoslavian firm on a 99-year lease. The manager, whose arms were marked with bullet scars, boasted to me they paid only a one per cent royalty, and there was enough good timber present to keep them going for the length of the lease. The yard was stacked with piles and piles of huge rotted trunks of giant forest trees, timber they had apparently cut before they were organized enough to send it down the river and which was now cracked and useless, riddled with the holes of giant wood-boring beetles.

I hired some of their pygmies to take me into the forest where the shy forest antelope, the bongo, abounded, and the lowland gorilla. Entering the cathedral gloom of the tropical forest we had not been going for long, following a narrow elephant path, when the leading pygmy started to complain. I inquired what was the matter.

"He doesn't like the dew on his body," was the reply. These indeed were the sons of nature!

It was not long, however, before we were obliged to wade up to our waists in water, for the tropical forest is a network of swamps and soon our way was repeatedly interrupted by it. The pygmies had spoken of a big salt lick in the forest depths where one would see lots of animals, and it was towards this we were supposed to be heading. But when my forest companions discovered the 'gun' they were carrying for me was nothing more than tent poles, they started procrastinating. They didn't know the way; it was far, etc., etc. Well, by this time it was evening and time to make camp in an open space shaded by a forest giant.

The next unpleasant surprise was that as the sun began to go down dense swarms of bees appeared and settled all over my water bottles. There was nothing else for it but to get inside the tent, zip up the mosquito net, and wait until just before dark when the bees would all disappear, and hopefully not be replaced by mosquitoes.

But before this happened the pygmies treated me to a display of calling up a forest duiker. We squatted down on the forest floor and one of the pygmies held his nose between finger and thumb and began to make a nasal sound, repeating it intermittently. Ten minutes could not have passed, less I would say, before a red-coloured duiker came hesitatingly picking its way delicately towards the sound. Someone made a slight movement and instantly it was gone.

The next day I didn't get very far with my reluctant pygmies; all they wanted me to do was to hunt for them. So I returned to the forestry camp in some disgust and went on down to Lidjombo, the furthest south one could get by track in the CAR, the track terminating at what had once been a flourishing coffee plantation.

I would not have been surprised to find Conrad's Mr Kurtz at this lonely outpost, but instead I found the equivalent of his enigmatic Russian. The plantation was now leased by a Czechslovakian firm (this was in the Cold War era), and the only occupant at the time, apart from some African staff, was a young Czech who had been flown out from Europe to fix the electricity and build a swimming pool. He could speak no English and almost no French, but somehow communication was effected.

"His very existence was improbable, inexplicable and altogether bewildering".[6]

He showed me some tiny diamonds which, with the aid of a soup strainer, he had sifted from a heap of sand he was using to make cement to build the swimming pool, announcing:

"Wife want. Me, ughh!" with a dismissive gesture of his hand.

The sand was full of them. Truly it would be a swimming pool fit for the Sultan of Brunei!

When he understood I was going into the forest to see what animals were there he became full of enthusiasm and made me to understand he would guide me in the afternoon.

At the appointed hour of 3 p.m. sharp, he appeared. Not dressed like Conrad's enigmatic Russian in multicoloured patched clothing, but not so very different, disruptive pattern camouflage combat fatigues complete with Fidel Castro camouflaged cap, and carrying a gun. He made it clear he was ready to shoot whatever I wanted. He would shoot a monkey. I tried to explain I did not want to shoot anything, but as with the pygmies, that appeared incomprehensible to him.

We trailed off reluctantly into the forest but it soon became apparent the monkeys had nothing to fear. We tramped around, shots were fired into the canopy, excuses were made, and finally we tramped out again. He explained, somehow in spite of the language barrier, he was a gun enthusiast and had a large collection in Czechoslovakia, even possessing machine guns. I suppose he had little opportunity to actually use such an arsenal, but what surprised me most of all was that it was allowed in the then Russian-dominated communist Czechoslovakia.

Exploring around Lidjombo I found another curiosity. A little whitewashed, tin-roofed chapel, perched on an eminence overlooking the river. It looked Portuguese to me, more at home in the hills of Alto Douro than in this incongruous setting of the humid tropics and the malignant brown river. It gave the appearance of having been plonked down unceremoniously in this lonely spot at some distant age, and now stood forgotten, alone in its pathos.

I pushed aside the thin weathered, creaking wooden door and peered in. The interior was almost bare, except for a raised floor at the far end on which stood a rough wooden table, which had served as the altar. Arranged upon it, one on each side, were two brown, dust-covered beer bottles, each sporting a handful of long-dead flowers. Somebody once had cared.

The sole other object was a faded and forlorn coster of the Virgin Mary hanging on a pole, the bottom half of which had long ago rotted and fallen away.

Where was Marlow? I half expected to turn and find him looking over my shoulder, contemplating the futility of it all.

At the turn of the century the dreaded ravages of sleeping sickness had caused the decay, depopulating the banks of these malevolent sombre rivers curtained by their dense, dark forests. The 'Rivers of Death' the French had called them. Now, it seemed, decay was simply the result of apathy – another kind of sickness pervaded these lonely outposts.

Notes

1. Negley Farson 1940 *Behind God's Back.*
2. W. D. M. Bell 1960 *Bell of Africa.*
3. M. Daly 1937 *Big Game Hunting and Adventure* 1897-1936.
4. A. Cureau 1915 *Savage Man in Central Africa.*
5. Thierry-Jacques Gallo 1988 *N'Garagba Maison des Morts un prisonnier sous Bokassa.*
6. Joseph Conrad *Heart of Darkness.*

Chapter 6

Tom-toms in my Nights

in the North of the Central African Republic

Oh! That infernal road to the north! With its endless police barriers. Sullen, arrogant, awkward gendarmes doing their utmost to be unpleasant with their questions, questions, questions. The laborious filling-in of grubby, tattered, school exercise books.

"Where are you going? Why are you going there? Where have you come from? How many are you? What is that you are carrying?" And then, always the punchline:

"Can you give this man a lift?" Meaning, give this man a lift or else I will make things unpleasant for you.

Once you succeeded in getting past the first of these barriers at Kilometre 5 on the outskirts of Bangui, there were 117 miles of good tarmac. When I first left the end of this tarmac road at Sibut in the company of Latakpi, the continuation of National Route No.8 was no more than two ruts in the grass.

"Is this the main road?" I queried apprehensively.

"Of course." Latakpi looked at me aggressively. The Central Africans were sensitive of any criticism of their country.

Well, it wasn't exactly like the curate's egg, good in parts, but rather worse in parts. There was almost another two hundred miles of it to Bamingui, and then thirty more to Bangoran; villages which were to be my field stations. It took me two days to reach Bangoran, admittedly somewhat quicker than the 132 days taken by the French scientist Auguste Chevalier in 1902. But one often wondered whether, on the next trip, one would get through at all.

At one point the rains had carved a deep gulley in the road. Some villagers were sent to repair it, but it was too much like hard work. When I passed they were, instead, cutting the grass on the bank at the side of the road. This served no useful purpose since the bank was too steep to allow a vehicle to divert onto it around the gulley. But satisfied they had done a day's work the villagers left it at that.

Latakpi had built a rectangular grass hut, or *boukarou*, for me at Bangoran. The only trouble was it was constructed right by the side of the main road, for the urban African is terrified of being away from others (because of the evil spirits which abound everywhere), and of being in the bush (because of the wild animals which abound everywhere). Passers-by treated it as a sort of public rest house.

In those days, with the roads so bad and the difficulties imposed by Bokassa's regime, few Europeans visited the north even in the dry season. The only regular transport was absurdly overloaded lorries bringing goods from the Sudan and returning with wood and illegal ivory. So overloaded they regularly broke through the flimsy wooden bridges. The bridges were constructed of no more than a few poles cut from the woodland at the side of the road, laid lengthwise across the gap so the wheels of a vehicle were in danger of slipping between them. Six people died when an overloaded lorry crashed through such a structure into the river bed beneath. The bodies were simply buried without ceremony by the side of the road. I frequently passed this grim memorial of 6 six-foot long mounds ranged in parallel on the verge, but after one season they were overgrown and forgotten.

When you came to a broken bridge there was no telling how long you might have to wait before it would be repaired. On one return to Bangui meeting such an obstacle to further progress I fished out some intact planks from the river bed about twenty feet below, laid them across the gap, and heart in mouth drove Land Rover and trailer across. The planks held, but as a Land Rover weighs over a ton it was not an experiment I wanted to repeat very often.

At Bangoran there had been an iron bridge over the river, but prior to my arrival in the country two army lorries had attempted to cross it simultaneously. The bridge was now a twisted mass of iron girders in the river bed and recourse had to be made to a ferry in the wet season. Even this could only operate for a part of the season because when the river overflowed its banks it was impossible to get to the ferry itself because of the mud. I was told the bridge would soon be repaired, but when I left more than six years later it was still in the same state. Indeed, I had thought I would never see the day when the road itself would be improved, but it was rebuilt with EEC funds as far as the village of Mbrès, within seventy miles of Bamingui.

There was only one drawback, the negotiations with the funding agency had only referred to rebuilding the *road* – it was taken for granted this would include repair of the bridges. But of course the contract did not specify that and bureaucracy being bureaucracy we thus had a fine road along which one could now drive at high speed, only to find from time to time it came to an abrupt end – at a bridge which could only be crossed with caution, or often at no bridge at all but a chasm.

Another hazard on the road to the north at the beginning of the dry season, when all was still green and moist, was butterflies! Millions upon countless millions of butterflies! White, brown and multicoloured, they fluttered inexorably across the road, always moving in the same direction, unceasingly, and in uncountable numbers, as numerous as the stars of the Milky Way. Driving through them the engine temperature gauge would suddenly shoot up, the engine boiling due to the masses of dead butterflies blocking the radiator. It was then necessary to stop and scrape off the baked bodies before one could continue.

* * *

On my first journey to Bangoran I stopped en route at Kaga Bandoro, 'the rock of the Ndoro people', formerly known as Fort Crampel. There was a very run-down Government rest house of which the toilet consisted of a hole in the ground – completely in the open. No doubt it once boasted some sort of screen around it but this had long since disappeared. I suppose the answer was to use it at night, but who knows what noxious beasts might be abroad then, to say nothing of the mosquitoes. So on my first visit I went out at dawn.

Squatting in the open, my shorts around my ankles, contemplating the lightening mists, I gradually became aware out of the corner of my eye of a crowd of giggling women huddled together, giggling at me! The reason quickly became apparent, for the original path to the toilet had been extended beyond and was now the regular footpath to the river. And these women wanted to get on with their daily washing. It was difficult to make a dignified retreat. I pulled up my shorts with indecent haste and hurried away, leaving the silly women to continue on their way laughing inanely.

Later I discovered at the village of Mbrès, sixty miles further on, a simple but excellent rest house at the Catholic Mission. Built by the Father himself it was replete with shower, flush toilet and electric light. What a relief that was! No more surreptitious visits to the hole in the ground at dead of night to answer a call of nature, wondering whether a prowling hyaena might not take advantage of one's undignified plight, but coming away anyway with a posterior swollen with itchy mosquito bites.

At Kaga Bandoro, the scene of my discomfiture, children were still named after Georges Toqué, the infamous young French colonial administrator who lived there from 1902 to 1905. Accused of executing a man by throwing him over a waterfall and of shooting men without trial, he was eventually brought to trial in Brazzaville by public opinion in France. At the trial it was revealed his assistant, with Toqué's agreement, had celebrated Bastille Day in 1903 by tying a stick of dynamite to an unfortunate native prisoner's neck and setting light to it like a firecracker. With stunning French logic the defence argued this was a quicker and more humane form of execution than was the guillotine in France. The assistant also cooked a woman alive in an oven, and forced one of his servants to drink a soup made from a boiled man's head.

Toqué, who when he did try people, conducted his court cases in grubby pyjamas, was first exposed in Europe by the American elephant hunter Marcus Daly through a letter to *The Times*, a fact for which Daly was never forgiven by the Oubangui-Chari administration and later arrested on a trumped-up charge. After much ill-treatment he was obliged to leave the country stripped of his possessions. Things hadn't changed much as far as justice was concerned.

Toqué, not an ignorant man, having published in 1904 a short book on the Banda people and their language[1] was however shot by a war tribunal in 1916 for alleged collaboration with a pro-German paper.

* * *

I saw some odd things on that road to the north. In one village there was a boy of about four years of age with a tail. He was crawling about in the dust together with some other children, wearing nothing but a short vest. One of the others, older than the rest, kept lifting up the garment, displaying the boy's tail. It was flat and triangular, projecting about two inches.

In the village of Danga Bordou on market day I saw a huge African, completely naked, standing in public in a sort of primitive stocks, his feet somehow secured around the ankles in a trunk of wood like that in engravings of slaves in 19th-century books. This was clearly some local method of dealing out punishment. He glanced at me shiftily with contorted brows. I tried to find out from my companions what offence he had committed, but they simply said he was mad. They never welcomed inquiries into their customs.

When the Director General of the forestry and wild life departments visited Bamingui, appearing never to have ventured beyond the urban confines of Bangui before, he echoed my remark of the strange things that one saw on the road. Pressed for an explanation he replied:

"Ah! But you are a white man. You do not understand these things. But to us Africans . . . " A pregnant silence left the sentence unfinished; the evils were too dreadful to speak of.

"But what?" I pressed him. I wanted to be aware if there were any dangers on the road I had travelled so often.

Well, he replied that, for example, he had passed a man standing by the side of the road wearing dark glasses, *at night*!

His emphasis was meant to imply volumes, but as a white man I just could not understand what there was to get so excited about over an idiot who chose to wear sunglasses in the dark.

* * *

Almost four hundred and thirty-five miles from Bangui along this road was Ndelé, former capital of the slaver Senoussi. Just before you reach it a sign tells you Ndelé is "*Pas Loin*" (Not Far). But what strikes one most about the place is that whereas in Senoussi's time it was fertile and productive, tilled by his numerous slaves, today the area is an arid desert of stony scrub.

Senoussi was the last great slaver in Africa. From his Ndelé capital he ravaged the surrounding country, depopulating the area to become known as the Bamingui-Bangoran National Park to the south, and the area to the north, which was to become the Manovo-Gounda-Saint Floris National Park. Senoussi refused to pay allegiance to the French and cease his slaving activities, so in 1911 a French military officer paid him a visit. The French had never forgiven him for the murder by his men of Paul Crampel, the first French Officer to attempt to penetrate the north, massacred at the Diangara river about forty-five miles north of Ndelé in April 1891. Senoussi came forward to talk to the officer, and when he was close enough the officer simply pulled out his revolver and shot him. That was, at the time, the end of slavery in the CAR. An alternative story put about by the French for their part in executing him, was that Senoussi was slowly torturing a man to death by cutting off little bits from his body each day and making the captive eat them, so the French administrative officer killed the tyrant.

The French government created a new capital at the foot of the hill on which Senoussi's headquarters stood, and forbade anyone to live at the old site. In my time it remained an overgrown ruin. But the descendants of Senoussi have never forgotten and, after the overthrow of Bokassa in September 1979, a hereditary sultan from the Sudan quietly reinstalled himself at Ndelé, despite the presence of government officials. It was some time before the government in Bangui realised what was taking place and chased him back to the Sudan, only for him to return again later.

* * *

In Ndelé there was a toilet, survivor of colonial times, with the old-style thunderbox used in a manner which would not have pleased Apthorpe at all.[2] My counterpart pointed out to me they called it the 'WC sportif', which translated means a 'sporting toilet'. It was so termed, he explained, because you had to climb up onto it to squat, and then jump down afterwards. The African was always mystified by the European's funny habits.

Yet further north, about one hundred and eighty-six miles beyond Ndelé, lies the Saint Floris National Park, named after a former French Inspector of Hunting, Henri Bouvard. Bouvard, winner of the Prix de

Littératur Coloniale 1930, was something of a novelist and wrote under the pen name of Saint Floris. Everybody talked about the Saint Floris National Park, created long ago in 1933, because it was here, in a 386 square mile triangle of floodplain, that the big game spectacle approached that of East Africa.

An open plain, inundated with flood waters from June to September, it carried large herds totalling some 10,000 Buffon's kob, 1,500 hartebeest, 700 buffalo, 630 topi, 275 roan antelope, and numbers of giant eland, waterbuck, reedbuck, oribi, duiker, bushbuck, warthog, ostrich, baboon, hunting dog, hyaena, lion, 50 elephant and about 1,400 hippo. In the dry season the hippo were crammed in serried ranks into one or two small pools, more tightly packed than the proverbial sardines.

When the plains dried out in December the tall rushes covering them were fired, to be soon replaced by a short green sward. But these open plains were not like the plains of East Africa's Serengeti or the Athi. For they are flood plains, and when the water recedes the clay soil dries out in dips and hummocks, and is pitted with the giant footprints of elephants which become indelibly cemented in. Driving over such plains is like trying to drive over a ploughed field, only worse because the ground doesn't give.

The headquarters of the Saint Floris National Park at Gordil comprised three stone-built houses, a rusting lorry, a Land Rover donated by the World Wildlife Fund with its front smashed in, a defunct bulldozer and a Fordson tractor with flat tyres bearing a faded American Aid badge. The buildings were scattered under a miserly canopy of shade on a floor of grey dust. Next to the long-abandoned foundations of some unfinished structure was a substantial building with a sign *Magasin* (Store) above it.

Two stone pillars reared up out of the bush on either side of the track marking the entrance to this dismal collection while incongruous signs informed the visitor everything was under control.

At the 'entrance' one sign proclaimed in French:

"Attention! It is forbidden in the park to exceed 50 km an hour, to chase or to frighten the animals. Obey the instructions. Good trip and thankyou."

Having passed this instruction one was confronted with another:

"Welcome to the friends of nature. In your interest you are reminded that driving is limited to the roads and tracks and the maximum speed is 30 km an hour. It is forbidden to leave a vehicle and to frighten the animals. We wish you a good stay at the park."

Intrigued by the sign '*Magasin*' I asked to see what was inside and it was opened for my inspection. I stood dumbfounded, feeling once more like Marlow when he saw the broken drainpipes. But this was even more absurd, for I was confronted with tier upon tier of neatly stacked porcelain lavatory bowls!

When I had travelled through rural France with a student party in the Sixties, sanitation was not one of the French strong points. At one village a girl in the party badly wanted to powder her nose and a sympathetic French woman, seeing her discomfiture, took the girl around to the rear of her house. The girl came back white faced. I never asked her what monstrous horror had frightened her in the privy, and like Great Aunt Ada Doom[3] and "something nasty in the woodshed", we shall never know. But once Paris had given up its *pissoirs*, French hygiene took a turn for the better with a vengeance. Now no Frenchman will be without his flush even in remotest Africa. But as any Englishman who has spent his life in Africa knows, a simple longdrop (a deep hole dug in the ground) is perfectly adequate and often more hygienic.

* * *

It was on this, my first safari to the Park, we got bogged down crossing the Vakaga River. It was only a narrow crossing but the driver took it too slowly and that was that. After half an hour I saw he was not going to get out before dark, and since he did not wish to listen to my advice I simply had my camp bed unpacked and a mosquito net strung from an overhanging branch. We were just getting ready for the night when an old man came wandering by. I asked him if there were many lions about and got the usual answer, "Lots." At this time I had a young cook called André, and as this was his first trip into the bush he was not too happy with the answer. So he and the driver proceeded to pass the night sitting awake on the river bank.

There was no moon that night and it was not long after dark when ghostly rustling noises began to be heard moving from the river towards them. André and the driver grabbed sticks and started to throw them into the undergrowth at the noises, but the stealthy rustlings continued. Fear changed to delight when, with the aid of a firebrand, they discovered the rustlings were caused by swarms of giant catfish, four feet and more in length, wriggling out of the river onto land. André greedily filled a large cardboard carton, having despatched a great number and hastily smoked them. But the smoking was inadequate and in a couple of days, much to André's chagrin, the carton became just a heaving mass of maggots.

* * *

In spite of the fact one of the principal pursuits in the CAR is hunting, it was not possible to obtain a tent in the country. As a German hunter complained in 1956, you could buy a crystal table service for twelve persons or a four-poster bed, and, I daresay, the latest Paris fashion, but not camping equipment. The French explained to me a tent was not necessary; all one required was a *bâche*, pronounced 'bash'. That is, simply a square of canvas which one stretched over some poles.

It sounded reasonable enough, and I arrived at Gordil, as the park headquarters was known after the name of the nearby village, with my 'bash'.

The first thing on arrival at the camping spot was to send André off to cut suitable poles from which the canvas could be hung. This was his first experience of camp life, and after a long and tiring journey, which had lasted the best part of a day, he was not expecting such vigorous exercise. Having cut the poles it was then necessary to dig holes in the ground for the central supports and it was thus some time before the canvas was stretched over a ridge pole in the manner of a tent and all was to my liking. By now a very tired and disgruntled André then went to collect firewood with which to start the camp fire and get on with cooking a meal.

Although it was the beginning of the dry season, at about three o'clock the following morning I was awakened by a tremendous squall. The wind blew like fury and soon the *bâche* was torn loose from its moorings. Then the rain came down in torrents. Clad in wet pyjama trousers and seizing a blanket, I dashed for the Land Rover and sat in the cabin, cold and wet, shivering until morning.

Everything was soaked, but soon the sun came out and by midday all was dry again and little the worse for its dousing. Except for the book I had been reading which had separated into its component pages.

Give me a tent every time!

* * *

The mystery of the lavatory pans was solved when I went to Dongolo in the extreme west of the park, near the Bahr Kameur River. Here a former French warden had been in the process of building a small lodge, which was to be the beneficiary of this modern convenience. But when he closed the lodge down in the rainy season, raiders came over the river from Chad and destroyed it. It was now a heap of ruins. So the lavatory pans were never installed.

Few Europeans pass the wet season in the north; the odd missionary, and I once knew of a French veterinarian who passed a couple of wet seasons there. He told me how the mosquitoes were so bad one had to get under a mosquito net before dark, and he even had to make a net for his dog. The Africans are sometimes obliged to construct platforms under which they light a smoky fire, and they pass the night lying on the platforms smoking themselves, the only way they can get any respite.

* * *

The Mbororo from Chad don't recognize the international boundary, which runs along the Aouk and Aoukalé rivers, and have traditionally grazed their herds on the flood plains of the Park. And little wonder they do not recognize it. A former senior French official confided to me that when independence was about to take place in 1960, the two chief administrators just put their heads together and chose an arbitrary boundary on the map. Previously, as the AEF or French Equatorial Africa, nobody had worried about such things as boundaries between the countries that made up this block of Chad, Oubangui-Chari, and French Congo.

Each year a team of game guards from Bangui would visit the area and make known their presence by opening fire on the herdsmen in the park, who of course poached as well as grazing their stock. Sometimes the guards even caught one or two, but if shots were returned then a hasty retreat was made. When I flew over the area and we came across some of these herdsmen deep in its interior, my counterpart Ndouté (pronounced N-doo-tay) was so furious he seized a shotgun and commenced to blaze away as the pilot dived the plane over them. We had taken the door off the side of the plane to facilitate observation. The little pops of the shotgun, drowned by the roar of the aircraft engine and lost in the slipstream, were, of course, completely ineffectual. All the same, I didn't much like the exercise when I saw the herdsmen staring up at us, remembering what had happened in northern Uganda when cattle raiders firing a gun had actually hit the plane and nearly killed one of the occupants.

When he was Minister, Patassé had a much better idea. He asked the United Nations Representative, a sort of Ambassador, to supply him with an aircraft equipped with rocket launchers with which they could attack the herdsmen, demonstrating by stabbing the air with his outstretched fingers how the rockets would shoot out killing them. At least the intention was good, to preserve the park, even if the method was a little unsuited to United Nations' sensibilities.

* * *

I had been flying over the park because one of my tasks was to get some idea of how many animals there were in the northern area, and the only way to do this was from the air. An aerial survey was called for. Getting an aircraft had been the problem, for Bokassa, paranoiac for his own safety, would not allow private aircraft to operate. Eventually he was persuaded to relent in the case of a newly installed American hunting company among whose directors was Neil Armstrong, the first man on the moon. A meeting with this famous man soon softened up Bokassa, for being the first man on the moon was something even Bokassa knew he could not aspire to, and neither did he have plans for building a rocket to go there. Although he did want an atomic bomb, but he never made clear quite what for.

The company promised to hire out their aircraft to me as soon as it arrived, ferried over from the United States. I planned my survey accordingly; almost seven thousand square miles had to be covered, an area nearly the size of Wales.

I waited impatiently.

The aircraft was on its way.

Why hadn't it arrived?

Nobody knew.

It had left the United States. That was all anyone could tell me.

Eventually, well behind schedule, it did arrive, the pilot simply having taken his time: perhaps wisely so, for it was rather an old aircraft. But at least it was a high-wing monoplane, perfectly adequate for doing air surveys, in which the high wings are necessary for an observer to get a clear view of the ground beneath. First of all, however, before I could start my survey some hunters had to be flown out to a hunting camp in the east of the country, and then at long last it would be at my disposal for the ten days I needed it.

Two days later a worried director of the company accosted me in the street. The aircraft had crashed on its maiden voyage to the east and had been completely burnt out. All of the occupants had escaped unhurt but understandably somewhat shaken. I was back to square one.

Never mind, I was told, we will get another aircraft, a new one this time. It was already ordered.

I waited.

Yes, it had left the United States.

Yes, it was coming.

No, they did not know when it would arrive.

But eventually it did arrive. It was a twin-engine low-wing. The least suitable model for conducting aerial surveys but I would have to make do as best I could with it. At least I now had an aircraft again.

The new aircraft had been in the country less than a week when the ferry pilot, while instructing a local French pilot in its use, landed the aircraft on the runway at Bangui airport – and forgot to lower the undercarriage! The aircraft slithered to a stop on its belly with two bent propellers. It would have to be repaired, and the engines would have to be sent to the Ivory Coast, the nearest place where work on them could be undertaken. At least a six-month delay was envisaged.

On January 2 1978 with the repaired aircraft I began my long awaited air survey, originally planned to take place a year before. It is remarkably difficult to see animals from the air because there is no relief, in spite of the fact the flying is done at the low level of about three hundred feet above the ground. It is like looking at a map and you often detect animals only from their shadows or if they move. Taking into account the fact therefore that aerial surveys usually underestimate what is actually there, the numbers of animals seen were nevertheless pretty low.

First of all I covered the 1,275 square mile Aouk Aoukalé game reserve, up against the north-west border with Chad, an area long ago virtually abandoned to Chadian herdsmen and their cattle. Although it was generally believed most of the game had been eliminated from this area I found some still existed – even an estimated 96 giraffes, a species greatly persecuted by black Arab horsemen, Baggara arabs from the Sudan, who prize its tail hairs for sewing thread.

Then I covered the Saint Floris National Park and the vast area to the south; then the 4,600 square miles of the waterless, barren wilderness of the Goz Sassoulko in the northernmost part of the country, where there was indeed hardly an animal to be seen after its ten years of drought.

While I was about it I covered the 656 square mile André Félix National Park on the eastern border with the Sudan, an almost totally unknown area, effectively abandoned since the mid-1960s. It was named after a former Inspector of Hunting who died in an accident with a buffalo in 1956. Here also, although Sudanese poachers had a free rein, I found more game existed than suspected. I estimated 426 giant eland, 414 hartebeest, 163 buffalo, 163 elephants, 121 waterbuck, 85 giraffe, 85 roan antelope and 22 Buffon's kob.

I never had time to get to this area on the ground, but the problem in the dry season, the only period of the year when it is accessible, is lack of water. Perhaps that served to keep the Sudanese poachers out as well. To my knowledge its steep thickly forested valleys running north-south into the mountains of the Dar Chala massif, and where from the air I could see a large herd of elephants, have never been visited. What treasures may await the inquisitive naturalist there! For the other nearest isolated highlands are Jebel Marra 350 km to the north-east in the Sudan, and the Adamoua Massif 1400 km to the west in Cameroon.

Finally I covered the Bamingui-Bangoran Park and its adjacent game reserves. In this park I estimated there to be some 6,480 buffalo, 4,240 hartebeest, 2,070 Buffon's kob, 820 giant eland, 290 roan antelope, 290 waterbuck, 90 topi, over 100 hippos, 130 black rhino and 1,160 elephants. All undoubtedly underestimates of the true numbers that existed, but even so relatively low numbers considering the size of the area. Some topi were still living in the adjacent Gribingui reserve where they had not been reported since 1936.

In 1985 the well-known elephant expert, Doctor Iain Douglas-Hamilton carried out a survey of the elephants in the same area and found only an estimated 587; a drop in numbers of 55 per cent (and 80 per cent for the whole area including the surrounding reserves) due to poaching in the eight years that had intervened.

I estimated also there must have been nearer 600 black rhinoceros in the Bamingui-Bangoran park than the calculated 130, previously thought to be almost extinct in this part of Africa. From my early, often hair-raising experiences on foot in the Aberdare Mountains of Kenya at the beginning of the 1950s, I knew the black rhino must be fairly numerous here on account of the frequent signs I came across on the ground, as well as the number of actual sightings. The aerial survey confirmed this was the richest pocket for this species, together with a smaller area to the east of the park.

But in 1982, following a radio programme in Kenya which announced the high value of rhino horn, the new military Minister began to take an interest in the rhino and sent Latakpi to shoot one in the Bamingui-Bangoran Park, because he wanted to "see what it looked like". Of course he could have looked at Bokassa's stuffed one. After an unsuccessful sortie into the Bamingui-Bangoran Park, Latakpi succeeded in shooting one in the Presidential hunting reserve, at least a more appropriate place. The carcase was taken to Bangui on an army truck where it arrived in a somewhat advanced state of decomposition. Rumour circulated it was wanted for witchcraft, and it was later reported the military regime had tried to poison one of the generals by sending to his house a gift of a leg of meat injected with a deadly liquid extracted from the stomach of a rhinoceros. No doubt the liquid from the stomach of a rotting rhinoceros would make one somewhat sick, but to poison somebody it would be much simpler to use the deadly poison of the *gounda* tree, a common enough tree along riversides in the north of the country. I had no doubt the objective in obtaining the rhino was simply to see how much the horn could be sold for!

After this there was a concerted onslaught on the rhino, so that by 1983 it had become, to all intents and purposes, extinct in the country. The 3,000 I had estimated to exist countrywide in 1977, vanished in the space of two years.

At the beginning of the century the rarer white rhinoceros, which was common in the north of the Belgian Congo, also existed in the east and north-east of the CAR. But by the beginning of the 1930s reports of it were already rare, and Saint Floris declared it to be "the Loch Ness monster of French Equatorial Africa".

But old stories die hard, and when I came to the CAR in 1975 it was still rumoured white rhino might exist in the 3,900 square mile Zemongo Reserve in the east of the country. There had been an alleged sighting about one hundred and thirty miles to the south-east of this area in that year, but the Zemongo itself had never been surveyed for its wild life resources. It remains today one of the least-known areas of the CAR, part of a vast, uninhabited wilderness extending along almost the entire border with Sudan.

The first known white man to visit this remote corner may have been a Greek doctor, Panaghiotis Potagos, who claimed to have done so in 1876. Some doubt has been cast on his account, but his sketch map, despite the misspelling of many names, suggests his knowledge of the area was authentic. If Potagos did not visit the area himself then at least he provided the first account of it, probably from Greek and Arab traders. We do know the English Governor of the Bahr-el-Ghazal Province in the Sudan, Frank Lupton, made a safari into the area about 1882. But he only crossed the south-west extremity; as the following year did the Russian doctor-explorer Wilhelm Junker who was working for Emin Pasha. Then in 1909-10 a French military detachment explored part of the area in the east where a route from the Sudan was reported, used mostly by Greek and Syrian ivory traders. This exploration was followed in 1922 by the Anglo-French boundary survey, which traced the north-east boundary with the Sudan. Neither of these expeditions reported rhinos in the area although making reference to them occurring elsewhere. But to this day no European seems to have explored the vast hinterland of the reserve, now overrun by gangs of Sudanese poachers equipped with automatic assault rifles, who penetrate with donkey and camel trains. No rhinos are expected to have withstood their onslaught, and the white rhino can be considered well and truly extinct in the country, even if it did exist until recent times in this remote corner.

* * *

In 1979 a vast new area of some six thousand square miles was added to the south of the Saint Floris National Park, creating the Manovo-Gounda-Saint Floris National Park. This area is mostly woodland, but with rich game densities along the Gounda River, which runs through its centre; while in the south-east is a little-known region of ravines and tall-tree forest. Part of it had formerly been a private hunting concession and game viewing area where people such as the former French President Giscard d'Estaing and the well-known French big-game hunter Lucien Blancou had hunted. Jean-Luc and his wife Annie-Evelyn had been camp managers in this concession and had the task of developing this huge park, a task later taken over by the EEC with disastrous results.

Karamojo Bell visited the western edge in 1919 when he hunted along the Aouk and Aoukalé rivers. He recorded meeting "extraordinary numbers" of rhino, and elephant were so unaccustomed to shooting they took no notice as he downed them. He was able to go "through crowds and crowds of them, getting a bull here and there."4 Five hundred elephant were seen in the same area along the Aouk river in 1977, but they have since been virtually exterminated. The last rhino footprints were seen there in 1983.

The elephant poachers in this area were Baggara Arabs from the Sudan, four hundred miles away to the east, who have traditionally hunted elephants right across to the Aouk, much to the chagrin of the French authorities who were always complaining the British in the Sudan did nothing to control them.

Although some poachers now carried automatic weapons, the majority still hunted the elephant as they had done so for the past two centuries or more, on horseback, with enormous spears bearing paddle-like blades a foot long, six inches broad and with razor-sharp edges. This method of hunting was first described in 1863 by a French ivory trader on the Nile, Jules Poncet, who perhaps reached as far west as Bangassou; and then in 1929 by Major Court-Treatt. He tried to make a cine film of a spearing but at the critical moment his helper ran away in fright taking the camera. The hunt has only recently been described in detail by Jean-Luc Temporal in his book *La Chasse Oubliée* (*The Forgotten Hunt*). During his time in the park in the Seventies he saw all stages of the chase and spearing, and was eventually wounded by the poachers in a less traditional manner by automatic rifle fire.

The hunt consists of galloping after the elephants pell-mell through the woodland, a hazardous enough task in itself considering the many obstructions: warthog holes, fallen tree trunks and branches, which might bring down the unwary. The Arabs use small horses, most cruelly treated, which when approaching an elephant for a kill are fitted with a spiked bit. With that in its mouth the horse will do whatever it is told. Getting an elephant on the run the horsemen throw their spears into its flanks. As the elephant continues to run the blades saw up and down, causing the animal's entrails to protrude. Brought to a standstill the horsemen surround it, plying it with more spears until it collapses.

There is one difference to the method of seventy years and more ago and that of today. Now the horsemen carry hypodermic syringes together with an antidote for sleeping sickness for the horses, allowing them to operate deep into the tsetse fly country.

For African horror stories this area tops the bill with the case of the rabid hunting dog. A young American Peace Corps Volunteer helping the Temporals, was sitting in the privy one day lost in quiet contemplation with the door open to the bush, when the entrance was suddenly blocked by a rabid hunting dog. Now hunting dogs, which are not known to attack humans, go for the nether regions of animals to tear out the soft parts, and as the horrified youth rose to confront it, that is exactly what this one tried to do, lunging at the man's loins and badly lacerating the insides of his thighs. The youth was fortunate in being large and well built. In desperation he succeeded in seizing the hunting dog around the neck with the superhuman strength born of fear and strangled it to death. Few would have survived to be able to tell such a tale.

* * *

Not far to the north-east of the Saint Floris Park a large lake is shown on the map, Lake Mamoun. But suffering the great Sahelian drought it had been dry since 1975. Formerly the home of many hippo it was now nothing more than a large bed of reeds. Flying over it no trace of water was revealed. From here I made my way by vehicle to the farthest outpost of the north, Birao. Cut off from Bangui for six months of the year it was Bokassa's punishment station, and it was not unusual to see people there with an ear missing, his customary method of marking a thief. I did not stop here; my aim was to reach the farthest northern point of the country, Lake Tizi on the border with Chad. The map indicated a track crossing the fifty miles of the Goz Sassoulko, shown as a sandy desert. Few people entered the area and I wanted to see if any animals still existed there, for at this time I had not yet been able to plan the aerial survey.

The track, opened up in French colonial times, had long since become overgrown but one could still trace its line. Alas, the whole area was drought stricken and many of the large trees were dead. There was no sandy desert like the map portrayed, it was entirely scrubby bush and dry woodland. The only trace of animal life I found was an old footprint of a roan antelope.

Lake Tizi was dry, and here we found a few abject villagers eking out a miserable existence. Their sole water supply was from a muddy hole they had dug in the dry lake bed. Even the game guards with me who asked for a drink refused to drink the water when they saw it. No rain came, and I suppose the people all eventually migrated to Birao.

* * *

Saint Floris wrote a book of verse he titled *Tam Tams de Mes Nuits* (*Tom Toms of My Nights*). After my first night at the roadside village of Bangoran, at the north-east corner of the Bamingui-Bangoran National

Park, I soon realized why he had called it that.

I had just fallen asleep when the tom-toms started to thud with a deep, resonant boom: now fast, now slow, unceasing on and on through the night, reverberating through the very ground under my bed. The sound of tom-toms at night is considered to be one of the romantic sounds of an Africa long past, in most places they are now played only for tourists in the same meaningless rhythm anyone might use. I had never heard real tom-toms before I came to this remote spot, an incessant, penetrating rhythm which went on until dawn, keeping me tossing and turning, sleepless for most of the hot tropical night.

Here they played them in the villages all night for three nights in succession if a man died, and two nights if it was a woman. And if nobody died, why, then they played the tom-toms all night just for the fun of it. As the noise continued on this particular night, I could hear even my African staff cursing. Coming from Bangui they were more used to the similar, but worse, discordant melody of the discotheque. The drummers, kept going by the drug called bhang, which is marijuana under another name, the drums only stop at dawn. In the morning, tired from my sleepless night, I asked a young woman from the village why they had been playing all night:

"Oh," was the answer, "just to amuse ourselves."

* * *

Auguste Chevalier, the distinguished French botanist sent out to make a study of the economic potential of Oubangui-Chari and Chad, took this route in 1902. Halfway between the villages of Bamingui and Bangoran is a massive whale-backed granite outcrop close to the road known as Kaga Poungourou, *kaga* being the Banda name for a rock. Behind it lies Kaga Kolo (giraffe rock). Both were marked on the earliest maps drawn from Arab descriptions. Chevalier climbed Kaga Poungourou, the height of which he gave as 1,992 feet: not a bad estimate since modern maps give it as 2,018 feet. It had been cultivated around the base for a long time and I found signs of ancient habitation with innumerable pottery sherds scattered about. Chevalier saw some huts on the kagas and others on the plain, inhabited by Banda who came under Senoussi. Before this point, Chevalier recorded, the country had been uninhabited. There had been no trace of cultivation or habitation at the Bamingui River, only wild animal tracks, "game abounds," he noted. At Kaga Betolo, further along on the right of the road, he recorded a water cistern said to be without depth, inhabited by bad spirits, which seized those who approached too close.

* * *

It was in the grass hut Latakpi had built for me by the side of the road at Bangoran I spent my first Christmas in the country. Somehow one cannot work up the same enthusiasm for the festive season in Africa that one can in temperate climes. December is the hottest time of the year, and it is difficult to get enthusiastic about tinsel and snow scenes when one finds oneself sweltering in the heat. The 'carol singers', ragged African children who wandered the streets of Bangui singing one line in French of a carol imperfectly learned from their mission school, and then holding out their hands for reward, underlined the grim annual parody of it all. Scrooge-like, I decided to get away from it and spend it on my own in the bush.

As I stood patiently in the hot sun at the road barrier at Bamingui on the day before Christmas, while the gendarme sitting at a little rickety table in front of his tumble-down thatched hut which constituted the police station, painstakingly filled in his grubby notebook with my details, I became aware the radio in front of him was trying to tell me something. The tinny, discordant crackle of atmospherics resolved itself into a barely recognizable rendering of "O come! All ye faithful." There was no escaping the parody.

Arriving at Bangoran I purchased a chicken in the village. At least I would have a good lunch tomorrow. Christmas morning came and I was awakened by the sun striking through the grass sides of my *boukarou*. There being nothing else to do I decided to have a lie-in, and went back to sleep. It was ten o'clock when I was awakened again, this time by my cook (I had not found Bernard then) announcing lunch was ready!

"What do you mean, lunch is ready?" I asked. "It's only ten o'clock."

"Well I haven't got a watch," was the indignant reply.

The roast chicken I had been looking forward to was at least well done by the time I came to eat it.

A couple of years later, when I was spending Christmas at Bamingui, Bernard, who was by then my cook, astonished me on Christmas morning by appearing clutching a bible in one hand and resplendent in a bright scarlet jacket that would have put Father Christmas himself in the shade, and gravely announced he was going to "Mess."

Like some reproachful Ghost of Christmas Present, no matter if it was in the middle of the pagan bush with the thermometer standing at 40° centigrade, Bernard was dressed in his very best and spending Christmas morning as it ought to be spent. By going to Mass. The red jacket had belonged to one of Bokassa's fancy bandsmen, looted after the overthrow.

Another Christmas at Bamingui was spent sitting around a campfire with a charming polite man allegedly wanted by the Swiss or Austrian police, I forget which, for an armed bank hold up. Under the guise of a hunter, he was looking for illicit diamonds.

* * *

I have recorded the dangers of drinking water in Bangui. But it was no safer in the bush. In March 1981, when in the remote interior of the

Bamingui-Bangoran Park, I returned to my camp at the riverside one lunchtime to find the Bamingui River had been poisoned. Dead and dying fish were floating past the camp in profusion. An enormous dead tiger fish was recovered weighing about ten kilograms. It was almost half the length of one of my workers, Kakumale, who paraded it before me. In the evening the sound of fish splashing was not that of the tiger fish chasing its prey, but of fish struggling in their death throes. Opha, another worker, together with some others, walked a long way upstream and didn't come to the beginning of the dying fish. They collected about fifty and insisted on smoking and eating them although I cautioned against it.

Opha (pronounced offa) had a theory that if people in one village wanted to kill those in another, then they fired a burning poisonous arrow at night at the village – if such an arrow fell into the river then that could account for the fish poisoning.

Of course the explanation was much more simple. The poisoning is done with pesticides, a cocktail of DDT and other chemicals banned in Europe but supplied here for cotton growing. It's much more profitable to pour it in the river and kill the fish. This accounts for the fact the whole of the rivers in the south and centre of the country are almost devoid of fish. This particular year there were three known instances of poisoning on the Bamingui, two on the Koukourou River and one on the Gounda, a small tributary, where others reported monstrous Nile perch of 65 to 110 pounds being killed.

Expatriate fish biologists in Bangui, never apparently having read Rachel Carson's *Silent Spring*, came to the remarkable conclusion the rivers are relatively unproductive because of the sandy bottoms! The real reason is repeated poisoning, which also accounts for the scarcity of fish-eating birds on the Bamingui, and no one has even started to consider what it does to the aquatic insect life. The people themselves will suffer eventually from eating the poisoned fish, which is smoked and sold on the market, but the *delirium tremens* which results and is probably mistaken for Parkinson's Disease, does not manifest itself until old age; by which time the cause will have been forgotten.

The poisoners took very little of what they killed and dead fish continued to float down the river for three days. On the fourth day it was the bloated corpses of those that had sunk and then floated back to the surface again. But on the third day I started to see a few live fish once more, so perhaps some escaped or they came from upstream. But it cannot be many more years before this is a dead river if it is not so already.

* * *

Long before the demise of the rhino, in 1976 Bokassa's financial situation was somewhat improved by the arrival on the scene of a Belgian woman, Madame Gilberte Van Erpe, sister of one of Bokassa's former wives Astrid, accompanied by a Spaniard appropriately named Dorado. Tongue in cheek they set up a firm called "*La Couronne*" (The Crown), after the infamous "*Domaine de la Couronne*", King Leopold's private sector which he had set aside for himself in the Belgian Congo and declared inalienable from himself and his heirs forever, and which exercised a monopoly on ivory buying over all of the Upper Ubangui.

Bokassa had a controlling share in "*La Couronne*", the objective of which was to annihilate the elephant for its ivory.

Between 1976 and the downfall of Bokassa in 1979 this firm, like King Leopold, had a monopoly on ivory, and set up collecting posts in the east of the country, the traditional haunt of the old-time elephant hunters and a region always renowned for its big tusks. It was one of the few places left in Africa where a hunter still had a chance of securing the coveted 'hundred pounder', an elephant of which each tusk weighs at least one hundred pounds. The handful of old-time hunters in the Twenties and Thirties had little impact on the herds, and the Second

World War, together with the inaccessibility of the region – ten days by road and you had to take all of your fuel supplies with you – had meant the elephants, unlike in most other parts of Africa, had a chance to grow to old age and so grow big tusks. Thus lucky hunters were still getting their 'hundred pounders' up until 1977. One man obtained a pair weighing 154 pounds each, allegedly later stolen from him by the authorities. Bokassa was also alleged to have had an enormous pair in his palace, which disappeared during the coup.

In the year 1977 I was on leave in England, having an X-ray at the Radcliffe Infirmary in Oxford for kidney stones, brought about by not drinking enough water in the tropics. In preparation I had just been given a hefty injection and was feeling about to vomit when the doctor, a short, black-bearded man, asked me where I came from. I told him from the CAR.

"Ah!" he exclaimed, "that's the place for elephants."

"He's looking very white," the nurse interjected.

I murmured weakly, I really did feel as if I was about to be violently sick, I was in no fit state to talk about elephants.

"Oh yes, I go there hunting elephant every year. I know," continued the doctor, and hurried off to his next patient.

I never had a chance to talk to him again, but it's a small world.

That was before "The Crown" had really got to work organizing the massacre, encouraging the Sudanese poachers from the east who came in with their camel and donkey trains and their AK47 automatic assault rifles. It was said in some quarters that much of the ivory came from Zaïre. It is true some did, but the greater part of the Zaïrean ivory was floated down the river to Brazzaville in the Congo and never entered the CAR at all. Most of it nevertheless had documents purporting to show it came from Zaïre or the Sudan, but these could be obtained for a bottle of whisky. One French smuggler explained to a colleague of mine an elaborate ploy, how he obtained Camerounian export documents by tricking the border customs, the ivory never leaving the CAR. The CAR had enough of its own to exploit. One of *La Couronne*'s main collecting camps was near Djèma in the extreme east of the country, run by a Portuguese who later obtained a well-paid position with the EEC-funded wild life project.

On one occasion I was urgently informed by my counterpart we had to attend immediately a hunting conference at the Safari Hotel. Arrived there I found all the representatives of the hunting concessions were present, and Madame Van Erp. Soon after, Bokassa entered and took his seat behind a table on a small dais at one end of the room. Madame Van Erp jumped up and began to talk, but then saw that Bokassa was staring into the distance with a dream-like quality on his face taking no notice of her. Suddenly we all realized he was listening to a crackly recording of his national anthem. We all leapt up and stood in respectful silence until it had finished and then sat down again. Madame Van Erp jumped to her feet once more and began to apologize but Bokassa dismissed the apology with an indulgent smile. He was in a good mood. Madame then began to outline a plan to build a hunter's clubhouse where hunters could get together and swap tales. An elaborate building was proposed which she suggested all the concessionaires could contribute towards the cost of. Bokassa listened and without making any definite commitment told her to look into it. One concessionaire, Daniel Henriot of Haut Chinko Safaris in the east of the country, was bold enough then to stand up and deplore the poaching of elephants, passing up to Bokassa some colour prints of slaughtered elephants. Bokassa spread his hands widely and sighed, "But what can I do?" he asked, "I just haven't the people or the resources."

Of course the biggest poacher of all was in the audience, but what none of the French and Portuguese concessionaires seemed to realize was that Madame Van Erp knew they could not afford to contribute the amount required for the clubhouse, and it was clear to me that when she met with refusal she would then go to Bokassa and complain of their indifference to his wishes. At her urging he would then close down the concessions and *La Couronne* would have a free rein to slaughter their elephants without fear of hindrance. But in the end we heard no more about the clubhouse.

It was in 1977 I estimated the number of elephants in the CAR to be about 70,000. Like early estimates of elephants in East Africa previous estimates had put them at less than one tenth of this; but there could have been more even than 70,000, for it is a vast country, much of it uninhabited yet with a good rainfall and well-watered in parts. Then from 1979 to 1984 Japan alone imported 430,369 tons of ivory from the CAR, equivalent to about 30,000 elephants. By 1985 the number of elephants left in the country was estimated to be 40,000. After Bokassa's fall from power the ivory entrepreneurs very wisely skipped the country, but a whole system of poaching had now been set up and this continued to operate.

The scandal was exposed in an article in the *Sunday Times* in February 1981, but undaunted by this exposé, which was repeated in the Paris press the following April, President Dacko exported to Paris the same month 16 tonnes, representing at least five hundred elephants. This time the shipment was refused, not being accompanied by the required international documents, and returned to Bangui. Dacko then got rid of it, together with another 15 tonnes, by sending it to Belgium via Sabena Airlines.

After Dacko's usurper President Kolingba tried to sell 300 tusks in Paris and had them sent back, an arrangement was then made to route the ivory to Khartoum through an office allegedly set up to co-ordinate cross-border anti-poaching activities. This resulted from a conference in Bangui in December 1981 called the "First Ministerial Conference of Central African States on the Organization of the Anti-poaching War". The whole thing, held up by the International Union for the

Conservation of Nature as a great example of African initiative, was an elaborate hoax, designed to sound out which countries the CAR could use to dispose of ivory and rhino horns. Chaired by the Minister Konzale, and attended by delegates from Gabon, Congo, Sudan, and Zaïre, the delegate from Gabon was so amused at the effrontery of it all that he could not refrain from smiling at the proceedings. I was obliged to participate as a part of the window-dressing, being required to give a talk on wild life management in the CAR, while the French writer Michel Droit of the *Académie française*, who leased a hunting concession in the country, spoke on hunting. The minister finding a kindred spirit in corruption in the official who was sent from the Sudan wild life department, an office was duly set up by the CAR in Khartoum, staffed by an official from the CAR nicknamed '*Tete à pointes*' or 'Tusk's head', who as a former Director had embezzled the ten per cent tax on ivory supposed to finance the "National Centre for Wildlife Management" in Bangui. His job was to organize the flow of illegal ivory and rhino horn from the CAR.

From 1985 to 1987 a further 135 tonnes were exported. But by this time average tusk weight had dropped by half, and this represented not 7,500 elephants, but an estimated 15,153; so by 1987 it was estimated the total number of elephants left in the country had fallen to just under 29,000, and by 1989 it may have been as few as 15,000. The year 1987 saw the first big drop in ivory exports, but the killing went on. The excuse offered by the authorities for the continued slaughter, despite an official ban on ivory sales, was that the elephants had been driven by the poachers into areas where they did not previously exist. This, the authorities explain, is why they are no longer seen in the parks and reserves; but their presence in these other areas brings them into contact with people, and they have to be shot in defence of crops.

* * *

At one time the greater part of the unforested land in the east of the CAR was inhabited by a variety of tribes believed to be of Sudanese origin, many of which became surrounded by other tribes or annihilated by the nineteenth century. At the end of the eighteenth century the Zande, their tradition asserting they came from the west of Chad, feared as the NiamNiam, cannibals who filed their teeth, conquered the region, founding the Zande empire in 1800. At the beginning of the nineteenth century every freeman in Darfur could obtain a special permit to hunt slaves in the CAR. In 1821 Egypt occupied the Sudan and about 1880 by setting up trading outposts attempted to extend its control westwards as far as Bria into what is now the CAR, and south of the Mbomou River in present day Zaïre. About 1840 a number of European traders in Khartoum, calling themselves 'the merchant princes of the Nile', had set themselves up to buy ivory in the eastern CAR, soon extending their activities to slaves as well. Eventually some explorers revealed their activities to the authorities and the "merchant princes" were forced to withdraw about 1860. Their place was then taken by the Sudanese Arab slavers Zubeir, operating from 1850 to 1875, and Rabah from 1880 to 1890. These slavers had already obtained thousands of slaves from the Kreich who ruled the eastern part of the CAR at the end of the eighteenth century. As a result of the removal of the merchant princes, Zubeir was able to ruin the whole of the eastern CAR and make a fortune for himself, establishing fortified trading stations and obtaining thousands of slaves from the Zande, who, through associating with other tribes, by 1890 had produced an east Zande principality which became the sultanate of Rafai. Eventually arrested, Zubeir was succeeded by his son Rabah, and between them in twenty years they caused more damage to the country than all of the previous operations of the northern sultans put together. The Muslims to the north called the country 'the land of fear'. The Upper Kotto was first overrun by Rabah and then by Senoussi, who Rabah appointed to succeed him, Rabah moving on to Chad. The Egyptian outposts were abandoned before they came into operation due to the Mahdi uprising. After the French occupation Senoussi was left to continue his slave hunts, until killed by the French in 1911. By this time the entire north-east of the country had been ravaged. Smallpox and sleeping sickness then took their toll of the remaining inhabitants, and by the 1980s the greater part of the country inland of the Mbomou River northwards, still remained almost totally uninhabited, except for a few seasonal camps of hunting organizations. Then in 1980 the Sudanese Arabs came back armed with Kalashnikovs, using their traditional routes from the north-east, to poach elephant and rhino. Having denuded the country of both in a short space of time, they then turned their attention to any other animal they could make money from, smoking the meat of antelopes and buffalo, using their skins, and making whips from the hides of hippopotamus. Becoming bolder and bolder they advanced further and further west, now ravaging and pillaging the country as their forebears had done, reaching the centre of the CAR without opposition. In ten years they created a desert as big as a quarter of the size of France,[5] today having effectively taken back control of the country after one hundred years and ravaging it as their infamous ancestors did, even to the extent of abducting girls and boys and using them as slaves, the captives never being seen again. And this goes on now, in the 21st century!

"Ivory?" said Marlow, "I should think so. Heaps of it, stacks of it. The old mud shanty was bursting with it. You would think there was not a single tusk left either above or below the ground in the whole country."

Well might we echo the cry of Conrad's ivory collector, Mr Kurtz: "The horror! The horror!"

Notes

1. Georges Toqué 1904 *Essai sur le Peuple et la Langue Banda.*
2. Evelyn Waugh *Men at Arms.*
3. Stella Gibbon *Cold Comfort Farm.*
4. W. D. M. Bell *Bell of Africa.*
5. Daniel Henriot 2004 *Au bout des pistes, le Chinko.*

Chapter 7

In the Unknown

searching for the caves of the Troglodytes

My assignment in the CAR was to explore, survey, and then develop single-handedly with the sole assistance of one clapped-out Land Rover, the immense and almost unknown area of the Bamingui-Bangoran National Park, an area more than half the size of Wales.

Created in 1933 and almost untouched since its creation, it is bounded on the north by the Bangoran River and Bokassa's former private hunting reserve the Avakaba (although he often preferred to cross over the river and hunt in the park), and to the south by the Bamingui River, or 'Much water' river. This river is joined by another called the Koukourou, the 'river of parrots', and eventually the Bamingui is joined by the Gribingui, finally becoming the Shari River where it enters Chad.

An immense, hostile wilderness, almost completely flat, much of it is covered with dense monotonous woodland of scrubby trees, offering little shade from the blistering African sun. Here and there this grim wasteland spawned patches of fine, tall, Isoberlinia woodland, or, near to the stream beds which were dry from March to May, the large attractive Daniellia trees which exude a copious resin and bear heavily scented white flowers. And then there were curious open flat plains of red ironstone: iron-hard rock forming a smooth plate on the surface, sometimes as much as a mile long by half a mile wide. And, more curious still, patches of grey earth dotted with myriads of toadstool-shaped termite mounds, a fairyland fantasy like something from the realms of the Hobbit and Middle Earth.

Here and there huge whaleback outcrops of smooth naked granite

197

rock from the beginning of earth's time, unchanged after five hundred million years of weathering, broke out through the surface to relieve the dreary monotony. Climbing the great dorsal curvature of one of these geological leviathans I was surprised to find several small rock pools – no larger than a suburban fishpond, and equally crowded with water lilies. Others were carpeted with dwarfed Nile cabbage, while green warty frogs splashed about in them, tadpoles cavorted and industrious water beetles bubbled to the surface.

When I began my task of studying this area I had only the use of the one broken-down Land Rover and a not very co-operative African driver. Due to the conscientious striking of the British worker there was an eighteen-months waiting list for Land Rovers, and so it was a long time before I could go into this hostile region with some confidence that I might be able to get out again.

The eastern boundary of the park was formed by the main road to Ndelé, and three tracks had been made in French colonial times from this road westwards into the park. One was at Bangoran, another roughly in the centre starting from a village called Yambala (the place of the elephant), and a third started from Bamingui where the French first created an outpost in 1902. None of these tracks went for more than twenty miles inside – after that the region was unknown. Even the villagers had not ventured further. This did not apply to the people of Kaga Bandoro, who had traditionally used a route travelling north-eastwards over seventy-five miles on foot into the centre to hunt; and the Sara who came up the Bamingui River from Chad in their *pirogues*, clumsy canoes fashioned from hollowed-out tree trunks.

Few visitors from the western world had been there. The first European to use the route from Kaga Bandoro along the ancient track to Ndelé, which cut diagonally across the heart of the area until the beginning of the twentieth century, was a trader by name of Toussaint Mercuri in about 1889. Then, in 1891, the French zoologist Dr Jean

Dybowski appears to have reached a spot some nineteen miles north of the Koukourou River, on the present-day road which forms the eastern boundary of the Koukourou Reserve; collecting on this journey a rat which was named after him, and naming 'Crampel Peak' a granite outcrop known as Kaga Nze (Leopard Rock).

The ill-fated Crampel passed this way in March of the same year on his way to his death on the Aouk River, while the second part of his mission, which had remained at the Koukourou River under his companion Biscarrat, was completely wiped out there in April by the son of Senoussi, and the bodies flung into the river. Dybowski came across seventeen of Senoussi's men at the river and massacred them all in revenge.

Specimen collecting then was not the same as in my day!

* * *

My first trip into the park had been from Bangoran to a salt lick and pool called Miangeti, a place much favoured by giant eland. There were many of these curious salt licks in the area, formed originally by animals digging for salt at the base of termite mounds or in seepages. Often they were marked by one or more large tamarind trees, sometimes veritable giants.

I had a driver with me on this occasion, and at the entrance to the park we picked up a game guard who was quite drunk, a not unusual occurrence. Leaving the Land Rover we walked about a hundred yards through tall trees to the salt lick. The guard, carrying an old rifle which I sincerely hoped was not loaded, staggered along in a pair of grossly oversized boots, with the laces undone trailing along the ground and threatening to trip him at any moment. Nothing was to be seen at the salt lick, which was hardly surprising in view of our noisy progress. But on the way back an old bull buffalo disturbed from his slumbers, suddenly jumped up a few yards in front of us.

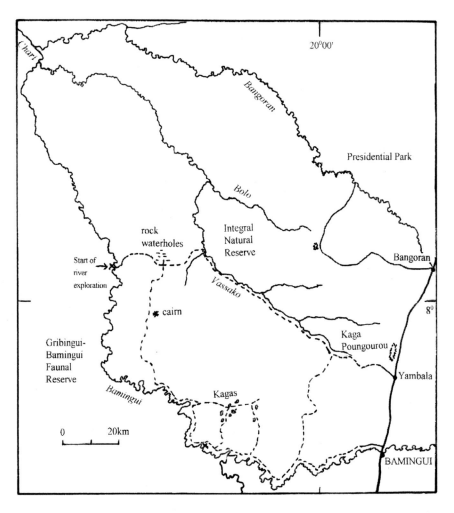

Explorations in the Bamingui-Bangoran National Park, Central African
Republic. Broken lines indicate tracks cut by the author.

The guard held his rifle pointed towards it in the attitude of a First
World War soldier about to make a bayonet charge, and we all froze,
myself heart in mouth at what the guard might do.

After glaring at us angrily for a second or two, with a snort the
buffalo tossed its head and turned and galloped away.

We all heaved a sigh of relief, and the guard said that perhaps the driver should carry the gun because he himself could not walk very well in his boots. We made our way back to the Land Rover without further incident so that the driver was fortunately not called upon to exercise his prerogative in the use of the gun.

A most curious structure not far from this point was a large circular hole in the ground with several narrow dark passages leading off, in which could be heard the rustling of myriads of bats. Called Krobo it was like a great subterranean bubble in the ironstone rock, which had collapsed, for the opening was circular and in the centre of the hole was a cone-shaped mound of earth which had fallen in. It made me always wonder when driving whether I might not find the earth collapsing under me and precipitating me into some similar underground chasm, especially when at one point the ironstone rock I was driving over gave off a hollow, ringing sound.

* * *

To enter the heart of the park I decided to first continue the track in from Yambala, through to the seasonal Vassako River, which formed the southern border of the Strict Nature Reserve. This was a small area of 330 square miles in the centre of the park, which no human being was supposed to enter. Of course such a rule was not observed by the poachers, and there was no more game there than in any other part of the Park; but the theory was that it would be the undisturbed core of the area.

I engaged the village headman to assist with the track cutting, an amenable enough, flat-footed fellow called Issaka. He was not old, although he hadn't worn well. Issaka would stump along in front of me, casually slashing ineffectually to right and left with a panga. He didn't really do anything, but he saw that the others worked, after a fashion.

The inhabitants of these villages, who were all Gbagga, a sub-group of Banda tribesmen, were not accustomed to hard work; an hour or two of casual light labour a day was their idea of a day's work, anything harder had to be done by the women. I subsequently had to keep frequently changing teams every week or so until I got a good crew together. Many of them would never volunteer a second time anyway.

We were clearing a passage barely wide enough to permit the Land Rover to pass, but even that required a lot of cutting in this type of woodland. I had, at my first arrival at Bangoran, tried to drive through the woodland to the river. Half an hour's tortuous weaving in and out of the trees took me an hour to return, with the sides of the Land Rover dented and scratched beyond all recognition. The scrubby Terminalia trees are just that much too close together, added to which the ground was littered with dead branches and fallen tree trunks hidden in the grass waiting to trap the unwary. A sudden jolt and a crunch, and before you knew where you were a tree trunk had dented the sump leaving you straddled across it. Walk? Well, portering was more or less a dead art, and the problem with that was lack of water. In the wet season when water was plentiful the grass was too high to see anything, and in the dry season when the grass was burnt off, by March all of the rainwater pools had dried out. By the end of the dry season the Bamingui River was the only permanent source of water. So to get anywhere you had to cut, cut, cut – mile after sweating mile. During my time here, with no more than half a dozen workers, I hand cut a track as far as from my home in Oxfordshire to London and back again, a distance of a hundred and twenty miles.

Apart from the heat, there were two major tribulations: bees, tiny sweat bees, no bigger than a grain of rice, and the vicious African honey bee. Sweat bees occur over much of Africa, they live in cracks in old tree trunks reached by a little wax funnel, and they have a honey store much favoured by Africans. In most parts of Africa they are not pests, but in the Bamingui-Bangoran they were unbearable. Swarming over one's face, crawling in an itchy mass over the back of one's neck, trying to crawl into eyes, mouth, ears and nose. Should you suddenly look skywards one would dive straight into your eye, its small, chitinous body, like a prickle on the eyeball. These little pests don't sting, but their persistent attentions drive one frantic. Particularly troublesome in the drier woodland areas, I was often forced to seek refuge from them by sitting in the Land Rover with all of the windows closed, until I was gasping in the stifling heat and driven out into their torment again. Of course the Africans didn't seem to be bothered by them at all.

Not so with the African honey bee which has a powerful sting it does not hesitate to use, flying out in a vicious swarm attacking anyone it detects near its hive. In most parts of Africa the Africans obtain its honey, which is usually in a hollow tree, by climbing the tree and smoking the bees out with a bundle of burning hay or elephant dung, then chopping their way into the hive. Here, they simply chopped down the whole tree, no matter how great its size. The bees, for their part, seem to have associated the sound of chopping with an attack on their hive, so cutting tracks is even more hazardous than simply walking through bee territory. But I still break out into a cold sweat when I think of the occasion I was walking along and suddenly noticed out of the corner of my eye that I was within touching distance of a swarm hanging on a low bush! I steeled myself to keep moving at the same pace and fortunately they did not pursue me. I think that is one of the narrowest escapes I have ever had. Africans have died from the stings of a swarm's concerted attack.

Tsetse flies were a relatively minor annoyance here. That was something to be thankful for!Because the sound of the vehicle and the chopping tended to drive it away from our vicinity, not much game was to be seen. This made it all the more exciting when one did see something. There were plenty of signs of elephant, rhino and buffalo, while lions frequently roared at night.

The first track held out a promise of contacts with game, which was not fulfilled. We had cut our way to the Vassako River, which here was a narrow stream now dried up into small pools with steep-sided banks of about ten feet high. My camp was at the top of the bank, overlooking the stream into the 'Strict Nature Reserve'. We had just got the tent set up when a strange roaring noise began to manifest itself, coming from the direction across the stream. We all stood and looked, puzzled by the sound.

What could it be?

Louder and louder grew the noise as we stood mystified, and then I saw a great army of elephants moving straight towards us, their grey, curved backs just visible above the top of the swaying grass. It was the noise of the dry grass stems brushing against their leathery hides which produced a continuous roar, getting louder and louder as they approached. They were making for the pool right beneath me in the stream, and as they got close the younger elephants broke ranks and ran. Suddenly, the whole herd was running straight at us, but we were of course separated by the narrow divide of the stream. The sight was too unnerving for some of the workers, who turned and ran.

Bernard was halfway up a tree. Issaka, his true bush worth showing through, half turned to follow the others, but then realized there could be nothing to fear. The elephants were only coming to drink. When they got close they must have got our wind, for instead of rushing down the bank (then they *would* have been close), at the last moment they all wheeled smartly to one side and rushed off headlong upstream, disappearing in a great cloud of dust and noise of crashing undergrowth.

Bernard came down sheepishly from his perch.

Well, that was exciting enough. But there was yet more excitement at some early hour the next morning when I was awoken by the snorting of a rhinoceros within a few feet of my tent. I had that experience before many years ago in Kenya, and knew the best thing to do was to remain quite still and quiet while the cantankerous old beast waggled its ponderous head from side to side and thought things out. Eventually, satisfied I was not dangerous, it moved grumpily away and I was able to heave a sigh of relief and go back to sleep. In the morning I found a great pile of fresh droppings not more than ten yards from the tent.

I never experienced such close encounters again with these two species during my time there, although I did almost drive head-on into an elephant on the track. He stopped, ears out, and there was a scuffling noise from behind me as the workers precipitated themselves out of the back of the vehicle in frantic haste. The elephant took one cautious step forward, then backwards a couple of steps, turned, and ran. It was on the same stretch of track I came across two buffalo, which had obviously never seen a vehicle before in their life. One came up so near to sniff at me he was too close for my camera lens to focus on him.

When a pride of lions came into camp one night and prowled close by the workers who slept in the open on straw mats, I asked Opha the next morning if the lions were not man-eaters.

"Ah," he said, "that's something else."

Which cryptic response I took to mean that man-eaters were really revengeful men in disguise.

Eventually the track reached a point 35 miles in, where I calculated if I struck due west for nine miles I would arrive at what was marked on the map as a large floodplain about one and a half square miles in area. No one (other than poachers) had ever been there before, and its presence was known only from air photographs. Perhaps it would turn out to be a little animal paradise, tucked away in the heart of the wilderness. From there it was not far to the

Bamingui River and we would have completed a traverse right through the unknown heart of the Park.

When I indicated to Issaka he now had to cut due west, away from the river, he became uneasy and protested. He had no faith in a compass (there was no such thing as a GPS, Global Positioning System, in those days). Following a river was one thing, striking off into the unknown away from a water supply was another. I told him there was no option, the route lay due west, so he reluctantly agreed, and the cutting recommenced.

We would rise at a little after five in the morning. I partook of a hurried breakfast of uncooked oatmeal, and at six o'clock I would drive with the workers to where we had left off cutting the day before. Small trees and bushes were cut down, while tree trunks were slashed. The slashes would callous around the edges and leave a mark on the tree, which could be followed for several years afterwards. The team would cut until one o'clock, and then I would drive them back to camp. If we were camped near the river the afternoons were spent by the workers fishing to supplement their ration of manioc. But when we had cut some distance it might be three o'clock before we got back into camp, and then it was time to move the camp forward. I did this usually every three days.

My prediction proved correct, and after five days' cutting we reached the edge of a large open plain. In the fringing trees was a recently abandoned poachers' camp of three grass huts which we set fire to, although it was only a gesture for they would build fresh ones when they came back next year. There was evidence of plenty of game, but not much to be seen because the pools had now dried up and the animals had all moved south, several well-marked trails leading in that direction. Later I was to learn why, for there was a number of pools in the ironstone rock at the southern edge of the plain, which held water long after the clay pans had dried out.

What I did see was a small group of topi antelope, hitherto unrecorded in the park. The chief of the French zoological service for French Equatorial Africa had suggested in 1936 they might exist there, as they did then on the other side of the Gribingui River, much farther to the west. After forty years I had confirmed his prediction.

Like the dreadful plains of the Saint Floris National Park this was just as bad. Bump, bump, bump, bump, crash! There was not a single flat area larger than a dinner plate to drive on. So I made my painful, jolting way across, and the last stretch was cut to the Bamingui River; completing on 23 March 1977 what I had started on 5 February.

Ndouté, my counterpart replacing Latakpi, accompanied me for this last stretch because from here I was to sail down the Bamingui River to Chari, a trip I believed at the time no other European had accomplished.

Camp was set up by a large tree overlooking the river, and during the night I heard the quiet swish of many canoes passing, Sara fleeing downstream with, as we were to learn, their dugout canoes laden with wild honey, dried fish, and the spoils of whatever they could poach; such as leopard skins and small crocodile skins. There had never been anybody to stop them since the Park's creation.

On 28 April the boat, an inflatable four-seater rubber dinghy, was made ready. I had two volunteer canoemen to paddle it, the river being too shallow to use an engine. Being only the end of April it wasn't yet the end of the dry season, but we often had to haul the boat over the sandy bed through only an inch of water. Due to the long-running Sahelian drought, the water level was abnormally low.

I had calculated, by careful measuring of the meanders on the map, the stretch of river from the camp to the post at Chari, where the Chari River was joined by the Bangoran, was about seventy miles long; and that if I floated down it using the current alone I should reach Chari in three days. But perhaps it might take three weeks! I knew little about sailing boats down rivers. In fact, it did take three days, at an average speed of 1.9 miles per hour.

Apart from the tsetse flies, which here were more of a nuisance than on land because they zoomed out from the banks and bit one unmercifully, evidently thinking the black rubber boat was a big hippo, it turned out to be an unadventurous, bucolic trip. I then knew why the early explorers often had so little to write about.

The water was clear and very shallow, and we progressed steadily. From time to time we came across sandbanks showing signs of having been hastily abandoned by Sara fishermen. There must have been a veritable concourse of illegal immigrants hastening downstream before us.

Game was not common since it only comes to the water to drink, otherwise passing most of its time inland. I noted in all 114 Buffon's kob; 58 waterbuck; 19 roan antelope; 7 hartebeest; 6 warthog; 4 reedbuck; 3 bushbuck; 4 black and white colobus monkeys; 3 troops of baboons; 1 red duiker; 1 cane rat; and near Chari there were 15 hippo.

Passing the confluence with the Gribingui on our left, where the water became quite deep, on the third day we came to the 'rapids', a place where the river rushed through a narrow defile between granite boulders barely wider than the boat itself, but with no marked drop. This was the place where at the beginning of the century a French trader named Ferdinand de Béhagle, attempting to sail up the Bamingui, had his boat smashed and nearly all of his men drowned. We could have carried the boat around but it was easier to attempt the white water. I hadn't read about Béhagle then, nor that below the rapids the river was deep and there had once been huge crocodiles there, and perhaps still were. We took a chance, and rushed the gap without incident.

We then came to the mouth of the Vassako and not far from here were the hippos. Fifteen of them I counted, the only ones seen on the trip. Not far downstream beyond the confluence with the Gribingui the left bank was Chadian territory; a country in an uncertain state at this time. A native, sitting on a chair high on the bank, perhaps some sort of village headman, suddenly saw us and gave a shout.

"Keep moving!" I ordered the startled paddlers, who had momentarily stopped, and pretended to take no notice, while all the time keeping a careful watch out of the corner of my eye and edging the boat a little closer to our bank just in case, for Chad had a murderous reputation. But the man subsided back into his chair without further ado. I could see others sitting in the shadows under the bushes on the slope of the bank, quietly watching us pass; but there was no hail of arrows or gunshot, and soon we were at the confluence with the Bangoran and the post of Chari, hauling our boat ashore, the exploration complete.

Later I discovered another Englishman had already beaten me to it. Lieutenant Boyd Alexander had sailed up the Bamingui River in 1905, almost as far as the confluence with the Koukourou. Like me he saw little game: "once or twice a few kob or a solitary waterbuck", once a pig (warthog or bushpig?); and the country was uninhabited. After successfully completing his exploration, on a subsequent journey Boyd-Alexander was assassinated near Abeché in Chad by the slave raider Rabah. Rabah also had Béhagle hung. As the third explorer of this river I was somewhat more fortunate.

But the adventure did not end at Chari. The plan was that Ndouté would drive around the three hundred miles by road to collect me. I expected him to be there when I arrived, but he was not. There was nothing to do but wait, for there was no communication in this part of the world. A hunting camp at Golongosso, thirty miles away on the Aouk River, was no longer operating at the time. The town of Ndélé lay almost a hundred and thirty miles away along a road, which was little more than a sandy track for much of its length, boasting only a few small, isolated, poverty-stricken villages.

On the third day Ndouté arrived, much to my relief, as I did not have enough supplies to remain there much longer. It transpired that on setting out across that dreadful plain, perhaps with undue haste, the back wheels of his Toyota pickup had parted company with the rest of the vehicle. Together with an assistant, Antoine, they had walked back to camp, a distance of about eight miles. Antoine later confided to me that it was just about as much as they could manage, having, in his opinion, nearly died of thirst. The next day Ndouté tried again using my old Land Rover, and had eventually made it.

On the return journey, when we got into the thick sand on the road, the clutch started to give problems and we ground to a halt. Ndouté thought all that was required was a little brute force in moving the gear lever, and took over the driving seat from me to demonstrate how. There was a look of astonishment on his face when the gear lever broke off in his hand! The misadventures on dry land were rather more than those I had experienced on the river.

Here we were, stuck in deep sand in the middle of nowhere, with no gear lever and no gears.

I buried myself under the bonnet in a broiling sun with the vehicle bodywork already too hot to touch, and eventually got the clutch cylinder, the cause of the trouble, functioning again. A screwdriver served as a makeshift gear lever, and we were able to continue our journey. Passing through Ndelé we picked up an old government mechanic who, never having had any spares to repair vehicles with for many years, and having few tools into the bargain, was just the person to fit the Toyota's back wheels onto the vehicle again. This he eventually accomplished with the aid of large amounts of fencing wire, which I had learned always to carry with me in the bush for exactly such emergencies as wiring the wheels back onto one's vehicle.

During the two nights he had stayed at the river camp after my departure, Ndouté had captured seven canoes carrying over fifty gallons of wild honey.

* * *

The next stage of my exploration was to cut a track along the Bamingui River from the village of Bamingui itself, through to the southern end of the central plain. Some twenty miles of track already existed and promised variety. At nine miles it passed along the top of a steep, high cliff, bearing the romantic-sounding name of Mandabalé, reminding me of Kipling's "On the road to Mandalay". The face of the cliff was an attractive pink from the presence of salt, and at its base rooting for the salty earth, elephants and rhinoceros aided by buffaloes, had dug out small caverns. Just over a mile further on was a small open plain, known as Foubouloulou. At this time Foubouloulou boasted about sixty Buffon's kob and the odd visiting lion. And then finally, at the end of the track one came to a large U-bend in the river, forming a deep pool which one could look down upon from a rocky cliff. This was Bourkoungali, home to some eighty hippo.

* * *

I decided to keep a diary at this time. I began it one day in January 1980 on some loose pages of notepaper. Several years later, when looking it out at home in England, I found only two of the loose pages remained, tucked inside the exercise book I later used. I can only think that Bernard had taken the rest while I was out one day and used them for lighting the campfire in the mornings.

There had been a break of a year since I had cut the track in from Yambala, and apart from old Issaka, who wouldn't leave his village, the workers I had used then were no longer available. Getting together another team proved to be very difficult. No one wanted to work and no one wanted to stay in the bush for more than a couple of days at a time. Food was always a problem. The Central African adores that school meal horror manioc, better known as tapioca, and will eat nothing else for his staple diet although it is almost totally lacking in food value. A type of yam, it grows as an underground tuber, which is deadly poisonous on account of the prussic acid which it contains. The secret is to pound it up, leave it in a stream bed for several days to wash the poison out, and then dry it. The Amazonian Indians somehow discovered this secret and it was imported along with the yam from South America.

For any trip into the interior it was necessary to buy huge, hundredweight sacks of this stuff, and for a part of the year it was almost impossible to find any surplus for sale in the villages. Of course the Africans do not like simply eating it by itself. It is mixed with water and eaten like a sort of musty porridge, but it must have what the French call a 'sauce' with it: a gravy with meat in it. Since all of my work was inside a national park there was no question of shooting anything, so the workers had to forego meat other than what they brought with them (which had probably come from the park anyway), and use instead what fish they could catch. But fishing was seldom profitable. Poisoning of the rivers was the cause of that.

I picked up a team on one occasion from the village of Kaga Nze. One of the number was a large well-built African, but with a frowning, sullen face. I should have known better than to take him, but he insisted he was prepared to work. In order to try to help catch fish for the team, whenever we were camped near water I often set a handline at night. This unpleasant character, assuming I was trying to catch fish for myself and determined I should not have any, would creep out after dark and deftly cut the nylon line almost, but not quite, through. So in the morning when I tried to pull the line in it always broke. Or had a fish taken the bait of course it would have got away with it. It takes a pretty devious mind to play such a trick!

As so often happened, long before the planned stay in the interior was finished, the team reported they hadn't anything left to mix with their tapioca. I said the job had to be finished before we returned to Bamingui. I knew the big sullen one was acting as an agitator. The next day he led a deputation before my tent after the morning's work and announced with threatening demeanour they had no food. I repeated we were not returning (it was about two days' journey to the road) until the sector was finished, and they would have to make do with what they had.

He adopted a menacing look and stood before me with knitted brows. I didn't feel too comfortable. There was no other white man literally within hundreds of miles in this savage wilderness. He certainly looked as if he was prepared to do me in without a qualm, and who would ever know what had happened? One's remains chewed beyond all recognition by some hungry hyaena, even supposing somebody would actually come and look for them. They could easily invent some tale to account for my disappearance. I found myself in the traditional position of the lone explorer confronted by hostile and rebellious natives. There was a rifle in the tent, but it would never do to show fear. A stiff upper lip and a firm chin were called for. I faced him squarely, and after a moment's hesitation he snorted his contempt and turned away.

After I had finished that sector, it was only a day or two more work. I made sure I never employed him again. He had the look of a madman about him.

Eventually I got together an excellent small core of willing workers, or at least Kakumale did. Kakumale (pronounced Ka, as in kat,-koo-ma-lee) was living in Bamingui at the time and I don't know why he hadn't turned up for work before. He was very short, with an ugly toothy face, full of self-importance and infinitely bossy. When in Bamingui he was always drunk on douma. Kakumale was what Dickens's Mrs Gamp would have called "an imperent young sparrer". Always strutting about giving orders to everybody else and telling me how everything should be done. Like most Africans here he sometimes affected odd forms of dress. One day I saw, peeping above the waistline of his ragged shorts, the pink, frilly edge of a pair of ladies' panties. No transvestite Kakumale, to him they were just as good as any other underpants.

Another member of the team was Opha, a young man who had his eye on a buxom young girl in his village and wanted to make enough money to marry her. He turned up for work one morning sporting a pair of knee-length French pink silk camiknickers over his shorts, which gradually disintegrated into shreds as the work proceeded. Opha turned out to be the most reliable and most intelligent of the bunch, and I eventually made him supervisor in place of Kakumale.

Then there was little Sali. A pleasant-faced little chap who always worked quietly and uncomplainingly, and one day constructed a marvellous hat for himself from the large leaves of a Terminalia tree. On one occasion he fell out of the back of the Land Rover when it started forward and Opha thought it so funny he repeatedly collapsed in hysterical giggles for the rest of the day until even Sali thought he was carrying it a bit too far.

But it was Kakumale who stood out as a character, for he was the most unlucky person I have ever come across. If anything unfortunate happened, then it happened to little Kakumale.

We were cutting towards a thicket in a drainage line when I sent Kakumale ahead to reconnoitre the best way through the bushes to avoid too much cutting. Cocky Kakumale strutted off, puffed up as usual with self-importance at the task he had been given. The thicket was about fifty yards ahead and I watched as he disappeared into it. Shortly afterwards a rhinoceros charged out to one side and crashed off through the trees.

There was silence. The others continued cutting, then Opha began to look worried. Kakumale had been quiet for too long. Opha called out. There was no reply. He called again, more vigorously. A small, weak voice echoed back. Opha started to giggle.

"What is it?" I queried.

"He says that he's tree'd by a rhino and can't move," laughed Opha.

At that moment a second rhino crashed out and followed the direction the other had taken into the trees. After some time a crestfallen and rather frightened-looking Kakumale came towards us. He explained that, pushing through the bushes he had stumbled upon a pair of rhinos lying asleep, but not so asleep that they didn't awake immediately, jump up and give chase. Kakumale just managed to scramble up a small tree, and while the cow ran off the bull stood snorting beneath the tree refusing to budge. Kakumale was terrified to make a sound in case it made the angry beast attack his slender perch. But when he finally answered Opha's call, the sound of his voice put the rhino to flight.

Then there was the occasion I sent him off with Opha to see if there was any water in the Yolo, a stream the line of which I could see in the distance from the trees along its banks. Too tired myself to accompany them I sat on a rock in the sun about half a mile away and waited. Time passed and then a very frightened-looking Opha and Kakumale came back. Walking unconcernedly into the trees they had come face to face with a herd of elephants, one of which had promptly charged. Running for their lives they had almost run into a rhino asleep under a tree, which promptly took up the chase in place of the elephant. Opha said it was a close-run thing. The rhino had nearly got them, but instead had given vent to its anger on a bush, which it promptly smashed to pieces. I was rather glad I had not gone with them, being the least agile.

The Yolo proved to be dry at this point, but after he had recovered from his fright I sent Kakumale off on his own to follow the stream down a little way to see if there were any pools left in the bed. I was beginning to get used to a rather fearful-looking Kakumale returning from these excursions, and I was not to be disappointed this time.

In his usual self-important manner Kakumale had swaggered off down the stream bed, when, he related, he had come across a 'grey lion' with two cubs. The 'grey lion' had gone for him and he had run for his life, but turning, saw it was pursuing him so he scrambled up a tree, dropping his only weapon, a machete. The animal halted at the foot of the tree, and unable to get at its victim, had seized the machete and bitten the handle. Kakumale showed me the teeth marks on it. Heeding the cries of its cubs, the 'grey lion' had then walked off and, after what he deemed to be a prudent interval, Kakumale descended from the tree, picked up his machete and began to make his way back. Great was his horror when he turned to see the creature coming after him again! Once more Kakumale ran for his life, and passing through some dense dry grass, he set light to it. This put a stop to the 'grey lion's' pursuit and Kakumale lived to tell the tale.

But what was a 'grey lion'?

When I showed him the pictures of animals in my big game handbook he insisted it was a striped hyaena. Nothing else indeed fitted his description. But it must have been an extraordinarily aggressive striped hyaena, a species generally known for its timorousness. I had never before heard of it going for a man. I suppose it was because Kakumale was so small.

Kakumale was the only worker to get stung on the finger by a scorpion when clearing rocks from the track, and it was by one of the more deadly small pale brown species. He bandaged the end of his finger tightly and didn't seem too much affected by it. But more serious was when he got the tips of two of his fingers caught in the Land Rover winch, practically severing them. He didn't lose them, they grew back together again somewhat hooked.

Then there was the occasion when we finally reached the southern end of the central plain after having cut 85 miles of track. Here I found there were five pools in the ironstone rock, full of beautifully clear water from rain the night before. It was to these pools the animals came when the rest of the waterholes on the plain had dried up towards the end of the dry season. They were not very large, about three feet deep. My team couldn't resist them; they had to celebrate by having a bathe before we drove back to camp. So each worker stripped off and washed in his own private pool.

It was a long journey back to camp, for much of the route lay through relatively open country where it had not been necessary to cut. Kakumale was sandwiched between myself and Opha in the front of the Land Rover.

We had been driving for about half an hour when Kakumale began to scratch himself. First his sides, then his woolly pate.

"Hell!" I thought, "I wish he would stop scratching or I am going to catch his fleas."

As we drove, Kakumale's scratching became more and more frantic until he was almost in a frenzy, wriggling and squirming in his seat. There was something seriously wrong.

By the time we got back to camp he was in a really bad state, covered with swellings and his face puffed-up. I gave him some aspirins and told him to lie down. There was no other treatment I could think of. Of the five rock pools, clearly Kakumale had picked the one that was infected. But infected with what? My guide to health for travellers in the tropics had nothing remotely resembling his symptoms. I could only wait and hope that by morning he would be better.

Thankfully, he was.

But did Kakumale's misfortune end there? No, it did not!

When we got back to Bamingui after six weeks in the bush, Kakumale found his wife had been imprisoned. For trying to poison her lover!

* * *

I let Opha bring his girl friend with him on one trip as he said she would be useful in camp. Arrived at the campsite Bernard quickly had my tent set up and Opha's girl friend, not knowing the custom, plonked down her three cooking stones nearby. Now the workers always camped a little distance away from me because they liked to sit up talking halfway through the night. Opha came up and explained to his girl friend that she should put the stones elsewhere. She looked at my tent, then at the stones, and flatly refused. In the end Opha had to move them himself. There was not much evidence of the downtrodden African woman here I noticed.

It now being evening-time Opha's girl friend, who had plenty to show off, promptly stripped to the waist displaying her fulsome breasts as she would do in her village. Opha again came up and remonstrated with her. Nubile young girls did not strip off in front of white men. At this she regarded me with sudden interest sitting in front of my tent, regarding her with some interest on my part, but this time obeyed Opha's injunction and retired from view. Central Africans appeared to believe that white men had rapacious sexual appetites, based on the experiences of colonial days when people like Toqué simply took their pleasure of any young girl they fancied. Such was the legacy that driving along one road in the north, at the sound of my vehicle approaching a village all of the women rushed into their huts and reappeared hastily fastening on their bras.

* * *

The track wound inexorably into the interior. I followed the Bamingui closely for the first fifty-five miles through constantly changing scenery. Floodplains when close to the river, woodland away from it, ranging from the gaunt forests of Anogeissus, said to be the only wood that termites will not attack, to the magnificent thick-boled Daniellia and woodlands of stately Isoberlinia. The latter tree, when young enough that its leaves can still be reached, together with the heavily-scented flowers of a species of Gardenia known as 'Jove's thunderbolt', provide favoured foods for the Giant eland, then commonest in this part of Africa.

At times the route passed over the ironstone plains, solid red rock covering the surface and often devoid of vegetation except for a few tufts of wispy grass anchored in the crevices. One theory was this ironstone formed on the surface after shifting cultivation exposed the iron in the soil causing a chemical reaction, but I found beds of it exposed deep in the banks of the Bamingui River, showing it had formed a covering probably long before man came onto the scene.

Signs of man's former historical presence were everywhere, especially in the shape of the slag heaps of early blacksmiths. Blacksmiths were always considered in Africa as a race apart, shunned as some sort of magicians; but perhaps they were really no more than a kind of prototype trade union, surrounding their profession with mystique and secrecy to keep it to themselves. Usually one found only one small slag heap at a time, but at one point I found eight together, three of which were of large size, signifying what must have been a very important and long-standing smelting site. Often also there were round plugs of slag that had formed in the clay drainpipes of the primitive smelters. I found one of these smelters almost complete, because the interior had been filled by a termite mound. A simple clay structure, hardened by fire, it had stood for at least seventy years and may have been a century old. I also found many sherds, the fragments of broken baked-clay pots, some of the decorative patterns of which had probably remained the same for several hundred years if not thousands. Some patterns were very similar to those dating back 6,000 years in the Sahara desert.

The track had to cross many tributaries, which flowed into the Bamingui, most of them dry but usually steep-sided. There was the Kaha, the Bingou, the Maia, the Biankourou, the Yolo, the Yalo, and many unnamed ones. At one high point I found a large cairn of stones, such as a traveller might make. Yet there was no record of any white man having been here before. It was on the flat summit of a piece of the highest ground around, about eight miles from the Bamingui River and almost two-and-a-half miles south of the first large tributary after the Vassako. It was the sort of thing an explorer might have done sailing up the Bamingui, and making a day's march inland along the first big tributary that he came to in the interior, then climbing to the highest point that he could see (not that he would have seen much from there except trees). Perhaps it had been Boyd Alexander in 1905, but he didn't mention it in his book and his diary gave no details. I never had time to dismantle it to see if there might be a message inside. My workers dismissed the idea it might be a chief's grave.

Having followed the curve of the Bamingui westwards to a swamp called Bido, about twenty miles before the river turned and flowed north, I then struck away from the river in a north-westerly direction, then north and north-east, looking at the country away from the river for thirty miles until I came to the five pools at the end of the floodplain.

It was usually only when on foot that one saw game, as Kakumale had so often discovered to his discomfiture, although a fine leopard did bound out and run along in front of the vehicle on one occasion. Leopards seemed common, as also were the cruel traps set for them by the poachers. These consisted of a wire noose attached to a bent-over branch or sapling, the noose inserted into a sort of cage made of two-inch-long Acacia thorns, the inside of which was baited with meat or fish. The leopard would come along, push its head inside the thorns to seize the bait, and then having done so try to shake the thorns free. In doing this it would spring the snare, which would jerk into the air and hold the leopard suspended, strangling it to death. I came across one such trap, which had obviously just been sprung. Bloodstained rocks littering the ground showed the leopard had been stoned to death, probably because it had not been suspended high enough to be strangled. There was always a ready tourist market for the skin.

Having sent the team off on some errand on one occasion, I was sitting in the shade of a thicket bordering a dry rivulet when I heard the sound of cautious footsteps coming along the bed, rustling the dry leaves in their passage. I waited tensely, ready to run if it was a cantankerous rhino or a prowling lion, when, to my delight, a rare yellow-backed duiker passed unwittingly within a few feet of me, picking its way delicately along the stream bed. This rarely seen creature is the largest of the duikers, for the most part a very small breed of antelope. But the yellow-backed duiker is as big as a goat, with a glossy black coat and bright contrasting yellow triangular patch on its back. I did see others in the Park, but none as close as this.

* * *

Most of the time I travelled by Land Rover, because only in that way could one cover the long distances quickly enough. But at the very beginning of my second season's cutting of this track I was very nearly reduced to walking. I had finally obtained a brand new Land Rover after a wait of eighteen months, and it was my first trip of the season with it.

The rains fall in this part of the world mostly from May to October, it then dries out rapidly in November and December. By the end of December the first grass fires have already started, roaring through the ten-foot high tinder-dry straw and reducing it to smoking ashes in seconds. Before the grass has been burnt off it forms an impenetrable screen. With a rainfall of almost fifty inches a year, just about twice that which London receives, the grass grows thick and dense. I always had my heart in my mouth when driving through it at the beginning of the season in case the heat of the exhaust pipe set the grass alight beneath me. So having driven through a particularly dense stretch and emerged onto an open ironstone shield, I told Kakumale he could set light to the grass behind us since the fire could not cross the ironstone. But the story is best told by my diary entry for February 18 1981:

"A new camp site near the junction of the Biankourou (a small stream, almost dry except for some pools) with the Bamingui, fifty-eight miles from Bamingui. Reached it at 0800 hours after two very hard days' work, having entered the Bamingui gate at 0730 on the 16.2.81. Spent the first night at Bingou camp (stream still flowing and very cool), arriving there about 1500 hours, exhausted, the track very difficult to follow, much of it having disappeared after the Gounda river. A rhino came to drink at the Bingou during the night – saw its fresh prints the next morning. I just slept under my mosquito net under an Irvingia tree. After Gounda much was unburnt – I don't like driving in this long, tinder-dry grass. At one point I was waiting for Opha and the others to find the route when Kakumale, of course, suddenly shouted:

"Avancez!"

"He had set fire to the grass just behind the Land Rover. We had to move a bit faster after that. I felt exhausted when I reached Bingou. The next day, with only twelve or so miles to go, the route was even more difficult to follow and again took us until after 1500 hours. At one point, having crossed some bare ironstone, I told Kakumale he could set fire to the grass, but while we made a deviation to the south, the fire cut across, very quickly, to the north. We came to the Maia, a small stream, dry, with a sandy bed and very steep sides. I hadn't recalled that this obstacle was as early as this. While the gang searched for a crossing, I ploughed through the ten feet high, tinder-dry grass, looking anxiously all the while at the huge pall of dense smoke to the north – the direction I was following the stream bed. Kakumale, who had remained with me,

222

suggested an impossible place to cross, but at his next suggestion since I could hear the crackling of the fire, I decided to try, for the fire was now coming ominously close. Opha and the rest had disappeared. The manoeuvre comprised a very steep descent with the Land Rover and trailer, with a left turn along the stream bed, and then a sharp right turn up the other side. Alas! Once in the bottom it was impossible to turn, the Land Rover just has no manoeuvrability. We detached the trailer and I tried all sorts of manoeuvres without success.

"The fire was now very close making a great roaring and crackling sound. At this juncture the others appeared, saying they had found the crossing and had been waiting there for us! After an exasperated exchange, there was no time for arguing, I set them to work cutting the grass at the top of the bank above us, but soon saw that this was not going to be done quickly enough, so I told them to light a counter fire and control it from burning back onto us. This they did, and only just in time, for it must have met the advancing wall of flame only some fifty yards distant. To our right the distance was much less and there was a sudden huge roar, with flames leaping high into the sky. But it looked as if we were safe. Then came the smoke, I hadn't thought of that. Dense great billowing grey clouds which suddenly sank into the gulley, and crouching in the bottom with my face against the ground I wondered for how long I could continue to breathe without being suffocated. But it suddenly lifted just as abruptly as it had descended and I was left with a very dry throat and smarting eyes. I tried again all manner of ways to get the Land Rover out, and then, suddenly, I got into a position where, very gently and at an alarming angle, I was able to ease it out by the place that I had descended. It only then remained to haul the trailer out with the winch. After more sweat through long grass (no more burning for me!) we got to the night stop (camp 2) at 1520 hours. I was so exhausted that I drank a whole litre of red wine straight off and got a fairly good night's sleep."

I wonder what my employers would have said had my brand new Land Rover for which I had waited so long gone up in smoke!

The first new camp of this season was made the next day at the junction of the Biankourou and the Bamingui, as recorded in my diary:

"A quiet night in the first camp [new] of the season, with a pleasant temperature. About 0545 hours, while breakfasting, I saw a fairly large wake move along in the river below me [my camp was right on the river bank]. Most likely a crocodile. Started track cutting again, but I must say without much enthusiasm. Dry, uninteresting woodland – Isoberlinia on laterite – Terminalia – dry woodland – recently burnt. Opha said he had heard a rhino in the bush just after we started."

Having reached the five pools at the southern end of the central plain at the end of the last season, my next plan was to cut my way through to the Kaga Bazou complex, a large group of granite outcrops, the biggest in the area, through which the ancient route to Ndelé had passed at the beginning of the century. There were thirteen main outcrops in the group. Firstly came Kaga Yangatou ("small chick"), then Kaga Rima and Kaga Zou; Kaga Kamangare ("if one comes with much manioc it is finished there"); Kaga Bazou, the biggest of the group, named after an edible root; Kaga Baglia (name of a Chief); and Kagas Mandouka, Bringui, Dargo and Balidjia, were all named after people, but who they were is no longer known.

In 1897, a French military officer, Captain Pierre Prins, followed the route from Kaga Bandoro to Ndelé through the Kaga Bazou complex. In an account of his journey published in 1909 in the French journal *La Géographie*, titled *The Troglodytes of Dar Banda and of Djebel Mela* (Djebel Mela is in the east of the country) Prins related (my translation):

"Some kilometres further towards the northeast, after having crossed the Bamingui . . . Between the river and the first summit, called Kaga Baglia, fresh water is more rare . . . The inhabitants of Kaga Baglia have thus perfected the work of nature in adroitly developing the folds and fissures of the granite to channel the water from the outside reservoirs, which is brought by this means towards the basins hollowed out partly by themselves in the interiors of their caves.

"The water stays thus as little exposed to the air as possible, jealously guarded in the deep caves, inaccessible from the outside without permission of the host . . . The Sultan Senoussi, who does not lack intelligence and who owns the whole of the country for slave raiding, knows the danger if he allows his soldiers to destroy these precious 'guardians of the water'.

"He has thus left them to exist, to grow would be a better word, because the troglodytes, who seem to be good cultivators whose plantations of millet cover with their stems the fertile plains from which emerge the rocks, only use a modest part of their harvests, the senoussistes stealing the rest.

"The ascent of Baglia and its slopes takes one and a half hours…it is completely bare from the base to the summit . . . the troglodytes have sown tobacco, sweet potatoes and the eternal *Hibiscus esculentus*, obligatory condiment for all local sauces from one end of the Congo to the other. It is on the flank of one of these folds which opens into the cave of the G'Bagas of Baglia . . .

"Behind a solid barricade of tree trunks, thick as a thigh, their bows and arrows in their hands, those who had never seen a white man, as soon as they saw me, dived into the depths of the rock and disappeared.

"However, with patience and perseverance we succeeded in obtaining, as water was indispensable, permission to slide between two tree trunks lightly moved aside and replaced behind us.

"The entrance corridor was three metres high and ten metres long, and only one metre wide, gently curving, and the first chamber was thus completely hidden by the elbow thus formed. This room, almost circular in form, measured ten metres diameter and four high, at the north angle of the ceiling a narrow crack easily blocked left visible the daylight sliding between two monoliths which formed the summit of the kaga.

"The base of this crack was worked in some manner that a large jar of sun-baked clay could be placed there to capture the water conducted by the funnel thus formed, from the watershed of the summit of the kaga.

"About five metres of rock thickness separated this basin from the higher platform.

"On the south side, a passage worked between the point of two blocks led to two miniature chambers, hermetically sealed; those were the storerooms containing strips of dried meat, baskets of millet, salt and arms. Finally, we arrive at the most curious, from the central piece and through a narrow passageway polished by the passage of bodies, one reached by climbing, a cistern dug out of the flat rock, of a capacity of about a thousand or twelve hundred litres, full, or nearly so, with limpid fresh water towards which converged seven channels like that in the main room and corresponding to other basins of the summit of the Kaga.

"A rapid examination showed most of these channels and the cistern itself had been reviewed and enlarged by the troglodytes . . .

"The closest and the most important is mount Bazou, which is the only one shown on certain maps from reports.

"Another group of troglodyte G'Bagas inhabit it . . . The naked saddle is crowned with enormous blocks, cubic and tabloid, some almost suspended in the air, others shading with their strong shoulders the rudimentary constructions in thatch and tree trunks, some of which are built like towers eighty metres high. One reaches there by ascending the long undulations from the west, or climbing the goatpath which runs along the abrupt eastern face.

"Midway on this wall almost eighty metres from the peak, a crack allows one to reach a corridor of some metres, defended by the solid palisades the reservoir of this mountain; this basin, containing about five hundred litres, is fed by infiltrations and not by channeled rainwater . . .

"The work of man seems limited to the barricades at the entrance, the roof of the cave is sufficiently large for a man to stand upright, but it is not large enough to be lived in, and the G'Bagas seem only to hide there when circumstances are critical . . . As for the habitations of the troglodytes, they were grouped on the platform of the mountain in the shade of the rocks, offering the most miserable look that one could imagine . . . "

After reading Prins's account I was consumed with curiosity to see the former homes of the troglodytes of Dar Banda, their secret caves and their remarkable water tanks. Since Prins's visit in 1897 no other white man had visited the area, apart from a botanist who had landed by helicopter on one of the kagas but had not explored the region.

I reached the first kaga on 22 February 1981 from my camp on the Bamingui River.

My diary takes up the story of my exploration of the kagas:

"Workers say there was much lion roaring near camp last night . . . Saw a leopard and four hartebeest on the way out. Reached the first kaga – although I had made a mistake and was cutting north instead of north-west, but saw it when two kilometres distant. It and the scene do not seem in any way to fit Prins's account. It will take quite a lot of searching to find whether any do have caves.

"23.2.81. . . . Began to get in among the kagas, but it is very confusing - they don't seem to match either the map (because only ones of a certain size are marked) or the air photos (which greatly exaggerate their height) –let alone Prins's account! It is amazing how you do not see them until you are right on top of them – due to the trees and slight undulations of the ground.

Despite their size one could easily miss them!

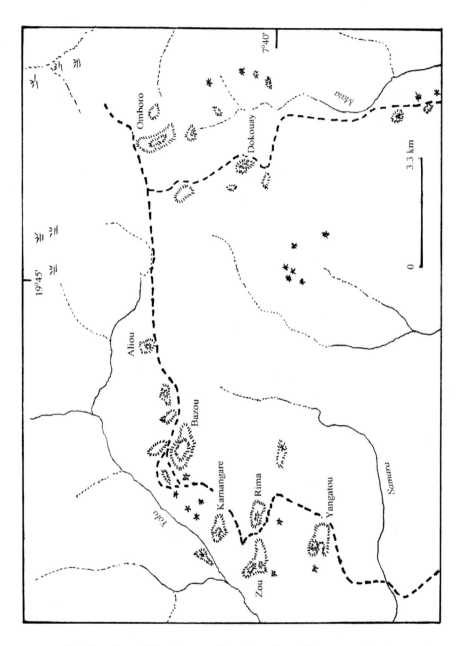

Exploration of the kagas of the Bamingui-Bangoran Park.
Broken lines indicate tracks cut by the author.

"24.2.81 . . . The kagas are still a confused mass to me, fitting neither the map nor the air photos. Opha's sharp eyes spotted an old iron finger ring lying on the ground – close to an animal path - probably from the beginning of the century. It won't fit my little finger. At the same place he unearthed a nest of black scorpions – about an inch long, half a dozen or more. Giant eland have been in the area within the week . . . The bees are a terrible nuisance in camp, I have now been stung twice.

"26.2.81 . . . Spent today searching some of the kagas for Prins's elusive caves of the troglodytes. There was nothing at the first - Kaga Yangatou. On the summit of one with a water-filled cavity on the side there was a tent-shaped cavern that would take about four men, and a few pottery sherds. A large varanid lizard crept out of the cistern and hid in the rocks . . . Searched some three other kagas, hard work climbing up and down as they are up to three hundred feet high. Very little sign of human use, only a few sherds here and there. They are mostly occupied by porcupines whose droppings are everywhere – and one had dragged a gnawed elephant femur quite high up. Otherwise they are very bleak and bare . . . there is no indication of any former cultivation now. The valleys are occupied with mature woodland – Anogeissus, Terminalia, Parkia, etc. I felt too tired to look at Kaga Bazou so sent the team. They came back reporting a large cavern full of bats, of which they brought three. I'll have to look at it tomorrow, also Kaga Rima which is the last chance for finding Prins's Kaga Baglia . . .

"27.2.81. Another search of the kagas . . . Still no luck, no sign of anything resembling Prins's description, yet it is so detailed, is it *all* imagination? Went to see the place where they caught the bats yesterday – little more than a cleft in the rock. But on the way back I found quite a large cavern, full of bat droppings and smell, but so many crevices that no bats were to be seen. It was about six feet wide, twenty-five to thirty feet long and very high. A few sherds there. Also close by there was a small shelter with some sherds. The valley below was very flat and mostly bare but with scattered spear grass (Imperata), said to be a sign of former cultivation . . .

"6.3.81. . . . Heard the lions again during the night and this morning came across a large adult lioness on the track only a quarter of a mile from camp . . . Found this morning's scrape of a rhino the other side of the Yolo river. Cut through to the last two major kagas of the group, the penultimate appears to be the highest. I climbed to the summits of both – the first white man to do so? On the side of the penultimate (Kaga Aliou?) there was a hole with a natural archway over it, and the entrance had at one time been covered up with two flat sheets of granite. A tree had grown up in front and died, and was now a charred, twelve-inch diameter stump. Some animal had long ago forced the covering aside, and peering in I could see what looked like a human skull in the dust. After much manoeuvering with a stick Kakumale succeeded in hooking the object out, and it was a human skull. I put it back to come back again tomorrow. On the other side of the same kaga I found a cavern which I will also investigate tomorrow. When I looked in, I heard the whirring of thousands of bat wings although I could not see any flying about. Lots of pottery fragments here. On the summit of the last kaga there were also some pottery fragments and iron slag . . . I couldn't see any sign of the cistern at the foot of the north face which Prins recorded. The area seems to be absolutely waterless but there may have been more water in Prins's time which kept the many shallow basins in the rock full. Quite a lot of elephant and buffalo sign in the area so Opha says there must be water somewhere.

"7.3.81. The frogs and toads were very noisy again last night (I was camped on the Samara river). They have a disconcerting habit of making sudden rushes through the dry leaves – disconcerting until you know what it is, that is. The lioness was roaring away again – a rather croaky old roar. Decided to spend the morning searching the last two or three kagas. On the way out saw a large herd of (fifty?) giant eland.

Pottery sherds from unnamed kaga at 07° 45'N / 19° 42'E.

Pottery sherds from Kaga Bazou.

Black glazed pot fragment from Kaga Bazou.

Storage pot from near Kaga Bazou with impressed pattern.

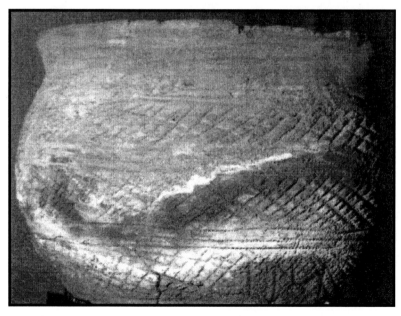

Cooking pot from the Kagas with inscribed and roulette pattern.

Explored the tomb first where I had found the skull yesterday. It was a triangular-shaped hole in the solid granite, about fifteen feet long, just able to take a man but I could persuade neither Opha nor Kakumale to wriggle in. Eventually, with some dexterous work with a long pole, and half inside the hole, Kakumale hooked out three more skulls, making four in all. All just the cranium with the upper jaw missing. The oldest, as determined by the lack of cranial sutures, was the smallest, a mere, pygmy-sized skull. Of the other three, two were young adults, all much larger skulls, and one did not have the sutures closed. My guess is that the old one was that of the chief, who must have been of pygmy-like stature; and at his death his three wives, including one who was still a young girl, were put to death and buried with him.[1] There was one leg bone but I could see nothing else. I replaced all of the remains and covered up the entrance again.

"In the small kaga to the south of Kaga Aliou I found another blocked hole. When we cleared the entrance we found a smaller chamber but quite empty. I expect porcupines or hyaenas had taken the bones a long time ago. Next I examined the cave on the other kaga but there was nothing inside except bats . . . Went on to the last kaga but found nothing. Went on to a low granite ridge to the north which is probably that mentioned by Prins to the north side of his Kaga Fagui. If so, the five metre deep cistern was only a narrow fissure about three feet deep and quite dry . . . On the way back to camp we noticed vultures behind Kaga Aliou and the team went off to investigate and reported finding a bushpig killed by hunting dogs [you never *saw* a bushpig] . . .

"8.3.81. Continued the exploration of the kagas, one to the east of Kaga Bazou and Kaga Bazou itself. No sign of Prins's caverns . . . there is nothing resembling his description of Kaga Baglia. I found a hollow under a flat rock, room enough for one man to hide, with the two ends more or less blocked up with stones, where some frightened savage had once no doubt hidden from Senoussi's slavers. To the south-east of

Kaga Bazou is a very broken ridge in which I found the large cavern [see entry for the 22nd of February]. There are several small shelters here and quite a lot of pottery, it seems to have been the most inhabited part of the kagas. In a shelter on the top of one rocky knoll, Kakumale found an almost complete earthenware pot – it had the most common pattern, made by pressing a strip of coarse woven fibre material on the wet clay . . . Sali found an iron finger ring on the ground (like the other one but more weathered). On one side of these rocks there was a dry "cistern" which would hold five hundred to a thousand litres, but completely exposed . . . Frogs and toads very noisy again last night, Opha said lions were roaring everywhere but I didn't hear them.

"12.3.81. . . . Spent two days cutting through to Kaga Omboro (not a Banda name according to Opha). Sweat bees an appalling menace . . . reached it at about 10.00am and almost 16 miles . . . came across fresh tracks of two rhino. The kaga a disappointment as usual. I saw only one piece of pottery . . . there were no suitable living places . . . The kaga has more bowls in the granite than any of the others, and the largest. Most were dry and the water in some of them was probably from the other night (when it rained). One had a water tortoise in it. There was no sign on its flat top (nor on any other) of people having arranged stones as walls. No sign of a large population having once lived here . . . The other day Opha found the *bazou* plant on the penultimate kaga, which Kaga Bazou is named after."

Having explored all of the kagas I then returned to a camp on the Bamingui. I had searched every single one of those rock outcrops, but there was no sign of Prins's mysterious cavern with its hidden water cistern and the seven channels leading into it. Was it all then a myth, or did that secret cavern really exist somewhere in the rocks, hidden from the sight of man for almost a century?

I fear it must have been a figment of Prins's imagination and that he must go down in history with the other great fabricators of African travels. The giveaway is the use of the magic number 'seven'. He had probably read Rider Haggard's *King Solomon's Mines*, which had been published in 1885, and I suppose he thought he would dress up the mundane facts with a little fiction, thinking no one was ever likely to go to that remote place again. So with the passing of time the granite bowls, often rounded in form, which are common in these rock outcrops and which do hold water for a part of the dry season, became romantic images.

The only sort of water cisterns I found in the Kagas.

Prins did then march eastwards and probably came to the Kaga Poungourou group, described six years later by Chevalier as being inhabited. But again, nothing fitted Prins's descriptions of the caves, and I explored all of the group: Kaga Kolo, Kaga Bongolo, Kaga Bouka, and Kaga Ichi. Rabeh camped a whole year here in 1880. One of Senoussi's leaders had laid siege to the place for three months, one hundred and fifty people hiding in the rocks allegedly being killed, mostly by being asphyxiated in the caves when the Senoussistes tried to smoke them out. But I found no large caves here, and no human remains. There were yet other kagas further east, outside of the Park, including Kaga Betolo, which I had no time to visit. There was a report of a cave on Kaga Kouvou, but as we approached it there was a scuffling sound and my companions fled – me with them – announcing it was a lion. So I never did get to see that one.

But who was the pygmy chief whose skull I had found? Was it Baglia, after whom one of the kagas was named? A chief of the G'Bajia who died in that rocky fastness hiding from Senoussi's slavers, or perhaps even slain in battle with them?My companions seemed to know nothing of history or tradition, it was a closed book to them. They only expressed horror that people had apparently lived in caves, "like animals," as Opha put it.

* * *

My intention had been to pick out the main points of interest to develop tourist circuits to them; the central plain with its waterholes, the caves of the troglodytes, interesting salt licks, woodland waterholes and other features. It now remained for me to make linking tracks to join it all together into suitable circuits. But cutting north-east of Kaga Omboro I ran over a granite boulder hidden in the grass, which the workers hadn't bothered to remove, and damaged the Land Rover sump, denting it as if made of tinfoil. Gone were the days when you could roll a Land Rover with impunity over rocks! It was now the beginning of June and the rains would soon start making exit across the numerous watercourses impossible, some of which swelled with the first rains from a mere fifteen feet across to rushing torrents of a quarter of a mile in width. So I was obliged to pack it in for the season.

I started again on February 1 1982:

"This time I am camped on the Vassako . . . Have found a nice shady place but there is not a drop of water in the vicinity, hence I am plagued with bees, sweat bees, and a fair number of tsetse flies. The bees are the worst, making it impossible to wash until sundown since they swarm all over the water bowl. The trip out gave good game viewing – I saw seventeen elephants from the Mandabale bluff (the first time I have seen elephants from there), and a curious, unafraid herd of about fifty buffalo near the end of the track. I have Opha with me, who has changed his name to Azouka alias (Azouka being the name of his dead father). Kakumale I have not brought this time as he has a hernia!"

On the fourteenth my diary records that I should finish the track tomorrow (which I did) and then ends abruptly, for I was informed the project was to terminate at the end of March.

Is there any hope of ever achieving anything with such policies? A year later there was probably not a rhinoceros left alive in the park. Four years later the number of elephants had been reduced by over fifty per cent and now they are reported as rare. Six years later, the eighty or so hippos at Bourkangali had been reduced to twenty; and the sixty kob at Foubouloulou had been reduced to twenty-seven; while buffalo were now only seen in small furtive herds of six or eight. A huge investment by the EEC apparently did nothing to stop this tide of destruction and the interior of the park has been abandoned. But even the main roads are no longer safe to travel in the CAR because of bandits armed with Kalashnikovs.

Now I understand what the cynical Frenchman meant on my arrival in Bangui, when he said it was a country *sans espoir*.

But it is worse than that. It is a country that has had its heart torn out. There is nothing left to bleed any more.

Notes

1. This was known to be the custom in the east of the country at the beginning of the 20th century. When a chief died a number of girls were strangled and buried with him.

Chapter 8

Voyage to the Congo

interlude in a Marxist Regime

"I take no pleasure in describing a place I am already wanting to leave", wrote Andre Gide in 1927.[1] I felt like writing the same. Gide would not have recognized Brazzaville in 1978, capital of the former colony of French Equatorial Africa. But he might have approved the monstrous faded scarlet hoardings in the city centre bearing their hammer and sickle emblems and the giant crude portrait of Lenin. " . . . I realize that it is impossible to get into contact with anything real", he wrote.

In spite of its communist takeover the country still retained the name of Brazzaville for its capital. Named after the first white man to explore the country, Pierre Savorgnan de Brazza, an Italian who was, after all, a libertarian and disliked by French colonialists for being so, the capital's original name was N'tamo, where Brazza built a fort in 1880.

I was lodged in the 'government' hotel. A five-storey ugly cement-block, built, owned, and controlled by the Russians. As usual it was sited close to the Zaïre River, overlooking neighbouring Kinshasha on the other bank. They did the same at Bangui, but there they called it an embassy. The latter building was never occupied before events overtook the Soviet plans, the Russians being expelled after the overthrow of Bokassa. In the Brazzaville hotel the second floor and above, with the exception of a rooftop bar frequented by prostitutes, was out of bounds, permanently occupied by Russians.

The only other residents in the hotel appeared to be two drunken English sailors on a visit from the port of *Pointe Noire*, and a Russian ballet troupe touring the country. I wonder what the Africans though of Russian ballet? I have no doubt they were completely mystified.

As a ballet troupe it seemed a little unusual to me in that it was composed of about a dozen hulking great men with massive shoulders, and one diminutive woman who minced with tiny steps wherever she went. As Gide said, it was impossible to get into contact with anything real.

In the evening when I retired to my room, or was intending to do so, a prostitute jumped out at me from behind one of the pillars on the first floor landing and stood in front of me giggling. It seemed these ladies watched the residents leaving the lounge and then regularly played this entertaining little trick.

In the morning, while waiting in the dining room to be served breakfast, I observed that as the waiters bustled out from the kitchen swing door, breakfast tray in the left hand, they passed a large sideboard. Yanking open a drawer with the right hand, with a deft movement that would have done credit to the magician Paul Daniels, half the contents of the breakfast tray were swept into the drawer, which was then slammed shut with a flick of the hips. Consequently the diners' breakfast helpings were rather meagre.

Fortunately I did not stay long in this dismal place but went down to Loubomo, the town halfway between Brazzaville and the coast. Here I lodged with two Czechoslovakians who were carrying out a forest survey. The elder of the two was one of those charming, good-looking Czechs, probably in his late thirties, named Ota. It seemed he had been putting his charm to good use for we were seated in the lounge discussing our programme of work when the door was abruptly thrust open to reveal a tearful young African woman, who suddenly threw a pair of high-heeled shoes into the middle of the room and stood there crying. I wondered whether this was some quaint Czechoslovakian custom she had learnt; it could not have been African for shoes were something of a novelty in this part of the world.

"Excuse me," murmured my host, rising quickly and going to the door, shutting it discreetly behind him.

Shortly afterwards he returned and continued our discussion as if nothing had happened. The object of my mission was to visit the forest north of Point Noire on the coast to see whether it was a suitable site for a national park. Allegedly the forest harboured lowland gorillas and chimpanzees.

The next day my hosts threw a handful of tins of food into a Land Rover and we drove off.

"But shouldn't we take bedding and other camping equipment?" I queried.

Ota looked at me amusedly.

"Ah, there's no need. These French foresters always live in style. Wait until you see. They will have a magnificent guest house."

By the time we had waited to cross the rather ancient ferry over the Conkouati River, a ferry which was always breaking down causing long delays, time was getting on, but we pressed forward unconcernedly along a road into the dense forest. The afternoon wore on and a heavy drizzle began so that soon we were slithering along with the wheels spinning in the slippery red mud of a forest track, the road by now left far behind. It was late evening and almost dark when the track led up a circular mound in the forest which the Land Rover only just succeeded in making to the summit in the now glutinous mud.

In the dank forest gloom I could discern a small clearing, to one side of which were two rather worn and tattered tents. We had arrived!

A short, dumpy, annoyed-looking man stood in front of one of the tents. He inquired shortly as to what we wanted.

Easing himself from the Land Rover Ota, full of charm, explained.

"But messieurs, you cannot just come into the forest like this. There is nothing here, nothing!" exclaimed the dumpy man emphatically, adding as an afterthought:

"I have no beer."

So this was the luxury in which the French foresters lived! I could see that one tent, with the ends flapping open in the drizzle, was packed with a disorderly jumble of stores. The other was the Frenchman's meagre quarters.

Ota turned on more charm. The drizzle of rain stopped and things began to look a little brighter. The Frenchman began to thaw.

Well, there was only room for two. I could sleep in the store tent, Ota would find room with the Frenchman and Ivan, Ota's young colleague, would sleep on the front seats of the Land Rover. This settled the Frenchman invited us to join him around the camp table in front of his tent. There was no campfire; it was too wet for that. As is often the case with our Gallic friends his initial hostility to strangers had softened and he began to warm visibly. Beer was miraculously produced and he beamed pleasantly, glad of company in his lonely forest retreat.

"And from what country do you come?" he asked Ota.

Ota's reply made him beam even more with friendliness.

"*Et vous m'sieu?*" he inquired, turning to me.

"*Je suis Anglais,*" I answered.

The Frenchman's jaw dropped so low I thought it would hit the table. The smile on his face vanished abruptly and he stared nonplussed at the table with downcast eyes.

"Umph!" he grunted.

Well here was an unforeseen setback, an anti-English Frenchman. But gradually he thawed once more and soon we were talking together like old friends. He confided I was the first Englishman he had ever met (he was in his fifties) and obviously they were not all as bad as he had been led to believe. His conception was not one of football hooligans (they had not been invented yet), but that all Englishmen were arrogant aristocrats who spent their Sundays eating cucumber sandwiches with the vicar on their immaculate English lawns and looked down their noses at working Frenchmen.

In the morning the only toilet facilities available were the surrounding forest.

"Mais c'est terrible, c'est terrible!" the Frenchman cried, "that an English gentleman should be treated like this!"

We parted the best of friends. Ota was quite unperturbed at leading us into such a situation; these things were just a part of life in the Congo. Arriving back at the ferry another setback awaited us for the ferry was broken down on the far bank and would not be repaired until the next day. We prepared to pass the night sitting in the queue of vehicles with mosquitoes for company. The only sustenance we had were some bottles of beer purchased from a nearby kiosk. But luckily, just before dark, the engine was got going and the ferry came across.

Before we left *Pointe Noire* I visited the local market. It was with difficulty I refrained from being sick. Whole roasted monkeys were displayed for sale, which the vendors chopped up for customers, the gut contents shooting out in a green, foetid mass. Roasted rats were another delicacy displayed, likewise cooked whole without first removing the guts. And there was fresh snake too, puff adders or pythons chopped up into succulent bloody portions. In one part of the market, where charms and other products were sold, there were dried black fingers, whether chimpanzee or gorilla I could not determine. *Pointe Noire* (Black Point) seemed an apt title for the town.

Back in Loubomo I inquired among the local people as to whether there were gorillas in the neighbouring forest. Yes, there were, someone actually had a captive one somewhere on the outskirts of town. This was too good to be true and we drove off in search. Everybody seemed to know about the captive gorilla. Yes it was this way, no that way, no not here, over there. Eventually we were directed to a hut which we were assured was the place we sought.

A dejected baboon with a string around its waist tied to a pole, sat on its haunches and eyed us miserably . . .

* * *

The Congo was the only African country I know of which, at Independence, shot out the animals in one of its reserves. This was in the Mount Fouari Game Reserve into which the army moved to celebrate independence by shooting all the buffalo and taking the carcases away for a feast. I was on my way there to see if there was anything left, for now the government wanted to reopen it as a place for tourists to visit.

Two ragged guides were still employed and they took me on a stalk through the long elephant grass to where I got a quick glimpse of a small group of frightened waterbuck. Some elephant apparently dared to venture into the fringes of the area in the wet season but soon retreated back into Gambia when they were shot at.

The Congo was a land of disappointments.

Notes

1. André Gide 1930 *Travels in the Congo.*

Chapter 9

Land of the Moro Naba

journeys in Upper Volta

"And what do you do, besides banging your head against a brick wall?"

Although the number of Brits in Ouagadougou, capital of Upper Volta, was far greater than in Bangui, it still amounted to no more than a couple of dozen. Thus when Her Royal Highness Princess Anne paid a visit to the capital in 1984 I was included in the select reception of aid workers gathered to meet her.

Introduced as the director of a wild life project, Her Royal Highness's immediate response was:

"And what do you do, besides banging your head against a brick wall?"

Indeed, I found it hard to describe any other activity with much conviction. Her Royal Highness's percipient frankness outshone by far the ponderous burblings usually emitted by pompous officials, trying to ask penetrating questions, which would reflect the questioner's acumen.

After leaving the CAR I had come to Upper Volta rather unexpectedly to replace a Frenchman who had been thrown out. A not unusual circumstance in this country, its predominantly Muslim black Arab influence producing a particularly intransigent people. The country was a remarkable contrast to the CAR. A former French colony like the latter, it was, on the contrary, one where the French authorities had seemingly not interfered with the traditional structures and customs.

But then, there had been few Frenchmen here in colonial times. Like Oubangui-Chari it had been one of the less attractive outposts to French administrators. Despite the fact the southern two-thirds of the country is heavily populated, even in the 1980s it remained one of the lesser-known African countries to the English-speaking world.

Invaded by black Muslim Arabs from the north in the 15th century it still guarded its ancient customs, a part of those found throughout the pagan countries of western Africa, and it had not suffered the same ravages of the slave trade as had Oubangui-Chari, or at least not as recently. It was rich in fetish worship, which, unlike other African countries of my experience, was practised openly and without embarrassment. Many villages had their fetish pole at the entrance covered with a motley junk of bones, dog skulls, giant snail shells, old broken earthenware pots and what have you.

Shortly after my arrival in the dusty capital of Ouagadougou (pronounced Wagga-doo-goo), I passed a rainmaker being led along the road by a guide: led, because his face was hidden by a grotesque painted wooden mask and he probably couldn't see where he was going; while his whole being was draped from head to foot in lengths of string. Such was the successful integration of the traditional with the modern that his guide hopefully held out a hand for a coin in case I wished to take a photograph. A small cloud had appeared in the sky the day before signalling the end of the dry season, and the rainmaker's real purpose was to go around the villages making rain – for a fee of course. Perhaps greater than that for having a snapshot taken!

Every Friday I saw stately old men in their djellabahs, the ankle-length nightgown of the Arab, muzzle loaders slung over the shoulder, incongruously pedalling slowly along on old bicycles, their sandalled, calloused oversized flat feet stuck out at right angles to the pedals. They were making their weekly pilgrimage to the palace of the Moro Naba, 'Ruler of the World', hereditary chief of the Mossi, the most powerful tribe in the country. Later during the day a gun would be fired in salute.

During my time there, the incumbent, Moro Naba Kougri, died. One of my staff confided to me he had taken poison. It was the custom, he explained, that if the chief did not behave as was expected of him, and this one had apparently failed in this respect, then the elders obliged him to drink a poisoned chalice.

Ouagadougou, unlike Bangui, which was founded by the French, was probably founded in the 12th century. It was the dirtiest African town I had ever lived in. A jumble of mud-walled African houses, side by side with modern-type buildings with tin roofs, a favourite roosting place for vultures which awoke me in the mornings with their clatter on the corrugated iron as if they were checking whether the inmates were dead or just sleeping.

From October to March the harmattan blows in from the Sahara desert, causing smarting eyes and covering everything with a fine, red dust. Leave your house for a week, with all the doors and windows securely fastened, and when you come back a thick layer of red dust is covering everything.

When cholera broke out I discovered, with some alarm, my injection was out of date. By the time I had become aware of this the chemists' shops had sold out of supplies of the antidote. It wasn't a surprise to me when André my cook caught the disease. It was a public holiday and I was having a late lie-in when he came banging on the door. Although I did not know what was the cause of his banging at the time, I pretended not to hear, and my watchman took him to hospital on the back of his autocycle as the taxis refused to carry cholera victims.

Three days after the day on which André had last served me a meal, which is the standard incubation period, I awoke with a forehead so hot I could hardly touch it, and an upset stomach to boot. I had an uneasy time thinking of those accounts I had read of cholera in old England, the victims dying convulsed with pain, their faces contorted in hideous grins with their lips stretched back in a horrible grimace of death. Going to the hospital here was as good as a sentence of death. It was a country where, if you got sick, you were flown to Europe. But not cholera victims!

See a doctor? Well, when a newly arrived assistant fell sick I telephoned one of the few Voltaïque doctors who were recommended, and he refused to turn out to see the patient. The patient would have to come to the surgery like everybody else I was told. So I took him to one of the few European missionary doctors, an Italian who ran a gynaecological clinic. My sick companion sat in a waiting room full of pregnant African women giggling and squirming with embarrassment while he sat moaning and groaning. The doctor reckoned there wasn't much wrong with him.

I also survived, and so did the cook.

* * *

I often wished I had faithful old Bernard with me (at least I liked to think of him as faithful). André was a young man, short, and not very intelligent. He had come to me without references, which usually means there is something to hide. It turned out he had really been a blanchisseur, a laundry boy, and had picked up some knowledge of cooking on the side.

While on home leave I had purchased one of those small Christmas puddings wrapped in scarlet paper with which the supermarket shelves in Britain are filled from September onwards. It was in early December I had some guests to supper. The meal passed off well enough and we came to the cheese course.

André bore in the cheese-board. Reposing among the Brie, the Camembert and the Danish blue, was a round, brown object. It was the Christmas pudding!

Well at least he hadn't cooked it.

As was customary André did all of my housework, including making the bed. When I went on my first safari and lodged in a small guest house, André prepared the bed. First he laid a sheet on the mattress.

248

Then he laid a blanket on the sheet. Then the other sheet on the blanket. Then the other blanket on top of that. A year later, on the first safari after the rainy season, he did exactly the same thing again. But yet he never executed such a curious arrangement when making my bed in the house at Ouagadougou.

* * *

Doctor Heinrich Barth, a German explorer who spent seven years travelling in northern Africa without a break, was the first European to visit Upper Volta, reaching the northern part in 1853. It was to be 33 years before another German, Gottlob Krause, followed, reaching Ouagadougou in September 1886. Next came Gustave Binger in 1888, who was to be the country's first French governor. He passed near to present-day Po National Park through which Krause had passed, but otherwise it was to be well into the twentieth century before the park region was to be visited again by Europeans.

Entering in February 1888 from what later became known as the Ivory Coast, Binger followed the main route along the northern boundary of the Diéfoula Forest, crossing the Comoé River near to its present-day crossing point, a collapsed bridge. The village of Ouangolodougou was more important then than it is today, but apart from noting the presence of hippos in the Comoé, he had little to say about the region. The normal route farther west through the middle of the area had been abandoned on account of war between the Ivory Coast chiefs.

After being threatened by warlike natives at Dessi, just before the present 'Two Balé Rivers' forest reserve, Binger followed the length of the present Po National Park a few miles south of its southern boundary, which follows the Red Volta river in a south-easterly direction. Its bleak woodland was hostile country in those days. First he was threatened by the inhabitants of Kalarokho village who turned out armed with bows and arrows "shouting cries of beasts" but eventually left the party alone as Binger, with great coolness, held his fire. Then arriving at Tiakane, just east of the Nazinga experimental game ranch, the chief tried to intimidate him, raising difficulties over the supply of guides to Kapori, some fifteen miles south. When he got to Kapori he had difficulty with the chief there, who demanded bigger presents. Continuing towards Paga, about half a mile further on, he was accosted by some two dozen people armed with bows, sent by the chief of Po to stop him and bring him back. But Binger was undeterred, and after threatening them was allowed to continue on his way.

I was told of a village not far from Po where there was a hut commemorated by a sign, the occupants of which were alleged to have hidden Binger in the roof when he was pursued. To this day the family of Binger is said to pay an annual pension to the descendants of the family which hid him. But Binger makes no mention of this in his book of his travels *Du Niger au Golfe de Guinée*. Perhaps he considered it would appear too ignominious for an intrepid explorer to have to admit to hiding in a roof, and preferred to pretend he stared his enemies out of countenance.

In spite of the fact the country was well populated, away from the major towns it had almost stood still in time since Binger's day.

Slightly less than half the size of the Central African Republic it has three times the number of people, the majority concentrated in the southern half. But there was still some game there because the most wooded areas along the rivers in the south had been devastated by sleeping sickness at the beginning of the century. River blindness, transmitted by a small black midge, was also very prevalent. These areas now held the last remnants of the West African fauna.

On the border with Ghana, an enterprising Canadian missionary's son had set up an experimental game ranch known as Nazinga. An area of almost four hundred square miles, it was to be protected from poaching, and when the animal populations had recovered their numbers sufficiently they would be systematically harvested and the meat sold to the surrounding villagers on a sustained basis. When a trial harvesting of the animals eventually began the local people had been so well schooled in the idea of protection they complained bitterly that the animals were supposed to be protected, not killed! Not only that, they refused to buy the meat and it had to be sold to a butcher in the capital.

A young American girl working as a Peace Corps Volunteer decided that at Christmas something should be done for the workers and their families in the surrounding villages other than the religious observances conducted by the missionary's son. I well knew of course that 'doing something' for Christmas in Africa usually led to disappointment.

Firstly she decided to organize a football match among the workers, but before this could happen the weed-covered football pitch had to be cleared. She asked for volunteers. None were forthcoming. That was work; they didn't work without being paid for it. If she wanted the football pitch cleared, then she would have to do it herself.

Somewhat disappointed she abandoned the idea of a football match and replaced it with a better one. She decided to buy a goat and have it barbecued for the people for Christmas lunch.

Now this really did interest them. On Christmas morning a huge crowd appeared, eager to partake of the feast. But one small scrawny goat does not go far, and the Christmas day feast soon turned into a near riot as the disgruntled crowd complained it had been promised a feast and most had got nothing.

Poor girl! She should have read Mooning's attempt to celebrate Klismas dinnel at Mambango, an imaginary outpost in Tanganyika based on the ill-fated Groundnut Scheme station.[1] It would have saved a lot of heartache.

It was she who told me about the knickers. Another American girl Volunteer working in a remote village observed one day the young boy she employed about the house was wearing her knickers.

"Goddammit man!" she yelled, "what are you doing wearing my knickers?"

"Well madam," the boy replied apologetically, "since they looked clean, I thought I would make them dirty first before washing them."

* * *

Clem, as I shall call the young missionary, was a stocky, powerfully built person who shortly before I made his acquaintance with true missionary zeal had floored one of his workmen with a straight right to the jaw, finding the old methods were still the best to command respect. It reminded me of a nineteenth-century missionary's arrival in Tanganyika. Entering a canoe with his wife to be ferried across a river, the quite drunk African oarsman leered across at the young woman and drunkenly began to warble a hymn, whereupon the missionary, being an Irishman with a quick temper, knocked the welcoming native senseless.

But strangest of all were Clem's beliefs in ghosts, related to me in all seriousness with the strict undertaking I tell no one. Later I learnt he had already told just about everybody else. Firmly believing in ghosts and the supernatural, he related how one night he and his wife were awakened by the goose in its pen making a loud noise. Looking from the window they saw the chickens, apparently terrified, all trying to get under the goose's wings. The reason for their fright was a pulsating blue light in a tree looking like a gelatinous pulsating blob about the size of a football. Nothing loath, Clem went out to investigate and as he approached the pulsating blob it descended abruptly to the ground and disappeared by bouncing away into the surrounding woodland. The following morning, one of his workers, who had a reputation for witchcraft, appeared with a limp, claiming he had injured his leg while working the previous day. But he had not been working the day before!

Clem was convinced it was he who had been practising magic in the tree and fallen out in his haste to escape when Clem made his appearance.

Then there was the occasion he was out after dark on a visit to a nearby village with one of his staff, when he saw a dancing light following them among the trees. Pointing it out to his worker the latter agreed he could see it also, probably thinking it best not to argue with a madman. The dancing light followed them to the nearby village where it vanished before the door of an old woman who had a reputation as a witch. She had this reputation presumably because she was disfigured with a goitre.

Yet another mystery was when he was riding his motorbike along a deserted road after dark (most African roads are deserted after dark) and saw a very bright headlamp coming towards him in the middle of the road. Pulling over he stopped and waited but the light never reached him, suddenly vanishing. Well that was spooky enough, but then there was the story of his father who was also travelling on a motorbike when he came across a large baobab tree with the crown aflame, but no sign of fire around the base of the tree! Shades of Moses and the burning bush! His father got away from there as if the devil himself was at his heels. But that one is easy to explain. Honey hunters had probably been smoking out bees in a hole near the top of the tree and the rotted interior had caught fire.

Another mystery related to one of Clem's best converts to Christianity whom he trusted never to tell a lie. The man had told him he had been walking along the road one day when an old woman with skirts down to her feet came along – an unusual dress for women in that part of the world. When he greeted her she asked him if he would like to see her 'karangas', and lifting her skirt several creatures like small warthogs ran out. She was a witch and these were her imps.

"How could one explain that?" Clem asked. I think the answer is straightforward. The man had dreamt it and many backward peoples firmly believe dreams are real events, so he was quite right in his own way of thinking to state the event had actually taken place.

* * *

In spite of the fact the country was fairly well served by roads, very little seemed to be known of what went on in it. The best-known game area was the Arli region in the south-east along the Pendjari River, called a national park but legally it wasn't. A floodplain area, it was characterized by open grassy plains dotted with clumps of stately borassus palm trees and herds of russet-coloured Buffon's kob antelope. Although game densities appeared high in the dry season, the months when tourists visited the area, the hartebeest, roan antelope and buffalo, all came in from a very large surrounding catchment zone. Because of the persistent Sahel drought this surrounding zone was now completely waterless in the dry season, forcing the animals to concentrate along the Pendjari River.

Not only did the animals have to contend with drought, but poaching was rife everywhere. A factory in Ouagadougou produced almost three million twelve-bore cartridges a year, and although a percentage was exported, most of them seemed to find their way back into the country again. I even found an English-made Eley cartridge in one poacher's camp. In addition, there were probably more home-made flintlock muzzle loaders used than there were twelve-bore shotguns.

But in the area around Arli spiked-wheel traps were also common, a method used throughout Africa since time immemorial. The manufacture of these cruel traps was described by the Ancient Greek, Xenophon, in his book on hunting written about 390 BC. The trap consists of a ring of sharpened sticks pointing inwards (sometimes porcupine quills are used), which is laid over a small hole in the ground. A wire noose is laid on top of the spiked wheel, attached to a log of wood. Any animal unfortunate enough to step through the centre of the trap then attempts to shake it off, at the same time pulling the noose tight around its leg. Xenophon recommended alternating the sharpened sticks with iron nails, which would hurt the animal's leg more, thus making it more anxious to shake off the trap.

Giant iron gin traps, like the man traps once used in English game preserves, were also common, and hazardous to anyone walking in the area. Cleverly camouflaged, they could smash your ankle if you were unfortunate enough to step on one.

I wondered how any animals managed to survive at all.

The Bontioli Reserve, much farther to the west, was close to the town of Diébougou, a stronghold of Vichy French during the Second World War who had fortified some caves in the area against possible attack by British troops from the Gold Coast. The Reserve was now practically devoid of game and overrun with cattle. Fifteen to twenty Buffon's kob, one roan antelope, signs of a few hartebeest, one warthog; and signs of one or two elephant and hippopotamus in the rainy season, were all I encountered.

On the way to this reserve I passed a chief's funeral taking place by the side of the road. The body, half-mummified, was arranged in an upright sitting position in a sort of three-sided cubicle made of dirty awnings, perched high up and looking like a macabre seaside Punch and Judy booth. Cooking pots were piled below. Bila, my driver, said it was the custom that all the relatives must see the body before it is buried. I got a glimpse of the corpse's face as I passed, and there was a grisly shrunken foot sticking out at the bottom. Not exactly the sort of thing one expects to meet with on the side of the road, but then, anything could happen in Africa.

Each house in this area was built like a fort: a square, mud-walled complex, with a narrow entrance. All had flat roofs and a central tower, or round second storey. Like Norman castles, small holes in the surrounding wall were for shooting arrows through. Bila told me the Lobi, a tribe further south, being a very warlike people, had lots of holes in their walls. Some of these people lived in caves and would have nothing to do with authority. They were spoken of with fear because not many years ago they had shot an arrow into an interfering official who had been presumptuous enough to try to collect taxes from them.

A village I visited on the edge of Lobi country seemed deserted when I drove up. But as I sat in the Land Rover wondering, after a while first one head, and then another, peeped up warily over a parapet. Eventually two young men showed themselves, grinning. They were dressed in shirts and trousers and appeared quite westernized, but still maintained the cautious habits of their forebears of hiding whenever anyone came visiting.

It was in the Bontioli Reserve I first saw an ancient living mound that, from its height, must have been several centuries old. These mounds, of which I was to see many more in other parts of the country, are easily recognised by their smooth, convex shape, formed by centuries of living on the same spot. They are built up by the disintegration of mud dwellings, fire ashes and domestic rubbish: evidence of centuries of occupation. Pottery sherds are found on their summits, and excavating them would provide a wealth of material about the previous inhabitants, but there is just too much for the archaeologists to do and no money to do it with. And so these mounds remain, memorials to an unknown past. Just as in the Bamingui-Bangoran Park, so here everywhere evidence of iron-smelting sites was to be found.

* * *

I went with Suleiman, my young Voltaïque counterpart, on a tour of the extreme west of the country next to its border with Mali, since no one seemed to know whether there was any game left there or not. On our journey we passed people quite unconcernedly carrying shotguns or muzzle-loaders, they had never seen a game official before. Hunting without a licence was illegal, as most of them knew, but the law was totally ignored.

I asked myself once again, how could any game survive this continual onslaught? And yet, surprisingly, some did. But it could surely not be for much longer.

My diary for February 13 1984, records:

"There seem to be remnants of game left; warthog, roan. But very little is seen. Much of the habitat reminds me of the Bamingui-Bangoran Park; ironstone rocks littering the ground, dotted with dry thickets; open grey, clay plains covered with mushroom-shaped termite mounds. There is much cotton growing taking place, and so only isolated bits of natural habitat are left. The first night's camp near Kati was a miserable one, swarms of sweat bees and honey bees. Sweat bees are numerous everywhere, and tsetse flies are sometimes a nuisance also . . . We moved northwards along the border region and are now camped on the Groumbo, near its confluence with the Ngorolaka, in a patch of Anogeissus woodland which was once extensive, but is now being rapidly cut down to make way for cultivation. The Ngorolaka is dry, but there is plenty of water in the steep-sided Groumbo. There are extensive floodplains here which ten years ago probably swarmed with kob, and now only a few are left. I saw seventeen this morning, but there is undoubtedly ten times this number hidden in the long grass. An old man to whom I spoke, said that two years ago (he probably meant ten), you could count herds of a hundred roan on the plains; but the game had disappeared because of the drought since two years. Two years ago the swamp near his house had dried up for the first time (he must have been about sixty years of age as he said that he had planted the mango trees around his house and they were now big trees)."

But what had really destroyed the game in the region was a rice-growing scheme on the floodplains and the poaching which came with it.

"We found a poachers' camp this morning and recovered nine guns (shotguns and home-made muzzle loaders) and 148 shot-gun cartridges. (One gun was later returned to the owner as he had a licence for it). The poachers had five kob skins, two red duiker skins and had also killed a genet cat . . . Most of the poachers were from Mali, but the camp owner was local. The guns were draped with charms to make them shoot better; little leather phylacteries containing bits and pieces of the animals they were supposed to kill. Suleiman was afraid that if we remained in our camp, they might attack us tonight to get back their arms, but we will stay until morning . . .

"February 14th. Well we weren't attacked, but Suleiman stayed sitting up until half past two in the morning! I slept with one of the shot-guns (loaded) under my camp bed, didn't use a tent, just slept under a mosquito net . . . "

We continued north-eastwards keeping to the western side of the country, questioning villagers about game and especially if they had ever seen any elephants. Some reported odd elephants having been seen during the wet season. Finally we reached a place called Siapi where the map showed there to be a square mile of forest. It turned out to be a groundwater forest of which the last remnants were now being destroyed to make way for cotton and millet plantations. Three or four magnificent, smooth-boled *mvule* trees (*Chlorophora excelsa*) still stood, and some very large kapok trees with the buttressed trunks typical of tropical forest. In the cleared area, giant half burnt trunks lay on the ground; in another season or so they would have burnt them completely. What a tragedy in a land that has lost almost all of its forest! I knew of no similar forest elsewhere in the country. I remonstrated with an old man in the nearby village: Why did they cut the trees down, I asked, could they not see they were turning the whole place into a wasteland?

He agreed it was not a good thing, but the Peulh nomads, the West African equivalent of the Maasai, forced ever further southwards by the drought, just came in grazing their cattle everywhere, and so they had to find more land to cultivate.

Palms fringed a pool of water, which was covered with water lilies and sported numbers of waterbirds. There was a woodpecker in the palms, and some large bats roosting. It was a veritable oasis in a wasteland of cultivation. By now the water will have dried up, and the once grand forest remnant will have vanished without trace.

It was in this camp that some small boys came to see us. One had the heads of several young spurfowl poking out of his pocket. When he took the birds out I found he had broken their legs so they could not escape. Suleiman confiscated them to eat for himself. Tasty as they no doubt were, I could not bear the thought and told him to put them out of their misery as soon as possible. But my concern was not understood.

The next day we drove on to Soukoudiankoudi, a village as fascinating as its tongue-twisting name. Its setting was like something out of *King Solomon's Mines*. The village was reached at the end of a long defile. With a rock wall on one side of the track and a marsh on the other there was barely room for a vehicle to pass along the path, and this was only possible in the dry season. The marsh was thick with palms, the only water available in an otherwise arid wilderness of rocks and bush, which stretched for countless miles around. The village itself was perched on a hill at the end of the valley in an unassailable position. Behind it was an almost sheer rock wall, the whole valley being banjo-shaped. There was only one easy way in, along the defile; and a single steep footpath led up the rock wall. This I climbed with difficulty in the hot sun, for much of the ascent the rocks being like steps. At the top was a flat plateau with dry bush stretching away into the distance. There was no road, but the villagers carried bicycles up if they wanted to go to the next village some miles away.

The inhabitants of this remote habitation were friendly enough, but I noted on each footpath approaching the village was a broken earthenware cooking pot and some ashes – to ward off evil spirits. They were well protected indeed!

The last time they had seen elephants, the villagers said, was seven years ago.

We continued towards the Sourou River, a permanent watercourse where there might still be good game country. On the way, striding along in the heat of the day and to all intents and purposes in the middle of nowhere, we came across an old witch doctor. He was, on the surface, a kindly, pleasant old man, but nevertheless had that malignant look which I suppose all witch doctors must have. Over one shoulder he carried a flintlock musket, and over the other a leather pouch and a horn, perhaps a powder horn or something connected with the black arts. A live black chicken in a string bag completed his accoutrements. We stopped, and with a gulp Suleiman got out and asked him if he had a permit for his gun. The witch doctor stopped and smiled a polite thin smile.

Yes, he had a permit. He delved into a pouch and produced a paper. It was an old French Sudan (now Mali) permit dated 1973, carefully preserved. As Suleiman examined it, he fidgeted to be on his way. He answered our questions politely but with impatience. Well it may have been ten years out of date, but it was a permit anyway, so Suleiman handed it back. With a brief smile the old man carefully put it away and strode off. He had come at least twenty miles on foot that morning and still had a good many more miles to go to his destination, Weresse.

The Sourou when I got there was a disappointment. The banks were bare and overgrazed. There was a single tamarind tree, the only shade to be found in the area, under which I pitched my tent. It also was the home of all the gnats and mosquitoes in the area, which woke up in the evening just when I was preparing to relax in the cool open air and enjoy my supper.

It was here that, after the revolution which was to come, the government ordered a thousand mango trees to be planted, part of an effort to halt the southward march of the desert. A discussion ensued in the Ministry. The young Voltaïque forester informed the Minister he had inspected the area but the soil was not suitable for mango trees: it was too clayey. He had questioned people in the area who had planted mango trees and they all said they never had any fruit from them after many years.

"I don't know anything about forestry techniques," replied the Minister, "but you will plant mango trees."

Well at least they would provide good shade for the mosquitoes.

From here we struck north and west through little-known country. There were many ancient living mounds in the area, perhaps abandoned in times past because of wars as there was no tsetse fly, the usual cause of abandonment. Then following the Sourou we came upon a hunters' camp occupied by six old men, all with flintlock muskets. One had lost three of his fingers, these guns being more dangerous to the hunter than the hunted. He fired his piece off at Suleiman's request before handing it over for examination. The firing demonstration was done by holding it out in front of himself at waist height, closing both eyes, and pulling the trigger. A loud report followed accompanied by a thick cloud of smoke; presumably the reason for closing one's eyes. The men said they only hunted guinea fowl, but then, there was little else there.

Apart from a few hippo in the river, the banks were occupied by nothing except cattle, cattle, cattle, all the way.

* * *

In March I decided to explore the Leraba River with a team. Large gangs of poachers from the Ivory Coast were said to operate in the area (we never saw any) and it was considered advisable I should take a reasonably strong force with me. My diary reads:

"Arrived at the Comoé camp on the 21st of March. There had been heavy rain about ten days previously which had caused a fresh flush of grass everywhere and dispersed the game. There were thunderstorms at night in the distance. It is terribly humid and the perspiration pours off, all my clothes are soaking wet. The temperature in the tent goes up to forty-one degrees centigrade, but even when it drops to about thirty-one the perspiration still continues at the same rate.

"Went west along the Leraba for eight miles and camped. Several poachers' camps seen which had been abandoned about November last. All have remains of kob, hartebeest and warthog. Lions were noisy at night. Patrolled back east along the river the next day [we drove from camp to camp and then patrolled the surrounding area on foot]. It doesn't look like chimpanzee country to me, one of the animals that we are looking for in the area.

"Today [23rd] continued westward . . . numerous abandoned poachers' camps full of bones, this area greatly favoured by buffalo . . . Game was quite plentiful when we cut inland from the river; saw several groups of hartebeest, kob, and one herd of young waterbuck does. The animals are not very afraid of the vehicles - the first that they have seen.

"March 26th. Now in camp furthest west along the Leraba. By far the most difficult journey getting here yesterday, crossing the many small stream beds. The vehicles were at some crazy angles sometimes, at one stage I thought that Oumar [one of the drivers] would somersault the Toyota Landcruiser backwards going up a steep sandy slope when the rear wheels dug in. We had to winch him out once, and there were a few hair-raising moments with the Land Rover because Bila will not listen to what I say, but goes blindly ahead. Finally we came to a fishermen's camp at the spot which I had selected to camp. They had killed a small crocodile and there were hartebeest remains in the camp, but otherwise they were fishing. Poachers are near as we heard shots at night . . . My tent is pitched overlooking the river which has a very tropical aspect here with thick, fringing vegetation on the opposite [Ivory Coast] bank. There are lots of a species of tiger fish - I caught a half-pounder on a wet fly, but that frightened off the others and so I didn't get any more. The temperature last night dropped to eighteen degrees, and at midday rose to forty-five degrees in the tent."

Patrolling on foot the next day we came to a point at which the narrow river suddenly opened out into an enormously wide expanse, forming a long pleasant reach with hippos in it. It seemed this was a sacred place, and people were making sacrifices on the bank. We came across a witch doctor who had a rust-coloured bark cloth shirt with mirrors sewn all over it (he was not wearing it). Hubert, the hunting inspector who was with me, said that such coats were used in connection with making hunting spells.

While we were investigating, since there was also a poacher present with a shotgun, two young men in clean shirts and trousers rode up on bicycles. Taking no notice of us, they laid down their bicycles on the ground and proceeded to strip to their bathing trunks (Africans always prefer the colours of bathing trunks to normal underpants). Then, quite unconcernedly, they started to offer sacrifices.

I was amazed by the openness of it all, for in most African countries they keep such customs secret from the white man's prying eyes.

While one watched the other dropped some coins one by one into a gourd, to the accompaniment of muttered incantations. He then held up a grey pullet by the wings and, after muttering more incantations, cut its throat and poured the blood into the gourd. He then did the same with a white pullet. An unfortunate goat also had its throat cut, and lay gasping its last on the ground.

Occupied talking to a fisherman, I did not see anymore of this process, except to notice they drank from the gourd. At that moment an enormous crocodile surfaced a little way out in the river and swam slowly towards some rocks before submerging again. The fisherman said it always appeared when people were making sacrifices.

After the two young supplicants had departed we walked up to where they had made their sacrifice. The chicken gut contents had been thrown on the ground in offering, and with an exclamation one of the game guards delved into the mess and produced several coins, which he eagerly washed in the river and then pocketed with a chuckle. André looked horrified, but clearly not everyone was superstitious!

Whenever we came across hyaena or lion droppings in the bush some of the guards would stuff their pockets with these disgusting turds, regardless even of whether they were completely dry or not. I never asked what they intended to do with them. I knew I wouldn't get a straight answer.

* * *

In January I visited the Sirba River in the east of the country hoping to find game there. But it was a devastated land, everywhere overrun with Peulh cattle. The drought had driven them down from their already overgrazed lands in the Sahel, deeper and deeper into the country, destroying it as they advanced. At Oursi Lake, well to the north in the Sahel, it was reported a once thickly bushed and wooded country had been turned into bare sand dunes in the space of twenty years, the area of which had doubled in size in the ten years up to 1972.

Here, where the Peulh had invaded, was Gourma country; the Hausa name for the country on the west bank of the Niger River, part of the Mossi kingdom since the 13th century. At Diapaga, a sub-district office, they still used talking drums to pass messages.

"At Babongou in the east, having taken a day and a half to get here, the roads shewn on the map being no more than footpaths. The place is almost a desert . . . the country is for the most part ironstone gravel. There is plenty of water in the various branches of the Sirba River, but the surrounding country is completely dried out. It is baobab country, with a real forest of them at one place near Piéla. Several seem to have collapsed from the drought. Did seventy miles this morning south-east and north of the camp, all a desert, every *inch* has been trodden by Peulh cattle or sheep. They say there are a few rare, red-fronted gazelles, but not much chance of seeing them . . . Fourteen years ago there were elephant and buffalo here, especially on the Faga River; and elephants were known at Datambi twenty years ago. They say that the game has disappeared since the drought, followed by the invasion of Peulh cattle . . . It is a devastated country . . . "

Driving south the extraordinary thing was the people in the villages that we passed through thought they were in neighbouring Niger. They even paid taxes to Niger, one showing me his receipts. Yet they were some twelve miles inside Upper Volta as shown on the map. The Niger authorities had even installed a well in one village. Igori, a village I was trying to make for on the map, was wrongly placed, causing me much confusion.

Close to the village of Kodyeli I found a rectangle of ironstone rocks, forming an ancient wall about three feet high. An old man in the village said it had been built by a Gourma chief against the French, but I suspect it was the other way around, since Africans were unlikely to build such a regularly-shaped rectangle. It now remained a forgotten piece of history, undoubtedly a defensive position in some skirmish at the beginning of the century.

We went on to Nassougou where, it being market day, I bought a Maria Therèsa silver dollar from a merchant who had his wares spread out on the ground before him. Maria Therèsa dollars, originally minted in Austria and bearing the head of the Empress Maria Therèsa, all bear the same date – 1780, although they have continued to be minted long since then. After they were introduced as currency in North Africa in the last year of the Empress's reign, the Arabs refused to accept any with a different date or head on them, considering them to be forgeries. Hence they have been minted ever since bearing the same date.

Today they still represent the wealth of a Peulh woman. The richer she is, the more she displays; hung around her neck in necklaces, or draped over her head in a network. One Peulh woman in the market place, when I walked up to her and asked if I could look at her necklace, without demur very politely took it off and handed it to me for my examination. One would not meet with such politeness in an English market place!

* * *

During my time in Africa I lived through five coups d'etat. Two of them were in the Central African Republic and three in Upper Volta. On my arrival in this latter country the Head of State was Colonel Saye Zerbo, who had overthrown President Aboubakar Lamizana in a bloodless coup in 1980 (who in turn had seized power in a military coup in 1966). Zerbo, who had formed a "Military Committee for the Redress of National Progress", was removed in another bloodless coup by Colonel Gabriel Yoryan, who formed a "People's Salvation Council" and installed Major Jean-Baptiste Ouedraogo as President.

But then came 1983, and Upper Volta's first bloody coup when the Marxists seized power under the 30-year-old excitable young army captain, Thomas Sankara. He had been put up to the coup by an international Cuban terrorist who masterminded its operation and remained Sankara's behind-the-scenes mentor.

Sankara had been in charge of an army detachment not far from the Nazinga game ranch in the south of the country, and I first learned something was up when troops dug a slit trench by the side of a road leading to the ranch. This happened after Sankara had been placed under arrest in Ouagadougou in March 1983, but was released shortly afterwards by the President with an admonition to behave himself. Rumour had it the President had little option but to release him, for Libyan tanks had drawn up on the Ghanaian border, ninety miles away, ready to roll on Ouagadougou. The Nazinga game ranch lay right in their path.

Then came the rains, the slit trench filled with water, and the rebel troops retired to their more comfortable barracks.

The loyal troops also retired. But one, more careless than the rest it seemed, must have tossed his grenade into the magazine without first ascertaining the pin was secure, for at about eleven o'clock one night I was awakened, as was the rest of Ouagadougou, by an almighty explosion. At first I thought it was a thunderclap right over the house, until I heard rounds of ammunition going off like firecrackers. Windows were shattered all over town. It was rumoured only two people were killed, but actual details of the blast were never revealed.

I was reminded of the passage in Thomas Carlyle's *French Revolution*:

"But lo, in the Autumn night, late night . . . what sudden red sunblaze is this that has risen over Lyons City; with a noise to deafen the world? It is the Powder-tower of Lyons . . . which has caught fire in the Bombardment; and sprung into the air . . . with a roar second only to the Last Trumpet! All living sleepers far and wide it has awakened . . .

"Worse things still are in store . . . "

How prophetic were Carlyle's words, for when the dry season came round again, and conditions were less uncomfortable for effecting a coup, Sankara waited no longer. At 10.30 on the night of August 4 1983 he seized a fleet of ten-ton trucks belonging to a Canadian government-financed road-building firm, filled them with his rebel troops, and drove hell for leather to Ouagadougou, where he shot his way into the Presidency. The President himself was spared, no doubt because of his earlier lenient treatment of Sankara; but others were not so fortunate.

The director of the national hospital was shot while rushing to the hospital to succour the wounded.

By this time I was used to gunfire in the night and took little notice. But the next morning, when my puzzled watchman declared he could get nothing but music on his radio, I knew the worst had happened.

Most of the former government ministers were lined up in a courtyard and machine-gunned to death, the executioners becoming so carried away with their task they cut the bodies into pieces with their fire. The revolutionary government then set about its task of transforming the country with zeal into a shambles. Citizens were armed to defend the revolution, and the capital was full of people carelessly sporting brand new, Libyan supplied, AK47 automatic assault rifles. Naturally there were a few accidents, such as a woman and her babe in arms accidentally shot dead waiting outside a bank.

Things had to be done.

There was dig-a-latrine day. People came round to the house ordering me to assist in the digging one Saturday morning. I answered I had diplomatic immunity against such excesses. Well then, a contribution towards payment of the petrol for the truck to cart the earth away would do instead.

There was walk-to-work day. It was to apply to everybody, but *everybody*. Solidarity was the theme. International arrivals at the airport would simply have to walk the several miles to the hotel with their baggage on their heads one supposed, since not even buses were allowed to run. And those leaving via the airport would have to make do in the same manner. Protests arose from government departments. How could the government television crew cover this remarkable event if they had to walk with all of their equipment? There will be no exceptions was the answer.

So many remonstrances followed that it was quietly put off to a Sunday (walk to work on a Sunday?).

Finally we heard no more about it.

There was a competition to think up a new name for the country, and it became Burkina Faso. Translated this means "the man who walks proud". Unfortunate perhaps in some contexts.

There was a dusk to dawn curfew, which didn't worry me since I rarely went out at night, but two donkeys were shot for prowling the streets in defiance of the curfew.

All citizens were encouraged to receive military training in case of some imaginary attack; my secretary, a very large woman, volunteered. I told her that her contract terms did not allow her to take time off for such activities. She complained to the revolutionaries and I was visited in my office by a rather rotund, over-fed, sly-faced dissident game guard who had found an influential niche for himself in the revolution, as such unwelcome persons do, as an organizer of one of the Committees for the Defence of the Revolution. Behind a transparently false smile, veiled threats were made of a diplomatic incident if I did not allow my secretary to attend the military training. Well, I had been through this sort of thing before. I replied I was unable to give her time off for such activities.

Things began to look ominous for me, and then one participant dropped dead during the training. Suddenly nobody wanted to do military training anymore. My secretary, the two-faced bitch, said she had never wanted to anyway, she had been told she had to do it. Now she was on my side.

For my part, I now wished I had let her go!

* * *

I went on home leave shortly after the coup, and two days before I arrived back again two months later the Americans invaded Grenada to put down the Communist takeover there.

Consternation reigned in Ouagadougou!

All authorities were on the alert against an attack by the Americans. Long queues ensued at the arrival desk of the airport as papers were carefully checked and our passports taken away for closer scrutiny. I had a diplomatic passport but it made no difference. Americans came under the greatest suspicion and were kept waiting until last.

Why did they think the Americans might want to intervene in a country of no wealth and no strategic importance? Even the French were prepared to let them get on with it. The answer was, of course, that if there wasn't an enemy, then they had to invent one.

* * *

I had to help organize a great wild life conference to be held in the capital so that the people could participate in the revolutionary transformation of the sector. It took place in one of the most sumptuous conference halls of Ouagadougou.

The Minister, a small nondescript youngish man in casual dress, not in the usual obligatory disruptive pattern camouflage of revolutionary regimes, nor wearing army boots, was to read the opening speech. Seated on the grand stage he had just begun his delivery when the same fat game guard who had tried to intimidate me got up with great deliberation and swaggered ostentatiously to a lectern at the side of the stage. The Minister paused in his delivery and looked at him.

Ignoring the Minister, with deadpan face the game guard raised a clenched fist and shouted:

"Imperialism!"

Then, using the catchphrase of the French Revolution (À bas! – down with!):

"Down with imperialism!"

There was a half-hearted response from the audience.

He tried again, louder this time.

"Imperialism!

"Down with imperialism!"

The audience responded more noisily:

"Down with imperialism!" and clenched fists were raised in militant solidarity. All except mine.

The Minister regarded the revolutionary game guard with a bemused expression.

"Colonialism!" shouted the revolutionary game guard.

"Down with colonialism!" came the response.

"Neo colonialism!"

"Down with neo colonialism!"

"Racism!"

"Down with racism!"

"Puppet regimes!"

"Down with puppet regimes!"

"Corruption!"

"Down with corruption!"

Having exhausted his revolutionary vocabulary, there came the final fervent punchline:

"The Fatherland or death! We shall conquer!"

Abruptly he broke off, and sauntered back to his seat.

The Minister continued. He had not progressed much further with his oration when the revolutionary game guard once more rose from his seat and swaggered to the lectern. Not looking at the Minister, nor waiting for him to finish what he was saying, he raised his clenched fist and again shouted:

"Imperialism!

"Down with imperialism!"

The whole list of colonial calumnies was then gone through once again. The audience was beginning to enjoy the shouting. Perhaps the

Minister should have chosen a shorter speech, for he was interrupted yet a third time.

Exhausting his repertoire of imperial iniquities, the revolutionary game guard added a new slogan:

"Down with rotten game guards!"

The conference hall roared enthusiastically in response:

"Down with rotten game guards!"

Even I joined in that one!

* * *

During all this revolutionary fervour I met Sankara himself. I was visiting the Director of the Wildlife Department, when a surprise visit to the government block was announced by the President. The Director left his office to see what was going on, and I was left sitting waiting for him. Suddenly Sankara himself, in the obligatory disruptive pattern camouflage, strode into the room, sporting a revolver on his hip and carrying a small, ivory-handled pistol in his left hand. Clearly he was taking no chances.

He was more surprised than I was:

"*Bonjour monsieur*," he murmured.

I replied in similar terms and stood up.

Considering that he had issued a directive that everyone was to be addressed as 'comrade' on pain of serious punishment if the rule was not observed, his greeting was cause of some surprise to me.

Any moment I was expecting a bodyguard of thugs to rush in behind him and see that I could do him no harm, but after some delay, in which we both found that we had nothing further to say to each other, the Director came in and the Head of State was able to busy himself with issuing commands.

The calendar on the wall was out of date. It must be taken down.

Papers must not be left lying around on the tops of cabinets. They must be put away. Then he marched out again, continuing his revolution, setting his country to rights.

But they were ugly days. For at the same time the traditions of the country were being dismantled. The chiefs were dispossessed of their roles and replaced by young revolutionary councils representing 'the people'. Barely more than boys, the troublemakers and malcontents suddenly found themselves with power, presiding over People's Revolutionary Courts and Committees for the Defence of the Revolution, as ugly as the Revolutionary Committees of the execrable French Revolution.

On 15th October 1987, Sankara deservedly got his comeuppance in an even more bloody coup, with over one hundred people reported killed.

I had no regrets. I was out of it by then. Thank God!

Notes

1. Gerald Hanley *Drinkers of Darkness*.

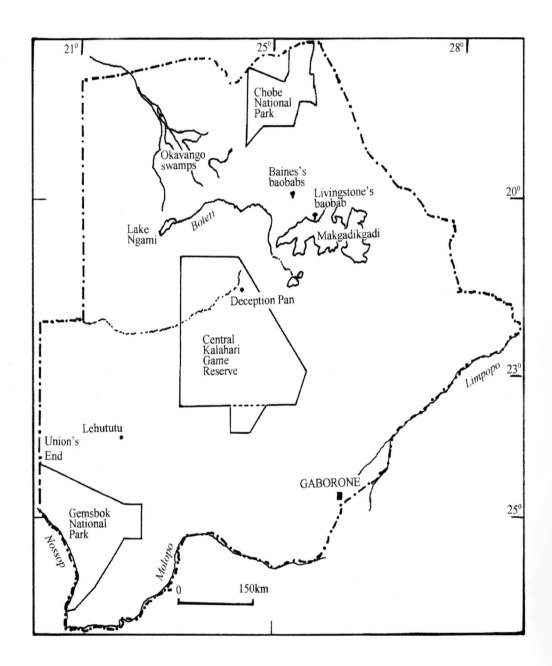

Botswana.

Chapter 10

Through the Chobe Wilderness

Botswana and its unknown corners

When I arrived in Botswana in the middle of 1986 I felt I had come full circle in my life with the animals of Africa, for here in southern Africa, the Chobe National Park and its surrounds in the north of the country bordering the Linyanti and Chobe rivers, which join with the mighty Zambesi, are home to one of the greatest remaining concentrations of elephants in Africa. In the evening, along the Chobe River waterfront you can count five hundred, perhaps twice that number, coming down for their sunset drink and a feed on the lush swamp grasses after their dry and dusty day in the interior.

The hunting of elephant was stopped in 1983, and despite the fact there must be more fencing wire for the taking in Botswana than in any other country in Africa, there is remarkably little snaring of game. Unharassed, these elephants have become the most docile that one could find anywhere on the continent. Contrary to some reports, elephants were numerous here until the post-war years, when numbers seem to have declined before building up again. The Government veterinary officer reported in March 1935: "Elephants were in large herds along the Chobe River all last winter as they used to be in Selous' time – the seventies". The Resident Magistrate at Kasane plaintively asked if he could be allowed to shoot elephants in self-defence complaining in a letter of August 1935:

"At present it is most difficult to be able to plan with certainty to go from Kasane to Kazangula in the afternoon. I have on three or four occasions had to turn back because of elephants on the road. They are quite peaceful; indeed I have walked quite close to them and taken photographs . . . They are not a menace but merely a nuisance."

275

And in October he again complained:

"I got into Kasane at 2.30 a.m. on Tuesday morning from Kachikau. There were elephants from Kabulabula to Kasane. They have dug the road to pieces and I could smell and hear them all the way."

Today government officials, with the accelerator pressed to the floorboards, drive the eight miles of tarmac road from Kasane to Kazungula in ten minutes.

But as the hunter Chapman showed in 1853, when he had a skirmish with a herd of five hundred at Shinamba Hills in the south of the park, the area has always been a stronghold for the great pachyderms. What I saw in Uganda's Queen Elizabeth and Kenya's Tsavo National Parks in the 1960s, before those great herds were brought to the point of extinction by poaching, could now be seen at Chobe. I don't expect it to last, with over a thousand tons of ivory on the hoof tempting the poachers. And what then? We shall never see sights like it again.

* * *

Botswana was where it all started, the opening-up of Africa. The young David Livingstone having converted Sechele, chief of the Kwena (the crocodile people) to Christianity (but it did not last for long), went on to discover the Victoria Falls, and then on to the heart of Tanganyika. Everyone knows the sequel to that, Stanley's famous "Doctor Livingstone, I presume?" and Livingstone's death and the transport of his body to the coast by his faithful followers. He, more than anyone, opened up the heart of Africa and set the foundations for change.

Perversely enough, although it started in the Bechuanaland Protectorate, or Botswana as it came to be called, the country then proceeded to almost stand still in time as one of Britain's poorest and most neglected Protectorates. The primitive Bushmen, eking out a Stone Age existence in the vast Kalahari Desert, only donned cast-off rags and became largely dependent upon government food handouts in the great drought of 1980 to 1987. Until a few years ago, because of the difficulties of travelling there were places still looking the same as they did when the first white men with their ox waggons visited them almost a century and a half before. But now there is no corner which remains unknown – the advent of the cheap Japanese four-wheel drive vehicle has made sure of that, opening up the remotest parts of the country to inquisitive tourists and their scattered beer cans.

Baines's baobabs looking exactly the same 136 years after he painted them.

What had kept many places almost inaccessible is that nearly the whole of the country is covered with thick, soft sand – the Kalahari sands, loose and deep, taking days of laborious work to travel through. And then the greater part of the interior is waterless for much of the year. That was why until very recently it seemed frozen in a time warp in many places, guarded by the desert sands and the inhospitable environment. The famous Baines's baobabs, a group of five giant baobab trees, still looked exactly the same when Prince Charles painted them in 1988 as when Thomas Baines did so in May 1862.

In 1858 the traders Frederick and Charles Green's expedition crossed the great Makgadikgadi salt pans and came to a giant baobab by Gutsaa pan. One of them carved his name and his emblem, a little beaver, on the tree. As I verified for myself in September 1988, this has survived clearly to this day, together with the initials of other early travellers. These include a cross and the date 1859 carved by one of the members of the ill-fated Helmore-Price missionary expedition to the Linyanti, the majority of whom perished there. H. van Zyl, a Boer hunter, carved his initials in 1851; while the earliest is an enigmatic date of 1771, a date preceding by almost a hundred years the first known European travellers to this area. But in the five years since 1981, all around Green's inscription has been defaced by modern additions, carved mostly by expatriate workers from the nearby De Beers Orapa Diamond Mine.

At least these vandals hadn't yet touched Livingstone's baobab, three miles away to the east. This is the first tree travellers see travelling north when crossing the blistering white Ntwetwe Salt Pan, a branch of the great Makgadikgadi Salt Pan. Although the signatures are no longer to be found, both Livingstone and William Cotton Oswell, Livingstone's hunter companion and guide, were recorded by the missionary Mackenzie as having carved their initials on this tree in 1860; and the missionary Roger Price the year before in 1859. Those which still exist are J. Jolley, who died of fever eight months later at Pandamatenga after carving his name here in 1875; James Chapman, dating from the 1860s; and the words LMORE, remaining from Helmore, one of the missionaries who died at Linyanti. Livingstone, although he did not mention carving his initials on it, recorded this tree in his diary on February 22 1853:

"At large Mouana [baobab] tree about two miles beyond pan Ntwetwe. It consists of six branches on one bole, and at three feet from the ground is 85 feet in circumference".[1]

Livingstone's baobab.

When measured in the 1960s its bole had apparently shrunk in size, although Chapman the year before Livingstone had recorded its circumference at the ground as 87 feet. But it is difficult to know how Livingstone measured it, since, as he records, it is not one stem, but six. I thought I would try, but do you measure each bole? Do you measure around the base at the ground at the widest points? Or do you measure at chest height, as a forester would do? I gave up.

* * *

279

Botswana, a country almost the size of France, was inhabited in the east along the upper reaches of the Limpopo River by five main tribes: the Ngwato, the Kwena, the Kgatla and the Ngwaketse. In the far north-west was the Tawana. The tribes along the Limpopo first attracted the attention of traders and hunters for ivory and ostrich feathers in the 1820s, but by 1850 they had already stripped the area almost bare. Rhinos and elephants had gone, and now to find the latter one had to travel to the Tawana country, across the inhospitable almost waterless Kalahari Desert. Unlike the rest of Africa south of the Sahara, and not counting the early Portuguese accounts, there is a rich literature from these first explorers, traders, hunters and missionaries, starting half a century before the first accounts of East Africa were written down.

Chobe (pronounced choh-bee) figures early in the exploration of the country, first visited by Livingstone in February 1853, who reached it by the Mababe route, which tourists use today, having cut across from Nxai Pan (Kamakama), now a national park; he was accompanied by a big game hunter, William Cotton Oswell. Oswell was really the leader of the expedition but deferred to Livingstone, allowing the latter to take credit for the exploration. These two had been the first white men to see Lake Ngami four years before, to them a legendary inland sea in the interior of the desert. Of his first visit to the Chobe Livingstone recorded:

" . . . toiled through a forest which daily became more dense, we were kept constantly at work with the axe . . . we moved along as much as we could, and came to the hill N'gwa [Goha] . . . This being the only hill we had seen since leaving the Bamangwato, we felt inclined to take our hats off to it. It is three or four hundred feet high and covered with trees . . . the valley on its northern side, namely Kandehy or Kandehai, is as picturesque a spot as is to be seen in this part of Africa. The open glade, surrounded by forest trees of various hues, had a little stream meandering in the centre. A herd of reddish-coloured antelopes (pallahs) [impalas] stood on one side, near a large baobab, looking at us, and ready to run up the hill; while gnus, tsessebees and zebras gazed in astonishment at the intruders . . . A large white rhinoceros came along the bottom of the valley . . . Several buffaloes, with their dark visages, stood under the trees on the side opposite to the pallahs . . . The game hereabouts is very tame. Koodoos and giraffes stood gazing at me as a strange apparition when I went out with the Bushmen. On one occasion a lion came at daybreak, and went round and round the oxen . . . "

I climbed to the top of Goha Hill in September 1988, and surveyed the grim, heat-scorched bush stretching into the blue horizon. Probably that scene is the same as Livingstone would have witnessed, one hundred and thirty-five years before. But his picturesque valley was some way to the north. One will still find wildebeest and zebra around the hill in the wet season, and a few impala and giraffe are to be seen; but the white rhino was exterminated in Botswana within fifty years of Livingstone seeing them. In 1988 there were believed to be over a hundred in the Chobe area, but they were reintroduced from South Africa and even those were eventually exterminated, although more have been reintroduced since.

Livingstone continued:

"As we went north the country became very lovely; many new trees appeared; the grass was green, and often higher than the waggons; the vines festooned the trees . . . We at last came to the Sanshureh, which presented an impassable barrier, so we drew up under a magnificent baobab tree . . . "

He then crossed over and followed the river downstream, bypassing the centre of what is today the Chobe National Park, to be the first white man to see Mosi-au-tunya 'the smoke that roars', so called by the natives after the noise of the water and the perpetual mist of spray that hangs over the falls. Livingstone promptly named them the Victoria Falls.

Things were already getting busy in the area. In August to October of the same year James Chapman, South African born trader turned hunter-explorer, was also at Chobe. In July 1853 he became the first white man to visit the Shinamba Hills, two little stony outcrops, but the only high ground for miles around. The next hills are either the Goha or the Gubatsaa, almost fifty miles to the west. Chapman made a camp near the waterhole and hunted from there, while his companion, Edwards, trekked west with some waggons to the Chobe.

"At sunset the Bushmen said they heard elephants by the water. The horses were saddled. We raced in the direction and saw three making off. I raced to get clear of a troop thundering down behind me. I selected an elephant . . . " Plenty more adventures with elephants in the area were to follow:

"21st. July. Myself and Thompson took up one bull spoor. We soon found him, when I gave him a shot as he stood asleep. The elephant turned and, my little mare Apple bolting, the curb chain broke and for two miles I could not hold her. I was at length compelled to throw myself from the saddle. Returned and found Thompson and my servant popping at the elephant on the same spot. He made up his mind for a start, and never have I seen an elephant run like him. I gave him nine shots, when I found myself surrounded by perhaps five hundred cow elephants, and saw six or seven cows crowd round the bull and dash water on his wounds. I did not know which way to get out, and those elephants below the wind smelt me. I was in danger of being run over. I mounted a tree and in a breathless state I contemplated the enormous number of elephants, and my escape, for which I saw no chance as yet.

"Thompson's gun broke and he stopped behind with my servant, who is glad to escape if he can. He fired a shot in the distance and the elephants made two files, one on either side of me, and marched off. I slid down the tree, mounted my horse, and fired at a cow . . .

our agreement being not to slay cows, I returned to camp, disgusted at my bad luck".[2]

Chapman and his companions continued to have adventures with the elephants, Thompson even being reported as "sick of elephant shooting."

On 11 August he left Shinamba setting off towards the north-west, eventually reaching at Komane the Ngwezumba valley which cuts across the centre of the Park. He then followed down the Ngwezumba for some way and then struck north-west up to the Chobe, returning later southwards via Mababe to the Boteti River; having lost all of his horses and oxen from tsetse fly. But in January 1855 he was back again at the Shinamba Hills with his companion Edwards, who went off to the Linyanti to buy ivory, while Chapman stayed at Shinamba to hunt.

"I felt a painful depression of sprits on being left alone and, climbing the pile of rocks, the view was of a dreary tract of country, the black forest beneath stretching away in every direction like a vast ocean . . . "

I climbed the hill in July 1988, but my view was rather more rewarding than Chapman's dismal picture. Chapman's pool could be seen shimmering in the sunlight to the south-east with two roan antelope and a family of warthog drinking there. Later, at three o'clock in the afternoon seven elephants came to drink, and the massive hulks of more could be seen slowly wending their way through the mopane trees from the east. In place of Chapman's black forest (evidently burning had taken place) there was a bright green colour to the bush together with a mixture of dry season tints.

Few people had visited the spot since Chapman's time, let alone camped there; apart from a party of mineral prospectors in the 1960s, and the trigger-happy Sub-Inspector of the Bechuanaland Protectorate Police, Arnold Hodson[3], in February 1909. I camped under a large baobab tree behind the main hill, called by the former inhabitants of the area 'Man Shinamba', in contrast to the smaller 'Woman Shinamba' a little distant from it.

Since the southern part of the Chobe National Park was the last remaining unknown part of it I decided to drive west, following the direction Edwards had taken over a century before, along a dry river valley marked on the map, a journey of some thirty-five miles, through quite waterless uncharted bush and forest. Thirty-five miles might not sound very far to those accustomed to covering such a distance in half an hour on a motorway, but there were three things I had to worry about. Firstly, whether there were patches of thorn bush to drive through, for one could exhaust oneself in the intense heat continually repairing punctures. Secondly, there was always the possibility of a major mechanical breakdown, particularly having a branch pierce the radiator; but having two vehicles helped lessen the risk. Thirdly, there was the possibility of catching fire from dry grass accumulating under the vehicle. Following good rains the grass was tall everywhere and there had already been several reports of vehicles being burnt out. I carried fire extinguishers just in case. The other vehicle did catch fire, but that was much later when we were on the way home.

Events subsequent to this trip showed my concerns were real enough, for in November 1990 six Africans, all local people, perished from thirst near the Shinamba Hills when their vehicle got stuck in the sand and they went to seek help, leaving their food and water in the vehicle, confident they could make the nearest post on foot. The bodies of two of them have never been found.

Unlike in Chapman's day there are no longer any bushmen in the area to guide you, and the valley which his bushmen had called the 'Dum', turned out to be indiscernible at this point causing me to go somewhat off course. Nevertheless, having set out from the Shinamba Hills at about 8.30 in the morning, by five o'clock we had traversed the wilderness and reached an old track, which took us to Tsotsoroga Pan, where we camped for the night. The only game seen was a cow and calf white rhinoceros when we came out onto the track.

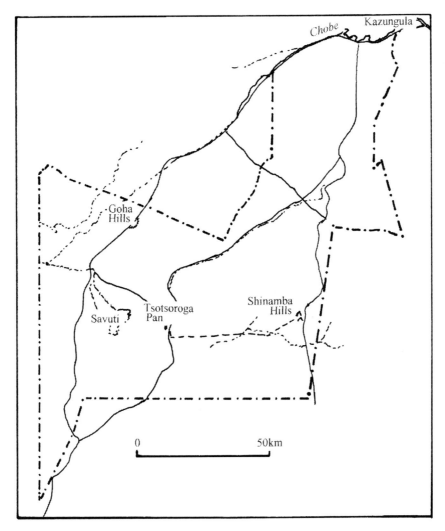

Chobe National Park, Botswana showing (broken line)
author's drive from Shinamba to Tsotsoroga.

There had been little to it, just an uncomfortable heat from the slow pace, the tiresome business of twisting and turning through the bush, rarely able to drive straight ahead; a brief stop at midday to open a can of pilchards and a tin of baked beans, accompanied by a hasty swig of lukewarm water from the water bottle. I never travelled with the comforts most of today's pampered travellers insist upon, cool boxes, ice, and other conveniences. My water bottle was the same old surplus First World War army bottle I had been issued with in 1953 in Kenya when I had first come to Africa.

Eight hours the journey had taken. Some difference to the anxious four days of toil Edwards made with his ox waggons traversing this hostile country!

Tsotsoroga Pan was at one time an important staging point but it nearly cost Livingstone his life, for when he arrived there in 1851 he found it dry. Years later, in 1877, an elderly Dutch elephant hunter, Martinus Schwartz, and ten members of his family, died there, allegedly of fever. While the famous hunter Selous in 1879 also nearly perished at the same place when he found it dry. Until the early 1960s the north-south road, track would be a more appropriate word, passed by the side of it. Now it has been realigned further west, and the pan's former role has been largely forgotten.

Selous recorded the problems he encountered in 1879 in his book *A Hunter's Wanderings in Africa*:

"About 2 a.m. having ridden along by the light of a glorious full moon for about five hours, we came to them, splendid, deep, pans, that one could not believe would ever dry up. Yet dry they were, and our hearts sank as we rode into the largest one, and found that although there was a little mud in it, there was no water . . .

"In the mopane forests beyond these pans the road became untraceable, so we returned to the last pan and waited for daylight.

"By the light of day there was no more sign than by moonlight . . . Though we found many pans, they were all quite dry . . . The oxen were now quite told out, and stood all in a heap under a cluster of mopane trees, trying to escape the fierce rays of the sun . . . Just before sundown [having abandoned the waggons] we emerged upon the great open plain known as the Mababe Flat . . . . We saw a great many zebras about the flat, and I said to old Jacob that there must be water nearer than the river, otherwise how could the presence of zebra and buffalo spoor be accounted for? The old fellow said that there were some pans just within the edge of the mopane, close to us, but that as the large vleis we had passed were dry, he did not think it likely that these little ones would still hold water. However, we went to look and found a long shallow vlei filled with water . . . "

Selous went on to hunt extensively along the Linyanti and Chobe rivers, "Puku flats" in the Park still bearing the name he gave to them:

"At the point where we struck the river on our way back – some three or four miles to the westward of our camp - stretched a large flat piece of ground, in some parts over a mile broad, lying between the steep forest-covered, jungly sand-belt and the bank of the river. This flat might be from six to eight miles long . . . The greater part of the extensive tract . . . was open, though here and there patches of bush were scattered over its surface, and near the river grew many very fine wide-branching camel-thorn trees . . . On coming down from the jungle, about an hour before sundown, and looking across the open ground towards the river, I beheld several herds of 'pookoo' antelopes, some impalas, and a small family of graceful striped koodoos – amongst them a grand-looking old bull – whilst far to my left the foremost ranks of a herd of buffaloes were just emerging from the bush, the fourth troop that I had seen that day . . . The number of pookoo on these flats quite surprised me. Sometimes troops of more than fifty of them were to be seen together...Owing to the great numbers of these antelopes, I christened this place the 'Pookoo Flats' . . . "

The numbers of puku there today are down to a couple of dozen or so, but one can still see the other animals appearing in the evening, the buffaloes in a herd of a thousand or more, covering the flats like a great herd of black cattle even more numerous than when Selous described them. Of his less pleasant experiences, we are lucky that today the tsetse fly is absent from the area, but the mosquitoes are still there:

" . . . in the early part of the evenings, huge black mosquitoes, as vicious as bull-dogs, already commenced to make their presence disagreeably felt: little did I dream what was in store for me during the hot weather later in the season! In the daytime, too, "tsetse" flies, whose numbers increased daily as the season advanced, were very troublesome. Nowhere does this virulent insect exist in such numbers as to the westward of the Victoria Falls, along the southern bank of the Zambesi and Chobe . . . along the water's edge they are an incredible pest, attacking one in a perfect swarm, from daylight to sunset . . . never had I met with them in sufficient numbers to cause so much annoyance; but along the Chobe river, during the months of September and October, hunger, thirst, fatigue, and all the other hardships that must of necessity be endured by the elephant-hunter, sank into insignificance as compared with the unceasing irritation caused by the bites of the 'tsetse' flies by day, and three or four varieties of mosquitoes by night."

Selous also camped at Gat-garra Pan, now known sometimes as 'Selous Pan', on the western boundary of the park, which forms the boundary with the Tawana tribal land. Three hippos occupied the drying pan when I visited it in June 1989, otherwise no game was to be seen. The area did apparently harbour one of the last remaining black rhinoceros in the country, a species that managed to hang on by the skin of its teeth in this area for more than a century after its white counterpart had become extinct. Now it also is extinct here.

* * *

The heart of Botswana is a hostile desert. Not a desert in the true sense of the word, for the ground is covered with grass and spreading acacia thorn trees. But there is no water. The shallow river beds have not carried water for perhaps four thousand years or more. Only the Bushmen had learnt how to survive in this forbidding place. Certain plants indicate the sand holds moisture and they exploit this by scooping a hole in it and inserting a hollow grass stem, packing the end around with fine grass or roots and then filling in the hole. This is left for an hour or more, after which they suck at the end of the straw for another hour or more. The reduced pressure then draws the moisture away from the sand grains and up the straw. How on earth did they learn to do that, I wonder?

This harsh habitat today forms the third largest national park or game reserve in the world, created in 1961. But its twenty thousand square miles, two-thirds the size of Scotland, carry little game, for even game must have water. In 1983 the area achieved notoriety due to the deaths of an estimated fifty thousand wildebeest, which, migrating north in search of water at the height of the drought, came up against an impassable veterinary cordon fence, which cuts the country in two. The animals were forced to move east along this fence, finally seeking water in the settled area outside of the reserve, but the area within a thirty-mile radius of the only water they could find had been overgrazed by cattle. So the wildebeest had the choice of food and no water in the reserve, or water and no food outside of the reserve. The majority chose the latter, and perished.

The Kalahari Desert has not, in spite of its formidable reputation, claimed many human victims. People other than the Bushmen avoided it, passing around its northern end to the Boteti River which, when I saw it at the height of the 1986 dry season, was no more than a few muddy pools lined by almost bare, overgrazed banks: a far cry from Livingstone's "beautiful river", as he described it in 1849, with its wide expanse of water and its huge herds of game along the banks.

I found numerous zebra and buffalo were dying. One half-grown buffalo was lying down, too weak to move at the close approach of the vehicle. An ear torn off by a hyaena, it lay there with bleeding stump, eyes closed in misery, a pathetic hump of black under the merciless sun. I came across three more resting under the scanty shade of a leafless thorn tree. They leapt up to run away at my arrival, but one fell down from weakness. There were vultures, vultures, everywhere; revelling in the stinking, gory feast.

Although the east bank was now a game reserve, cattle entering illegally from the other side of the river had denuded it of grass so that, as with the wildebeest farther south, there was nothing for the wild animals to eat when forced close to the water by drought.

In 1972, a Member of Parliament of the ruling Democratic Party, together with his brother, a Councillor and another Councillor, were caught having poached 52 zebra, 17 wildebeest and 5 gemsbok in the reserve. The romantic image of the 'Norfolk poacher', the peasant who poaches to feed his hungry family, is just as out of place in Africa today as it is in Great Britain. It is this insensate greed which has such an impact on the game, not the odd animal killed without a licence for food. Commercialized poaching will sound the death knell of Africa's game and impoverish the rural dweller, who simply took what he saw as Nature's bounty and his right when he needed it.

Livingstone followed the Boteti River on to the fabled Lake Ngami. He was not striking new ground but following a well-worn native route. However, thirty-two years after Livingtone's delight at the vast expanse of water he had found, in 1881 the lake was dry, caused by changes in the inflow of water from the Okavango swamps to the north. Livingstone got some hint of the existence of this vast inland delta when he was making for Lake Ngami and passed the Thamalakane River flowing into the Boteti. His canoe paddlers told him it came from a land full of rivers, "so many no one can tell their number". But he himself, after seeing Lake Ngami, went on to Linyanti, where he found they attached no value to ivory, which they called 'bones'. The tusks of dead elephants were left to rot on the ground. His arrival soon changed all that.

Within the next two years after his visit to the chief in the area, Letsholathebe, some nine hundred elephants were killed by, and for, the traders who followed. Much of the ivory which these elephants produced was purchased in exchange for guns. The slaughter was small beer by today's standards, but although Livingstone was not to know it at the time, the trader Wilson who accompanied him on that first journey, sowed a seed, which took far stronger root than did Livingstone's gospel teachings.

The Okavango swamps were only gradually penetrated here and there by early traders. Covering some six thousand square miles the area consists of a vast inland delta fed by the Cubango River, which rises in the highlands of Angola. Each year, after the rains swell its upper reaches, it overflows into this great swamp, breaking into countless channels. The current which has been flowing westwards, suddenly reverses and flows eastwards, carrying on to fill the Boteti. Infested with tsetse fly and mosquitoes there was little attraction for people to penetrate its depths. But this once fever-ridden area is the area now claimed by the tourist brochures to be 'the last wilderness', 'the last Eden', or 'the jewel of the Kalahari'.

Tourists travel its labyrinthine waterways in dug-out canoes, but I had no time for such a leisurely mode of travel and was taken to a private camp by motor boat. Squatting on a wooden stool in the prow I felt like a character in a book by Evelyn Waugh, sailing up some remote tributary of the Amazon. But here the banks were not lined with tropical verdure, and the channel was scarcely as wide as an English country brook. The aquatic vegetation itself also had a decidedly English look, with potamogeton-like plants floating on the surface. Mauve water lilies were in abundance, and a type of Canadian milfoil strained in the current. Flowing over a sandy bottom the water is crystal clear.

The swamps are noted for their aquatic bird life but there is little game to be seen. Once the home of numerous crocodiles these were over-exploited in the fifties and sixties, the number taken being put as high as 25,000 in twelve years, but good numbers probably still exist in the more inaccessible parts. I stopped off on one of the palm-fringed islands used by the tourists as an overnight camp. There was nothing to be seen except discarded toilet paper and a rubbish pit overflowing with empty beer cans.

The tsetse fly that had kept people out for so long has now been largely eliminated because the area has been soused with insecticide, usually of a type banned in Europe. But cattle have been prevented from entering by the erection of a fence to keep the buffalo in, for the buffalo is suspected of harbouring foot and mouth disease virus. Europe has a phobia concerning this virus, and will not allow the import of beef from any cattle that may have been in contact with it. Thus the impenetrable buffalo fence, which, for the moment, safeguards the area from being overrun with cattle.

But there is another threat. From the first proposal of a South African professor of geology in 1918, Professor E. H. L. Schwarz, that the waters of the Delta could be diverted to refill the ancient lake that once occupied the Makgadikgadi Pans, people have always dwelt on the idea of somehow using this water source to irrigate the Kalahari Desert, or parts of it. More than seventy years later schemes were finally going ahead to build dams to supply improved water sources to neighbouring areas. The experts assure us the Delta's character will be unharmed, the conservationists are not so sure, but for the moment the idea has once again been put on hold only to be replaced by another threat. This is a proposal for a hydroelectric dam to be built higher up on the Okavango River in Namibia at a site called Popa Falls. It is feared this could destroy the nature of the Delta if it goes ahead.

* * *

The second richest diamond pipe in Africa was discovered on the northern edge of the Kalahari Desert in 1967, transforming the country's fortunes from one of the poorest countries in Africa to the most prosperous. This has led to an explosion of mineral prospecting in the once unknown Central Kalahari Game Reserve, a previously virtually ignored area until made famous by two young Americans, Mark and Delia Owens, who spent seven years there studying the brown hyaena.

The first prospector's cut line, cutting straight into the heart of the area for fifty-five miles, had been made in 1972, providing a convenient access for motorised poachers who were quick to take advantage of it. Now the area is criss-crossed with a network of lines and tracks, so much so it takes only three days to drive the whole length from north to south of this once formidable wilderness. I did this in May 1987.

Although there are vast stretches of perfectly flat open country reaching drearily to the horizon, unlike the Athi and Serengeti Plains of East Africa it is sand, sand, sand, nothing but sand; and the going is tough as the vehicle wheels labour to grip. The only relief is provided by the flat, fossil river beds, expanses of white alkaline dust fringed by thorn trees. "Deception camp", made famous by the Owens in their book *Cry of the Kalahari*, is marked only by a stand of particularly dense thorn trees, offering welcome shade in an otherwise barren landscape.

Once there were elephant, rhino, buffalo and zebra, in the northern and western parts of what today constitutes the reserve. Climate and man removed the elephants and rhino long ago, but it was not until the erection of the Kuke veterinary fence in the north in 1954 that the zebra and buffalo disappeared. Springbok occur on the fossil river beds, and if you are lucky you might come across giraffe, gemsbok, wildebeest and hartebeest. But since the drought has taken its toll no longer are the latter two species to be seen migrating in their thousands. Indeed the wildebeest, once one of the commonest animals in the country, will be the next to go the way of the zebra in the reserve. But like the zebra it will continue to survive to the north outside of the reserve where it has access to water.

* * *

In 1885 an American adventurer, William Leonard Hunt, travelled from Cape Town into the southern Kalahari accompanied by his photographer son, Lulu. He claimed in the book which he published the following year to have reached Lake Ngami, but this has been found to be impossible. The Union Castle Line steamship bookings show he was in southern Africa for only 175 days, and not 255 as he stated. Allowing time for preparation, this meant he would have had to have travelled fifty miles a day, easy enough today but not when you are travelling by ox-cart, which averaged about six miles a day.

A contemporary witness records he got as far north as Lehututu, a village 280 miles before Lake Ngami, which is at approximately the map reference Hunt gave for the 'lost city'.

Hunt went under the name of G. A. Farini (perhaps it is only coincidence that *farini* means 'flour' in Kiswahili), and was an acrobat and entertainer, having crossed the Niagara Falls on a tightrope in 1864. In 1884 he had a show in London at which he exhibited pygmies as "Dwarf Earthmen from the Interior of Africa" with such turns as "Stalking the Lion" and "Exciting Torture Dances over War Captives". Perhaps when he published his book *Through the Kalahari Desert* with his claim to have found a lost city in the desert's depths, and followed this up with a "Lost City Exhibition" at the Westminster Aquarium in London, his claim should have been met with a little more circumspection. Nevertheless it fired the imagination of generations, and people today are still looking for this phantom city.

In 1990 a Member laid the following question before the Botswana Parliament:

"To ask the Minister of Local Government and Lands to brief this Honourable House on the current status/position of the "Lost City of the Kalahari", with particular reference to the following points:

– whether the "Lost City" is still in Botswana, if not where is it at the present time . . . "

A lot of people would like to know the answer to that. Farini's reference to it in his book is rather brief, he left the rest to the imagination: " . . . beside a long line of stone which looked like the Chinese Wall after an earthquake, and which, on examination, proved to be the ruins of quite an extensive structure, in some places buried beneath the sand, but in others fully exposed to view. We traced the remains for nearly a mile, mostly a heap of huge stones, but all flat-sided, and here and there with the cement plainly visible between the layers. The top row of stones were worn away by the weather and the drifting sands, some of the uppermost ones curiously rubbed on the underside and standing out like a centre table on one short leg. The general outline of this wall was in the form of an arc, inside which lay at intervals of about forty feet apart a series of heaps of masonry in the shape of an oval or an obtuse ellipse, about a foot and a half deep . . . some of these heaps were cut out of solid rock, others were formed of more than one piece of stone, fitted together very accurately . . . found that where the sand had protected the joints they were quite perfect . . . On digging down in the middle of the arc, we came upon a pavement about twenty feet wide, made of large stones. The outer stones were long ones, and lay at right angles to the inner ones. This pavement was intersected by another similar one at right angles, forming a Maltese cross, in the centre of which at one time must have stood an altar, column, or some sort of monument, for the base was quite distinct, composed of loose pieces of fluted masonry. Having searched for hieroglyphics or inscriptions, and finding none, Lulu took several photographs and sketches . . . "

The photographs were never produced.

Called upon to address the Royal Geographic Society on this interesting find, Farini gave a slightly different version: "While hunting we came across an irregular pile of stones that seemed in places to assume the shape of a wall, and on closer examination we traced what had evidently once been a huge walled inclosure, elliptical in form and about the eighth of a mile in length. The masonry was of cyclopean character; here and there the gigantic square blocks still stood on each other, and in one instance the middle stone being of a softer nature was weather-worn. A large stone, about six feet in length and the same in width, was balancing on this, and but for its great inertia would have been blown over by the wind. Near the base of the ruined walls were oval-shaped rocks, hollowed out, some composed of one solid stone and others of several pieces joined together. These peculiar basin-shaped ovals were regularly distributed every few yards around the entire ellipse. In the middle was a kind of pavement of long narrow square blocks neatly fitted together, forming a cross, in the centre of which was what seemed to be a base for either a pedestal or monument. We unearthed a broken column, a part of which was in a fair state of preservation, the four flat sides being fluted.

"We searched diligently for inscriptions, but could find none, and hence could collect no definite evidence as to the age and nature of the structure. The approximate latitude and longitude of this remarkable relic of antiquity were about 23° S. lat. and 21° E. long., near the tropic of Capricorn".

The description was, perhaps, not quite as exciting as that of Prins's homes of the troglodytes in Oubangui-Chari. Like Prins, Farini undoubtedly thought nobody would ever be able to check up on him, but since 1923 when Professor Schwarz drew attention to the account in support of his own theories of watering and populating the desert, many people have searched for the Lost City of the Kalahari.

One author wrote in 1963:

"It is generally believed that the re-discovery of Farini's Lost City will provide the missing clue that will probably solve the tantalising mystery which surrounds the origin of the great Zimbabwe and other spectacular and inexplicable ruins, now locked in mystery, throughout the continent of Africa".[4]

Of course, it is possible Zimbabwe-type ruins exist elsewhere, for in fact smaller related stone structures do exist in eastern Botswana, one in the Makgadikgadi Pans. But what Farini, or Hunt, to give him his proper name, probably saw was a calcrete rock outcrop, which fired his imagination. For calcrete, a hard, white, limestone rock does have veins of softer, cement-like rock, running through it. The existence of the Zimbabwe ruins was first reported in 1867 by a hunter, Adam Renders, but as elsewhere in Africa they were of dry wall construction. Calcrete, being a soft rock, is eroded by wind, and could easily assume 'fluted' shapes. But what no one has yet succeeded in doing is to locate a calcrete outcrop that Hunt could have used as his model for his "Lost City".

Although the area is vast and waterless, it has now been penetrated by mineral and petroleum exploration cut lines, and covered in detail from the air. But it is vast, and it is riddled with salt pans. There is still a chance of finding the calcrete outcrop, which may have inspired Hunt's legend, but not, I fear, a "lost city".

To the south-west of the mystery area, and through which Hunt claimed to have travelled, is the Gemsbok National Park. This is a waterless area of over nine thousand square miles, separated by a dry river bed, the Nosop River, from South Africa's Kalahari Gemsbok National Park, of a further five thousand square miles (now joined to form a 'transnational' park).

Although the Nosop River valley was inhabited by Cape coloureds from 1913 to 1934, and the South African side was farmland earmarked for coloureds before 1931, the Botswana side, declared a game reserve in 1940 and a national park in 1971, was almost *terra incognita* until recently, when the hungry tentacles of the prospectors' cut lines penetrated it. The centre has yet to be visited. Not that anyone should want to do so. One can imagine what it is like, an arid, barren wasteland of unfriendly bush with hardly a living creature to be seen.

In the summer, with the mid-day temperature soaring to over forty-two degrees centigrade, it gets too hot to be bearable; and in winter the night temperatures fall to almost ten degrees below freezing, as I found for myself when I visited the northern part in August of 1989. It is a burning, arid wasteland: "Here is no water but only rock, Rock and no water and the sandy road", to quote T. S. Eliot's *The Waste Land*. No different to the Central Kalahari Game Reserve, except that the area is one of undulating sand dunes which, as you approach the Nosop River, become closer and closer together, steeper and steeper, and higher and higher, until many are impossible to navigate with a vehicle.

The Coloureds were moved out of the valley, with their consent, and settled to the south of the Park. Their villages are now a signal lesson as to what the fate of Botswana will be where there is uncontrolled grazing by cattle, sheep and goats. For the farms are now bleak oases surrounded by bare dunes, without a scrap of vegetation on them; the area has become the Sahara of the south.

The Coloureds themselves, who range in colour from yellow to black, have developed an anachronistic culture of their own, isolated in this south-west corner of Botswana which maps do not show as even possessing a road, although several hundred miles of passable road exist. They speak only Afrikaans, the language of South Africa. The majority do not understand Setswana, the *lingua franca* of Botswana, nor English, the official government language. The men affect 1930s-style felt trilby hats, and the ladies' finery consists of Dutch or Victorian-type long dresses and petticoats. When they have dances, they dance the waltz and the polka.

I spoke to Paul Matthys, one of the original inhabitants who left the Park in 1938 as a boy of nine years old. He was born at Kyky, where his father Willem Matthys's old windmill still serves the gemsbok and springbok of the Park. He didn't seem to have any regrets; one area of land was as good as another, except that his cattle post was now in a sea of sand. His main complaint was about the lions, which came out of the Park and ate his cattle. He had recently shot an old male lion, which had killed his best bull.

There is no aura surrounding lion killing in Botswana, they are killed all the time as vermin, usually with nothing more than a shotgun. Unlike among many East African tribes no tradition of manhood is associated with such killing. If it once existed amongst the Tswana, it was forgotten when the possession of cattle became the only symbol of importance.

The Nosop valley was receiving twelve thousand visitors a year on the South African side. The single road, 152 miles long, as smooth as a billiard table, was tarmacked in 1991. Game is kept in the valley by the presence of artificially supplied water, using windmills to pump it which were originally installed in the First World War in preparation for an attack on German Southwest Africa, then used by the settlers who in turn left them behind over seventy years ago.

Thus what was once regarded as one of the most hostile of places, has for many years been one of the most artificial. People have come to accept the sight of springbok and gemsbok watering at farm troughs as if it were the natural way to view game.

In 1901 at the site of one of these windmills before a windmill existed, Groot Kolk, although it was in British territory the Germans set up a heliograph station in an operation to put down a rebellion by the Hottentots. But early one morning the Hottentots massacred the entire German contingent. Some modern tourists camping at the spot and hearing the eerie wailing of jackals at night, spread the story that the ghosts of the massacred men can be heard crying here. The story is good for tourism.

I went past Union's End, once regarded as virtually the World's End, along the game-proof barrier with Namibia, almost forty miles along the sandy track to the northern park boundary, and then drove down the latter on one of the roughest rides I have ever experienced. For the ground was riddled with rodent holes making driving a misery. In some fifty miles back and forth along this remote boundary I saw only half a dozen gemsbok, and the occasional little steinbuck antelope. But what was lacking in big game must certainly have been made up for by rodents!

Shown on the map traced from air photographs was a long series of connected pans, twenty-five miles in length. I wanted to see whether this might not be another sort of Nosop Valley with its great old gnarled acacia trees, hidden away in the north of the park. Perhaps even Farini's Lost City might be found in a place like that! Somewhere also in this area is the site of the final battle of the Herero-Nama uprising, fought between the Germans and Hottentots in 1908, when again the Germans were massacred. But like everywhere else in the area, I found only a bleak and barren landscape. The valley was open, with no friendly shade trees and few signs of game. The petroleum prospectors had made a track along its length. That made the going easier, but finding it in an area where no track was supposed to exist was also a bit of let-down.

Was there no unknown corner left, even in this bleak wilderness?

* * *

Until Independence in 1967 Botswana had the dubious distinction of being governed from outside of the country, the administrative seat

300

being at Mafeking in South Africa. This seat was moved to Gaborone in 1966, where a town for 20,000 people was planned. By 1989 the number of inhabitants was estimated to be about 100,000, and still growing rapidly. In many respects the creation of a new administrative seat was an advantage, for the city, as it has become, could be planned. Shanty-town buildings are at a minimum: the people housed in neat, whitewashed, brick and cement-block bungalows, with corrugated iron or tiled roofs. There is an efficient refuse collection, although the streets are littered with beer cans, cola cans, and plastic bags. The people are well-dressed in European clothes and they live a western-style life. The urban dwellers have, in fact, never had it so good: in stark contrast to the majority of their African brethren.

There are several smart hotels, one with a gambling casino full of fruit machines; the obligatory governmental 'President Hotel'; and an imitation English pub called 'The Bull and Bush', the brainchild of an Indian.

But one thing is lacking in this burgeoning metropolis – character. There is no remembrance of things past, no tradition and no history. Traditional dancing is kept alive in junior schools, but urban adults view it with disdain. Traditional crafts are few.

In Gaborone the De Beers diamond office block was not for long the tallest building in the city, now overshadowed by the glass-fronted post office building. The modern architecture is of the garish type that has come to be associated with developing nations spending money: monstrous carbuncles, as Prince Charles would call them, an incongruous affront to Kgale Hill, the landmark of Gaborone, rising majestically in the background.

As if in protest at the style, an Indian has built a lavish gin palace, a pseudo-classical, porticoed extravaganza, surrounded by a pink wall. At least it shows imagination.

Regularly, morning and evening, the long lines of bored commuters wind their way slowly into and out of the city centre, dozing to the hum

301

of their air conditioners, their smart cars nose to tail. Often, to add some sparkle of interest to the journey to the office, there is an upturned car in the ditch left by a drunkard of the night before, or an accident occurs when somebody, dreaming over the wheel, rams the back of the car in front. There is nothing of the sense of despair of Bangui, or of the souk-like bustle of Ouagadougou; but there is no character either.

Gaborone has become the Milton Keynes of Africa.

There is, perhaps, nothing wrong in that. But do not expect to find the old Africa where the new has risen in its place.

Or . . . is the old Africa perhaps still lurking there after all, hidden away from prying western eyes?

The following extract appeared in an article in the official Government newspaper in October 1989:

"He [Chief Sechele] also cited the sporadic cases of ritual murders, perpetrated by uncivilised people who still succumb to the idea of keeping their superiority through muti [medicine] prepared from human flesh.

"Kgosi [chief] Sechele said gone were the days when muti was regarded with high esteem."

It would seem not everyone agreed. Even the Milton Keynes of Africa has its dark secrets.

Notes

1. I. Schapera ed. 1960 *Livingstone's Private Journals 1851-1853*.
2. E. Tabler ed. 1968 *Chapman's Adventures in South Africa*.
3. A. W. Hodson 1912 *Trekking the Great Thirst*.
4. Fay Goldie 1963 *The Lost City of the Kalahari*.

Bibliography

Alexander, B. 1907 *From the Niger to the Nile* 2 Vols. London: Edward Arnold.

Baker, S. W. 1866 *The Albert N'yanza, Great Basin of the Nile* 2 Vols. London: Macmillan & Co.

Bell, W. D. M. 1960 *Bell of Africa* London: Neville Spearman.

Brown, D. and M. 1996 *Looking Back at the Uganda Protectorate, Recollections of District Officers* Perth: Douglas Brown.

Conrad, Joseph 1902 *Heart of Darkness* London: J. M. Dent & Sons Ltd.

Cook, A. R. 1945 *Uganda Memories (1897-1940)* Kampala: The Uganda Society.

Cureau, A. 1915 *Savage Man in Central Africa* London: T. Fisher Unwin.

Daly, M. 1937 *Big Game Hunting and Adventure 1897-1936* London: Macmillan & Co.

Davie, M. (ed.) 1976 *The Diaries of Evelyn Waugh* London: Weidenfeld and Nicolson Limited.

Farini, G. A. 1886 *Through the Kalahari Desert* London: Sampson Low, Marston, Searle & Rivington.

Farson, N. 1940 *Behind God's Back* London: Victor Gollancz Ltd.

Federick, A. Duke of Mecklenberg 1910 *In the Heart of Africa* Cassell and Company Ltd.

Gallo, T-J. 1988 *N'Garagba : Maison des Morts Un prisonnier sous Bokassa* Paris: Éditions L'Harmattan.

Gibbon, S. 1932 *Cold Comfort Farm* Harmsworth: Penguin.

Gide, André 1930 *Travels in the Congo* New York: Alfred A. Knopf.

Goldie, F. 1963 *The Lost City of the Kalahari* Cape Town: A. A. Balkema.

Hanley, Gerald 1955 *Drinkers of Darkness* London: Collins.

Henriot, D. 2004 *Au bout des pistes, le Chinko* Paris: Éditions Montbel.

Hodson, A. W. 1912 *Trekking the Great Thirst* London: T. Fisher Unwin.

Johnson, B. 1908 *Tramps Round the Mountains of the Moon* London: T. Fisher Unwin.

Melville, H. 1851 *Moby Dick* New York: Harper & Brothers.

Middleton, D. (ed.) 1969 *The Diary of A. J. Mounteney Jephson* London: The Hakluyt Society.

Owens, M. and Owens, D. 1985 *Cry of the Kalahari* London: Collins.

Perham, M. (ed.) 1959 *The Diaries of Lord Lugard* 3 Vols. London: Faber & Faber.

Potagos, P. 1885 *Dix Années de Voyages dans L'Asie Centrale et L'Afrique Équatoriale* Paris: Fischbacher.

Prins, P. 1909 *Les Troglodytes du Dar Banda et du Djebel Méla* Bulletin de géographie historique et déscriptive 11-26.

Saint Floris 1930 *Tam Tams de Mes Nuits* Paris: Berger-Levrault.

Schapera, I. (ed.) 1960 *Livingstone's Private Journals 1851-1853* London: Chatto and Windus.

Selous, F. C. 1879 *A Hunter's Wanderings in Africa* London: Richard Bentley & Son.

Stanley, H. M. 1890 *In Darkest Africa* 2 Vols. London: Sampson Low, Marston. Searle & Rivington.

Tabler, E. (ed.) 1968 *Chapman's Adventures in South Africa* Cape Town: A. A. Balkema.

Toqué, G. 1904 *Essai sur le Peuple et la Langue Banda* Paris: Librairie Africaine et Coloniale.

Waugh, Evelyn 1952 *Men at Arms* London: Chapman & Hall.

The Author

Clive Spinage first went to Africa in 1953 to Kenya but did not become a professional wild life ecologist until 1964 when he conducted antelope research in Uganda. Since then he has worked in Rwanda, Tanzania, the Central African Republic, Upper Volta and Botswana. He has been described as one of the world's leading authorities on African mammals. Author of many scientific papers his best known books are Animals of East Africa, The Book of the Giraffe, The Natural History of Antelopes, and Elephants. This partial autobiography is a generally light hearted account beginning with the author's attempts to gain a degree in zoology and then deals with his adventures as an ecologist, weaving together anecdote and history particularly of some of the lesser known African countries. His wide experiences range from helping the later Uganda dictator Idi Amin to take off at night in his private aircraft, the doubtful honour of attending Emperor Bokassa's coronation banquet at which it was rumoured human flesh was served, coming face to face alone in an office with Upper Volta's Marxist dictator armed with two revolvers, to his explorations searching for the caves of the troglodytes in a part of the Central African Republic previously unvisited by any European.